Britain alone

How a decade of conflict remade the nation

Liam Stanley

MANCHESTER UNIVERSITY PRESS

Published by Manchester University Press
Oxford Road, Manchester M13 9PL
www.manchesteruniversitypress.co.uk

British Library Cataloguing-in-Publication Data
A catalogue record for this book is available from the British Library

ISBN   978 1 5261 6438 4 hardback

ISBN   978 1 5261 5920 5 paperback

First published 2022

Typeset
by New Best-set Typesetters Ltd
Printed in Great Britain
by TJ Books Limited, Padstow

Britain alone

Manchester University Press

Contents

Introduction

In Autumn 2014, I was commuting from Birmingham to Sheffield. Each week I travelled through Birmingham New Street station, a year or two before its dramatic rebirth as a light and affluent commercial space. The new station was then in-progress, the concourse a maze of constricted and temporary corridors. Grey and narrow, it was not a stimulating part of the commute.

One day, with ten long minutes before my train departed, I had my first meeting with a set of automated holographic assistants. Positioned between the escalators that lead passengers down to their platform, they took form as smiling young brunettes. They reminded travellers about the dangers of escalators, the no smoking policy, and to stand back when a train approaches. They made awkward jokes ('our lift is like a pantomime ... it's behind you') and used positive 'body' language.[1]

The holograms provided novelty to my commute, gave me something to think about, mostly because they were so evidently absurd. What was the point of them? What purpose did they serve? With no obvious answers, my curiosity curdled into indignation – so much so that I approached and asked a Network Rail employee about them. He told me they cost £10,000 each. Surely that money could have been spent on something more worthwhile, we agreed, united against the holograms and the bosses and bureaucrats that birthed them.

I continued to think of the holograms as I glided towards Yorkshire, totting up costs and human labour as I went. The meetings to brainstorm, initiate, plan, administer, and finish this scheme. The negotiations with the hologram manufacturer. The purchase orders. The focus groups used to decide the content of the messages. Hiring an actor to read the messages. And so on.

Who was accountable for this? And who had paid for it? My instinctive answer was that 'the state' was responsible, and so that we – 'the taxpayers'? – had foot the bill. I even did some brief googling to find out, which only confused matters. I discovered that the automated holographic assistants were a Network Rail initiative. Network Rail do not run any train services themselves; rather, they oversee the UK rail network. And they are funded, I found out, through a mixture of rail revenue and government grants.[2] Does this mean that we, 'the taxpayers', paid for the holograms? I wasn't sure. I soon discovered I wasn't alone in my confusion. Over the last decade, statisticians have disagreed on the status of Network Rail. On one side, the National Audit Office argued that Network Rail is part of the state. On the other, the Office for National Statistics (ONS) argued that it is actually private.[3] In 2013, it was settled, the ONS changed their minds, and thus established an official consensus: Network Rail is part of the state. This statistical change instantly added £30 billion to the UK national debt.[4]

I became fascinated by this experience. At first, I thought it might tell us something about the experience of privatisation, and how it distorts the divide between public and private authority, thereby limiting democratic oversight. But later I started seeing this experience differently. Why was I so outraged? And so compelled to know? Why did I take so much pleasure in unearthing the apparent misspending of Network Rail?

I came to realise much later that in this experience lay an answer to the question of why Britain has gone through a decade of prolonged political and social conflict – and why it now finds itself alone, shorn of the European Union, and seemingly heading towards break-up.

Britain alone

It was not so long ago that globalisation seemed inevitable – or at least a particular version of it did. This globalisation emerged from the end of the Cold War, where the collapse of Soviet communism gave rise to a truly capitalist world order. Trade barriers lowered, global finance grew, and foreign investment increased. One result was increased economic interdependence: a mesh of cross-national transactions and obligations that wove a world of territorially bound states closer together. The nation-state, it was argued, would find it challenging to exercise authority over this new economic geography, and so would retreat in significance and power.[5]

The future seemed clear. So long as governments did not challenge economic interdependence, their main dilemma was how to share the proceeds of economic growth and promote competitiveness. Gordon Brown, the then British Chancellor and famous proponent of globalisation, used to regularly declare that the world was past the problem of boom and bust.[6] States were advised to hollow themselves out: open up to foreign capital, delegate decision-making to institutions like central banks, hand power downwards to regions and cities, and pool sovereignty into regional federations such as the European Union.

The nation was eroding alongside the state. One of Brown's pet projects as prime minister was promoting a kind of civic Britishness, whereby the nation would be united by a commitment to 'British values' rather than by blood and soil. Outside of British values, the only place for nationalism in those days was supposedly on the extreme fringes. In 2006, the then Conservative Party leader David Cameron famously described the United Kingdom Independence Party (UKIP) as a party full of 'fruitcakes, loonies, and closet racists'. Nationalism was seen as a sad relic, Euroscepticism a fringe concern, and both were considered in decline. With state and nation in retreat, politics was a one-way street, with the roads paved by liberal progress.

That imagined future is now lost. The global financial crisis demonstrated the downsides of interdependency, especially in global finance. The crash brought to the fore more challenging political dilemmas, such as how to deal with increasing fiscal deficits and stagnant economic growth. The election of Donald Trump and other strongmen indicated nationalism's return. The pandemic has slowed life and economies down, perhaps permanently. It has become legitimate to debate whether globalisation is in reverse or even ending. From one path to many, a different fate awaits.

Britain's arc in this story – past, present, and future – is intriguing and important. For it once had the starring role. The Industrial Revolution and Britain's embrace of free trade in the nineteenth century generated the so-called first wave of globalisation. It then moved to a supporting role as the US took up the mantle of maintaining global order. But then came the plot twist: Brexit. It is unusual for a state to withdraw from entrenched interdependence that was legally enshrined through an open, consensual process. A significant part of British identity is made through the conviction that it brought the world free trade and the rule of law, saved Europe from fascism, and is open to different cultures. Britain is going against both the grain of economic interdependence and its own history.

This narrative, which ought to be familiar to those with an interest in the politics of the global economy and Britain's role within it, is where this book is situated. It builds from the following observation: now Britain has left the EU and its customs union, Britain's formal boundaries of economic authority are as national as they have ever been.

This is not say that Britain's economy is no longer globalised. The City of London continues to host a gigantic global financial centre. This puts the UK at the heart of the offshore economy, including tax abuse and other illicit activity.[7] There are few barriers to foreign investment. The percentage of the UK stock market owned by foreign capital remains at least six times higher than it did in the 1960s.[8] The British state continues to participate in multilateral global governance, including the highest core voluntary contributions of any nation-state to the World Health Organisation.[9] A typical British resident can still cook some aubergines grown in Spain, on a stove manufactured in China, distributed by a Turkish conglomerate, powered by Norwegian gas. No one in Britain with sufficient resources will struggle to source any of those goods – even, it turns out, in a nation locked down because of a global pandemic.

Rather, the observation is specific: *the formal boundaries of Britain's economic authority are as national as they have ever been.* This observation only holds if one takes Britain's imperial history seriously, and so it is unsurprising that it has emerged from post-colonial scholars such as Gurminder Bhambra and Robbie Shilliam.[10] After all, the economic boundaries of England, and later Britain, were once transcontinental – and considered as such. As an influential eighteenth-century legal treatise put it:

> The meaning therefore of the legislature, when it uses these terms of *empire* and *imperial*, and applies them to the realm of England, is only to assert that our king is equally sovereign and independent within these his dominions, as any emperor is in his empire.[11]

England united with Scotland to make Britain. Britain's borders expanded through empire, which gave way to the Commonwealth, with British citizenship and therefore labour market access extended to subjects across the globe.[12] In the 1950s, 50 per cent of British trade was with its empire and Commonwealth, aided by imperial preference and the sterling bloc.[13] And then the pivot to Europe, with the single market and freedom of movement. Now that the Commonwealth is mostly irrelevant and Britain has left the EU, the markets for labour and trade that Britain can authoritatively shape and access without restriction will be as geographically limited as they have ever been. While there are alternative visions for trading blocs with the US or wider Anglosphere, these remain just prospects. For now, then, Britain finds itself alone. How did this happen?

This book's central argument is that Britain is going through a process of *nationalisation*. Nationalisation is typically thought of as the transfer of services or commerce from private to state ownership. But there is an equally important second definition that this book focuses on: making the state more national. In general terms, nationalisation can involve using the state for nation-building, gaining independence, or bringing the state in line with the interests of the national peoples. This latter option could, in turn, include distributing resources along ethnic lines, or excluding those other to the nation from resources. It can also entail state action that aims to legitimise those moves, such as encouraging a sense of imagined community within a territory. Although Brexit is its ultimate symbol and transformation, Britain's recent nationalisation cannot be reduced to just leaving the EU, as the book will show.

This raises the question of why this turn – and, in particular, why now? This book argues that the explanation for this nationalisation lies in the intensified social and political conflict that has characterised Britain over the last decade. As the Coalition government pursued austerity in the midst of sluggish growth, relative scarcity and inequality fuelled conflict over who gets what, when, and how. This intensified distributional conflict has manifested through these kinds of questions: What sort of country should Britain be? Who should have a share in Britain's wealth? Who is most deserving of national resources? This conflict is most clear in the build up and fallout of the Brexit referendum – especially in how that created seemingly new battle lines between Remainers and Leavers – but the book shows that this was the evolution and twisting of conflict, rather than the start of it. This is a book, then, about the how the relationship between nation and state is twisted and transformed by political and social conflicts.

Decade of conflict

Why has there been a decade of conflict? Read the opinion pages of newspapers, refresh the Twitter feed, or consult the latest academic journals, and one will find two typical explanations: the cultural backlash thesis, and the economic pendulum thesis. Both tend to focus on explaining populism as a widespread, contemporary phenomena that is encapsulated by the 2016 victories for Trump and Brexit. We will look at each in turn.

The cultural backlash thesis is associated with political science books such as *National Populism* by Roger Eatwell and Matthew Goodwin and *Cultural Backlash* by Pippa Norris and Ronald Inglehart.[14] The cultural backlash in question is a reaction by some to 'progressive value change' (to use Norris and Inglehart's phrasing) and 'hyper ethnic change' that results from 'mass immigration' (to use Eatwell and Goodwin's). Norris and Inglehart argue that 'the silent revolution in socially liberal values' has reached a 'tipping point' where those with conservative values feel threatened to the point of a counterreaction.[15] Although Eatwell and Goodwin are sensitive to overplaying cultural factors, they nevertheless position this backlash as emerging 'long before the financial crisis', to the extent that they imply Trump and Brexit would have happened with or without the biggest economic crash in a century or so.[16] Their argument against economic explanations include the observation that many of those who voted for Brexit were affluent rather than impoverished.[17]

To understand the cultural backlash thesis and its limitations one must understand the research methods that these political scientists use to reach their conclusions: sophisticated analyses of public opinion surveys and voting patterns. In these studies, political scientists look to identify and isolate the specific motivation behind an individual's choice to vote for populist parties or causes (or not). However, that data requires ordering, and that ordering requires choices, and so those political scientists will typically clump together possible motivations into different categorical divides. One of the most popular divides is between economic and cultural motivations. In studies of populism, question topics such as 'immigrants make country worse or better place to live' and 'important to follow traditions and customs' can be taken as cultural, while 'subjective economic insecurity' (reported difficulties about living on household's income) and 'ever been unemployed for more than 3 months' are taken as something different.[18] When studied in this way, cultural factors are found to be a better predictor of who will vote for populism than economic factors.

While helpful for statistical studies of voting behaviour, this divide between cultural and economic factors can lead to problems, especially as those explanations filter from statistical modelling and into public discourse. This way of thinking requires that the different but overlapping features of political and social life are sorted into either the culture box or the economy box. Race, gender, and sexuality tend to be seen as merely cultural, especially when accompanied with denigrating terms such as 'identity politics' or compared to the hard stuff of economic reality. There is no divide between economic and cultural factors in real life. Political grievances cannot be reduced to either.

The economic pendulum thesis contrasts this, and not just because it develops an economic rather than cultural explanation for Britain's decade of conflict. Instead of starting with the microlevel motivations behind voter choices, the economic pendulum thesis begins with the observation that capitalism is structured differently across historical periods. These historical periods can be characterised many different ways, but the most popular way is in terms of how liberal those periods are. Each historical period can therefore be characterised by a degree of liberalism with either the state or market dominating the organisation of capitalism – until there is a crisis. To resolve the crisis, capitalism requires reorganisation. When more liberal capitalist systems crash, the consequent harm generates a backlash for greater protection. And, vice versa, the problems of state-led order seem best fixed by free markets. Crises are thus the moments of 'great transformation' in state-market relations, a term that invokes Karl Polanyi's masterful *The Great Transformation*.[19]

This generates a historical narrative of British capitalist development based on a number of great transformations. The story goes something like: laissez-faire capitalism ushered in the first wave of globalisation during the nineteenth century, which Britain led with the Industrial Revolution and free trade; this system faced crisis through the Great Depression and the rise of fascism, which culminated in the Second World War; which generated a new global system of 'embedded liberalism' underpinned by the Bretton Woods system, or, in British politics terms, the Keynesian post-war consensus; this system faced crisis through the Nixon shocks and 1970s stagflation; which generated a new global system of neoliberalism that restored market power. The history of capitalist development is thus written, as the political economist Martijn Konings puts it, as 'pendulum-like': swinging between state-led and market-led forms every few decades or so, punctuated by crisis.[20] It is quite straightforward, then, to update this story to incorporate the events of the last decade or so: 2008 was the biggest shock to the capitalist system for a generation or more, and so the Brexit and Trump victories represent a backlash against market-led order.

Whether or not this kind of historical narrative is accurate or helpful is not a question this book directly addresses, although there are downsides to thinking of history as following a preset or preordained pattern.[21] Rewind, say, to 2004, and look ahead from that vantage point: the developments of the 2010s seem so profoundly unforeseen, crash or no crash, pandemic or not.[22] Rather than further critique this pendulum thinking, the aim of this book is to bypass it, and leave periodisation to future scholars. This book instead proposes to follow this decade of conflict in action – to crack open this seemingly automatic process, to peer inside, to reconstruct it, in order to understand it better. By doing so, we can leave behind the distraction of a seemingly never-ending 'interregnum' and the wait for a decisive 'great transformation'.

This book develops an alternative way to analyse this past decade without falling into the trap of pitting economic factors against culture, or presuming the pendulum swing. To show how requires explanation of the book's main building block: the concept of 'nationalisation'.

States and nations

Within the British context, 'nationalisation' has taken on a specific usage as the transfer of services or commerce from private to state ownership. This meaning was popularised by the post-war agenda of the Attlee government, who created the National Health Service and nationalised the railways, among other interventions. Any recent or mooted state ownership will inevitably be characterised as 'nationalisation' – as in, the Royal Bank of Scotland was 'nationalised' following its collapse in 2008, or Corbyn's Labour Party promised to 'nationalise' the railways.

The main issue with this usage is how it conflates 'nation' and 'state'. While nation and state often come together in the form of nation-states, it is important to recognise that the two constitutive elements are distinctive. Following Charles Tilly, we can define a state as 'coercion-wielding organizations that are distinct from households and kinship groups and exercise clear priority in some respects over all other organizations within substantial territories'.[23] In its modern incarnation, we can recognise 'clear priority' as the principle and practice of sovereignty. And, following Benedict Anderson, we can define a nation as 'an imagined community – and one imagined as both inherently limited and sovereign'.[24] A nation is therefore a self-identifying homogenous set of people with a shared culture, defined as against the difference of outsiders (i.e. ethnicity, defined properly), and thus a coherent political unit.

While the combination of nation and state may seem natural, we can observe how complex this relationship is by glancing around the globe. We will see nations without states, such as the Kurds; states without nations, such as the Vatican; and states with many nations, such as the United Kingdom. We can also look to the past, and see how European political history is driven as much by city-states and empires – Genoa and Venice, Habsburg and Ottoman – as it is nation-states.

From this, we can start to see why the popular British definition of nationalisation as state ownership is misleading. Surely it would be more accurate (albeit an offence to the English language) to name the process in which the state takes control of, say, the railways or healthcare as 'state-ification' rather than national-isation. After all, the process of state ownership is logically distinctive from national ownership. State ownership *can* be national ownership, if it was done with the purpose of democratising state services or nation-building – as it was with the creation of the *National* Health Service (more on this later). But it could also do the opposite: bringing resources into the hands of a corrupt elite or colonial powers who may be outside of the imagined community of the nation. So while it is possible to speak of 'national ownership' in the same terms of 'state ownership', there is no reason why the latter would necessarily entail the former.

Simply put, then, nationalisation means making the state more national. Although this is a simple formulation, it belies a complex foundation that requires further elaboration. The concept of nationalisation developed in this book has two inspirations. The first is in historical and sociological scholarship on nationalism, which situates it as a general feature of modernity. The second is Britain's unique history of capitalist development through empire, and its post-war and post-imperial experience of 'nationalisation'. We will look at both in turn.

The meanings of nationalism

One benefit of the historical scholarship on nationalism – especially by theorists such as Ernest Gellner, Tom Nairn, and Nira Yuval-Davis – is to show how nationalism has a dual meaning. Nationalism can, somewhat confusingly, refer to both specific nationalist ideologies *and* a feature of the modern world.[25] By specific nationalist ideologies, we mean, for example, Scottish nationalism or Indian nationalism, with their specific political demands which are justified through supposedly unique origin stories and symbols. As Sivamohan Valluvan has shown so clearly, there is nothing intrinsically conservative about nationalism, as it can also take liberal, neoliberal, and socialist forms.[26]

By nationalism as a general feature of the modern world, meanwhile, we mean something broader, from which we can draw out three principles. The first principle is that the population of the world can be divided – no matter how messily – into nations. As Gellner puts it, one can easily imagine a stateless peoples, but imagining a person with no nation is perplexing.[27] It is like trying to imagine a person with no identity, no background, no community. The second and third principles are that each nation has legitimate demands for its own state, and that each state ought to have its own nation.[28] Taking all three together, then, nationalism is the idea that each state should be governed by and for its own national people.

These principles are some of the most important and influential ideas of the modern world.[29] This is why it would be strange if France was governed by an Italian. It is also one of many reasons why colonial direct rule is so indefensible to modern eyes – even though this was historically justified through the racist assumption that non-Christian and non-white communities were not adequately civilised enough to govern themselves. Anticolonial struggles are and were themselves often justified and mobilised through nationalist ideologies.[30]

One way in which these two meanings of nationalism work together in this book is in the understanding that a specific nationhood or national identity does not necessarily lead to a nationalist ideology. This is because *the* key feature of any nationalist ideology is the political demand for some kind of power, most likely in the form of state control. Nationalism always involves, in Nairn's words, 'a demand for the Grail, or at least a bit of it'.[31] If we work with just the first definition of nationalism, we may fall into the trap of seeing nationalist ideologies where there may not be any.

This is significant for British political discourse, whereby the dominant usage of 'nationalism' tends to refer to just the ideological definition in its British/English manifestation, rather than the general principle. This leads to a preoccupation with the cultural politics of (British and English) national symbols and myths that are used to justify far-right positions. This preoccupation is understandable. The way in which the far right use otherwise banal national symbols such as the St George's Cross to launder dangerous politics and sometimes intimidating actions requires constant vigilance. Consequently, some of these symbols, notably the St George's Cross, have become imbued with that meaning. This is perhaps why nationalism gets muddled up with similar concepts such as national identity, patriotism, nativism, racism, xenophobia, and fascism. Yet, it is worth remembering that when people support the England national football team in the World Cup, for example, that form of patriotism does not automatically translate into political demands for greater powers for the English, even though it may be a basis for excluding parts of the British population from the imagined community (as is the case with Norman Tebbit's infamous 'cricket test').

To be clear, this sort of analysis – the cultural politics of British and English symbols and myths, and their exclusionary, racist, and intimidating effects – is necessary and urgent, and an important part of this book. However, I aim to show that it is more a potent and precise analysis when combined with the other meanings of nationalism as a general principle of the modern world. If one aims to take power of the British state, which is the implied purpose of the major British political parties, then one must also to some extent be a nationalist. One can campaign and do politics at any scale from the street to the earth, but the reason so many direct their energies towards the nation-state is because that is where the most power lies, and therefore the greatest capacity to transform. But that power is underpinned by nationalism. This is not to say that one must figuratively or literally wrap oneself up in the Union Jack (nationalist ideology), but rather acknowledge the complex terms in which the authority and legitimacy of the modern nation-state rests (nationalist principles).

If the principle of nationalism is that the state should be governed by and for its own national people, then this naturally raises the question of who those national peoples are. This is a complex question, which thousands of scholarly books and articles have helped answer. Rather than delineate and summarise all of that work, which is an impossible task, I will instead outline two scenarios from which we can then derive some conceptual precepts.

First, let us consider the example of a key public service provided by almost any nation-state to its residents: education. In the UK, the state requires all of its residents to attend some form of education from ages 4–16, at enormous cost. To concoct an example, let us say that the state will take some of the income from, say, a childless solicitor in Newcastle to help fund the compulsory education of children 400 miles away in Plymouth. The solicitor will likely never meet, know, or even think about or be aware of their contribution to these children's education. It is unlikely that the solicitor would challenge the authority of the British state to redistribute, to provide those services to those (imagined) people within the national territory. The allocation of those resources (education) to those people (residents aged 4–16) is generally consented to: it does not break the laws of the land, and it fits with the shared values of voters. It is entirely uncontroversial, to the point where it barely registers as a political act.

Now imagine, second, that the UK state decided to educate children in a different territory, perhaps by building and running a network of schools in, say, Austria. This could involve diverting public resources away from educating children who are resident in the UK or not. Never mind what those in Austria may make of such a scheme, it is self-evident that such a decision would be seen within Britain and by its residents as intensely political and likely very unpopular. Simply put, while children in Plymouth would be seen as included in the national peoples, children in Austria would not, as they are outside of the national borders. This second hypothetical scenario is deliberately implausible to the point of absurdity. Yet, in some senses, the first scenario is also absurd, albeit in an idealised way. Who are these children and who is this solicitor? What rights do they have? How deserving are they deemed in the arena of popular culture? Without taking these questions seriously, the first scenario is as idealised as the second is implausible.

Between these two scenarios of the idealised and the absurd is where one can start to explore the complexity of nationalism, the boundaries of which – as in, who are and who are not considered the national people – work on a more sophisticated basis than just residency. Take gender and sexuality, for instance. In not so distant British history, women were kept disenfranchised, with the feminised roles of biologically and socially reproducing the nation naturalised as private, and so made non-political.[32] Since for a while only men were bestowed with formal citizenship, women were provided with at least uneven access to resources such as formal education. While women are now formally included within the bounds of citizenship in places like contemporary Britain, they are often scrutinised and/or controlled because of their role in remaking the 'national stock'.[33] This can manifest itself as a wider political defence and cultural valuation of heterosexual couples that produce their own biological children, to the extent that female sexual freedom, miscegenation, and queerness can be considered a threat to the nation.[34] Gender and sexuality therefore gradate and modify one's inclusion in the nation.

Colonialism, empire, and race also make and interact with these boundaries. The formal economic boundaries of the British state once spanned the globe, but the redistribution of resources within that was vastly uneven. The school example, then, may seem absurd, but it has historical precedent, especially if one swaps twenty-first century Austria for nineteenth-century Australia. There was little consent about redistributing resources from the colony to the metropole. Resources redistributed in the other direction were typically in the coloniser's interest. As recent research by Bhambra highlights, the birth of the British welfare state at least coincided with intensified colonial extraction.[35] These relations were based on racial hierarchies that still structure British life and nationhood today – for example, the implications of how Black and Asian commonwealths citizens were racialised as 'immigrants', and therefore peripheral to British nationhood (see Chapter 3).

Nation-state boundaries

From this we can derive some conceptual precepts. States distribute and redistribute resources. Resources can be tangible and intangible: following Tilly, this includes 'not only wealth and income but also such various benefits and costs as control of land, exposure to illness, respect from other people, liability to military service, risk of homicide, possession of tools, and availability of sexual partners'.[36] The state redistribution of resources requires a boundary which includes some people and excludes others. The most important of these boundaries is the nation-state. It operates on two levels. The first level is a simple in-or-out line: one is either included and so eligible for those resources, or excluded and so ineligible. These lines include citizenship and residency, and typically have a legal foundation. These can be named as the *formal boundaries* of the nation-state.

The second level operates as an *informal boundary*. Rather than a simple line of inclusion or exclusion, this second level can be imagined as a series of concentric circles, like an archer's target. Those with the most characteristics core to the imagined community can be placed in the core circle, and those who do not have all of those characteristics are placed in the outer circles, increasingly closer to the edge the less characteristics they have. Some of those who are included in the formal boundaries of resource redistribution will be seen as on the periphery of the imagined community, and therefore less valued and deserving. These concentric circles are fluid, dynamic, and ever-changing. For example, those who are more peripheral and thus close to the edge may be close to crossing the line and thus being excluded from the boundary entirely – which is to say formally excluded from those resources.

If nationalisation simply put is to make the state more national, then this scenario and associated concepts elaborates that. Nationalisation, then, to reuse Gellner's wording, is *the process in which the boundaries of the state are made more congruent with the boundaries of the nation*. This process cannot be reduced to either cultural or economic forces. The redistribution of resources (which might typically be thought of as economic) cannot work or make sense without the formal and informal boundaries of the nation (which might typically be thought of as cultural). Nor can this process be reduced to an automatic reaction to capitalist crashes.

The relationship of nationalisation to nationalism is this: the general goal of any nationalist ideology is the nationalisation of a state. In practice, this will almost certainly involve taking (further) control of the state (or acquiring or establishing a new state). Nationalisation is often achieved through nationalist ideologies. If the principle of nationalism is that the nation-state should be governed by its own people, then the specific ideology of any nationalism is that some state ought to be governed by *its* people. Historically, this usually involves calls for self-determination and self-government. To mobilise as a forceful political project, nationalism requires a homogenous set of 'people' with a shared culture – i.e. ethnicity – whose relative lack of status or inequality can be narrated as the fault of an oppressor, mythical or otherwise.

The promise behind successful nationalist mobilisation is to prevent or take power away from that oppressor, install or support rulers who will govern for the people, and create a self-governed and secure future. The oppressor may be seen as providing supposed advantages to outsiders, such as immigrants, rather than the national peoples. But nationalist ideology usually needs to link those supposed advantages to the (potential) rule of oppressors to successfully mobilise, such as the 'metropolitan elite'. This is the basis of most historical nationalist successes, such as nineteenth-century state-building in Europe (e.g.

Bismarckian Germany) or twentieth-century anticolonial independence movements (e.g. the Indian National Congress). In these cases, the purpose of taking power in the name of a national peoples was simple enough: unification as a military and economic bulwark against foreign enemies, in the case of Germany; independence from colonial oppressors, in the case of India.

What this highlights is that while the general goal of every nationalist ideology is the same, it is also the case that every nationalist ideology is unique, depending on its context and purpose for seeking power. This is why, as we will see, English and/or British nationalisms are sometimes described as an enigma: if nationalism is about taking power or building a state for the national peoples, then what does that mean for nations whose state is already united and has no oppressors? This question sets up a discussion of the second inspiration behind the nationalisation concept: Britain's own history, and its complex and unique intermingling of nation and state.

From empire-state-nation to nation-state

Great Britain was formed in 1707, when Scotland was united with England and Wales to create a single, independent political territory on the island of Britain for the first time.[37] (The United Kingdom of Great Britain and Ireland was formed around a hundred years later, but the Irish Republic broke away in 1921 with Northern Ireland remaining part of the UK.) The union meant forging a new supranational British identity to bond the distinct nations of England and Scotland (and, to a lesser extent due to its forced absorption several hundred years prior, Wales). This national settlement was characterised by historian Linda Colley as a *state-nation* because state came before and therefore shaped the nation.[38] Britishness was forged *after* constitutional union through the forces of war, empire, and a shared Protestant faith. However, the union was and is lopsided towards England, both constitutionally and culturally. Britain was, as the political economist Andrew Gamble puts it, always 'a continuation of England and a vehicle for England'; about absorption rather than federation.[39] Significant Scottish moves against this lopsided union are bookended at its birth with the Jacobite rebellions and, since the 1970s, the rise of the Scottish National Party

(SNP) as a political force.[40] Otherwise, the union has been remarkably stable (although, as Chapters 5 and 7 show, two referendums in the 2010s and a pandemic suggest break-up is as plausible as it ever has been).

Britain has consistently faced outward. Its territory has extended beyond the island of Britain from the time of union. England was already an expansionist power before uniting with Scotland, and this intensified after union with full participation from Scottish elites. Britain's first wave of industrialisation was driven by exporting textiles. This economic model was underpinned by colonialism (such as slave-operated plantations) and imperialism (such as eroding domestic competition in foreign jurisdictions).[41] By 1900 the formal boundaries of Britain's economic authority were vast: it controlled over 20 per cent of the world's land surface and formally ruled over around 25 per cent of the world population. Its informal empire was wider still, and included British influence in Latin America, China, and the Middle East.[42]

When we look back, Bhambra points out, we tend to see Britain as a nation-state that *had* an empire.[43] This is an error. Britain *was* (and to some extent remains) an empire. Until relatively recently, British elites have consistently seen themselves as patriarch of an 'imperial family' that incorporated 'Greater Britain' – that is, the white settler colonies of Australia, Canada, and others – a sense that resonates today through the so-called 'Anglosphere'.[44] And, to many ordinary people in the early 1900s, the term 'Britain' marked the boundaries of empire as much as it did the isles.[45] For most of its existence, Britain has been a formal *empire-state* as well as a state-nation. An *empire-state-nation*, rather than a nation-state, if you will.

By 1950 the British Empire was retreating. Britain was deemed in decline, and in need of a new economic model that was not reliant on empire.[46] The typical story that follows can be told as pendulum-like: the British state reasserted its power over the market to protect the people, with the NHS its greatest achievement. However, as David Edgerton argues in *The Rise and Fall of the British Nation*, this settlement resembled conservative national statism in at least equal measure to social democratic Keynesianism. This was a turn away from the competing ideologies of liberalism and imperialism that had otherwise organised British politics. As a result, the British empire-state-nation started looking a lot more like a textbook European nation-state.[47]

The NHS is the central symbol of these changes. Both meanings of nationalisation apply here: it brought private enterprise into public ownership, but it also made the state more congruent with the nation. These two meanings of nationalisation give sense to that important founding myth of Britishness: how the Attlee government founded the post-war welfare state to reward the British peoples for their sacrifices that helped win the Second World War. Institutions like the NHS were *for* the nation, and were appropriately labelled as such.[48]

It might seem odd to describe the NHS as a 'founding myth' to a nation that has existed for centuries. It might be more accurate and specific to instead characterise the NHS as a founding myth to *post-imperial* Britishness. The shift from empire-state-nation to nation-state produced Britishness as the kind of national identity we recognise today. It is a national identity made through the Second World War – the so-called People's War, where plucky Britain stood strong as Europe fell, with Britishness coming to stand for anti-fascist, tolerant, and ordinary – and thereby conveniently placing colonialism and empire to one side and out of the picture. Post-war nationalisation was not just for the British people, then, as it also helped cement the British peoples, shorn of empire. This is part of the meaning and significance of a *National* Health Service for a declining imperial power: it was as much a post-imperial project as it was a post-war project.

Despite these nationalising moves, post-war Britain retained many colonial possessions. While the typical post-war Middle Englander probably did not consider Jamaica or its peoples to be part of Britain, Jamaica remained constitutionally part of Britain. In 1948, British subject status was granted to all former British subjects across the Commonwealth. And so someone born in Jamaica around that time might think of themselves as British, since they were a British subject. Yet it goes without saying that the distributional benefits provided through institutions like the NHS were not extended to all British subjects, as those services were only for those resident in the United Kingdom. Many Asian and Black subjects who travelled to the 'homeland' in the post-war years were shocked by the racism and exclusion they faced,[49] despite being told that they, too, were included in the formal boundaries of the British nation. As Chapter 3 examines, those Asian and Black arrivals were racialised as 'immigrants', placed in the periphery of or even outside of informal British nationhood, and thus conferred less value. The implications of this are crucial to the book.

Two relevant questions arise from this potted history of British nationalisation: What was and is the role of England? And what happened to that inward turn?

The inward-facing nationalisation project slowly turned more outward from the 1970s onward. The state's role was still geared towards securing the conditions for strong economic growth in the national economy, but whether that was driven by domestic or foreign capital – or finance capital – was no longer deemed so important. Throughout this period, Britain was entangled with Europe. In the 1950s, trade with Europe grew faster than trade with the Commonwealth, and post-war arrivals from Europe out-numbered those from the current and former empire. With Common Market membership in 1973, Britain could no longer be said to be inward-facing. Although Britain flirted with the idea of turning outward instead through Commonwealth preference, in the end the threat of European tariffs and the lure of stronger growth convinced British elites otherwise.[50] Under Thatcher and then New Labour, the national economy was increasingly displaced by an imagined global economy; the community of national peoples were governed instead as a population of economic actors and their families.[51]

Within this history is the puzzle or, to use Nairn's phrase, 'enigma' of English nationalism.[52] The United Kingdom is a strange set-up. The English parliament became British, and England's overseas expansion became the British Empire. Scotland kept its church and legal system. Power has been recently devolved to the UK's three other nations, but not to England. The four nations have their own national football teams, but compete as Great Britain in the Olympics. And, there has never been a significant, self-identified English nationalist movement. When we consider the account of nationalism outlined above, this should not be especially surprising. If nationalism is about gaining power and self-determination, then it is not imme-diately clear how that would manifest for a nation like England that has always seemed to dominate and does not need freeing from an oppressor.

Writing in 2003, Gamble argued that the future of British politics 'will be determined by the way in which the choice between Europe and America is finally resolved'.[53] Its wider analysis is as close to a prediction of Brexit as one can reasonably expect. Gamble's analysis was sensitive, too, to the role of England within Britain, past and present. As one political science study memorably puts it, Brexit was 'made in England'.[54] Like Scottish nationalism, English nationalism came to the fore in the 1970s through Enoch Powell's anti-immigration racism and in the 1980s through Conservative Euroscepticism. [55]However, it did not have any significant mobilisation or electoral success until English nationalist elites found a compelling way to link those two strands together. In this way UKIP is a bit of a misnomer: they are an English (and to lesser extent Welsh) nationalist party, as reflected in their political irrelevance in Scotland.

Post-crash Britain

If nationalisation is how this book characterises the last decade of British life, then the obvious question to ask is: why now? This book answers this through the intensified social conflict stoked by post-crash austerity, scarcity, and inequality.

Let us first consider this part of the argument in conceptual terms. Politics is about who gets what, when, and how – that is, the distribution of resources.[56] Social conflict over the (re)distribution of resources is thus a part of any socio-economic system, including capitalism. This is because resources are always scarce, and from this scarcity emerge lines that bound and limit their distribution (such as the nation-state). So long as there are boundaries, there will be conflict: some will contest for those boundaries to be broadened or narrowed; others will contest when resources are distributed to those outside of (or close to) those lines. The *increased* scarcity of resources will intensify and twist existing social conflicts, as well as producing new dividing lines. If severe enough, this conflict will extend to where the boundary lines of (re)distribution are and should be drawn.

The most important of these lines for a nation-state are the formal and informal boundaries of the nation. Hard times thereby produce a social impulse towards consolidation: to draw in those boundaries, to protect those who are conferred greater value by virtue of being core to the nation. Scarcity thereby creates the conditions for nationalisation, if consolidation means (as it does here) drawing in the boundaries of the state and redistribution to more closely match the boundaries of the nation. But this is not and never is automatic or organic. A number of steps are needed: to create and solidify the dividing lines; to mobilise people into participating in contesting those boundaries; and then to have the power to formally redraw them. Some will win, others will lose. Control and patronage of the state is the most decisive weapon.

This description of the argument is, however, somewhat abstract. Let us make it concrete and unpack how it directly applies to this book.

In 2008, the UK entered its worst ever recession. Dampened gross domestic product (GDP) growth created greater scarcity in terms of less jobs and lower tax revenue. Meanwhile, the state bailed out major banks, including taking some into emergency state ownership. The UK found itself with one of the largest fiscal deficits in the Organisation for Economic Co-operation and Development (OECD). Brown's promise about the end of boom and bust seemed the height of hubris.

The crash transformed the existing governing dilemma of how to share the proceeds of growth. The increasing fiscal deficit was a once-in-a-generation opportunity for the Conservative Party to strip Labour of their reputation for economic competence. The Conservatives abandoned their commitment to match Labour's spending, and rebuilt their political strategy around restoring 'fiscal responsibility'. In coalition government with the Liberal Democrats, the then Chancellor of the Exchequer, George Osborne, enacted his 'emergency budget' in June 2010. It combined moderate tax rises with the largest cuts to public spending since the Second World War. There is a lot that can be said about this period and the Conservative strategy that drove it. What is most relevant to this book is the following: that we can look back at that period now with the power of hindsight and see clearly that this period was nationalising in effect.

In this book, the term austerity will refer to the specific Conservative-led Coalition project of spending cuts. This project was justified as 'living within one's means'. If that sounds ambiguous, then that's because that is ultimately what austerity was and is: a moral decree that one ought to live one's life by not spending more than one has coming in. That this often does not make macroeconomic sense provides the basis for a powerful critique in economic policymaking circles. But, as Chapter 1 shows, those critiques are less helpful in understanding how this political project had a nationalising thrust.

If austerity is the moral decree to live within one's means, then foregrounding that moral narrative is key to seeing its nationalising effects. Austerity also came with an implicit promise to restore the nation after a debt-fuelled moral decline. By restoring to the state and society those British values of prudence and thrift, state and nation were made more congruent. As Chapter 2 shows, the values of the Second World War period were rediscovered as exemplary for these new hard times. This permeated many aspects of everyday life in sometimes unknowing ways, such as consumption choices over what to wear or eat.

This narrative was powerful. However, this power did not derive from the automatic authority of politicians or from the susceptibility of the electorate. Rather, this power comes from the situation and what was being enacted by the state. The Conservative-led Coalition governed as if there was a national emergency: the deficit posed a threat to British life, and if they did not act now, Britain faced a catastrophe in becoming like Greece. The Coalition government between the Conservatives and Lib Dems was publicly justified in terms of a 'great national challenge'. The agreement signed by both parties in May 2010 recognised 'that deficit reduction, and continuing to ensure economic recovery, is the most urgent issue facing Britain'.[57] In Prime Minister David Cameron's speech to announce the agreement, he spoke of how 'at this time of great national challenge, two parties have come together to help make it happen … Let's come together. Let's work, together, in the national interest.' This surprising moment of cooperation invoked wartime – it was indeed the first coalition government since the war.

Whether or not this was truly an emergency or not is, and has been, contested.[58] What is important for our purposes is that austerity was governed through, and justified by, a national emergency. By promising its population that there are not as many resources to go around as before, the state asked that its people come together and act as one in the national interest to resolve an emergency. The aim was to justify the harm this would cause and suppress resistance, but it also mobilised the nation – that is, the imagined community of Britain – in a warlike way: you are with us or against us. In this way, the austerity narrative was nationalising.

Austerity was also nationalising in the way that it stoked social conflict over the distribution of resources. In short, existing conflict over who gets what, when, and how – including struggle over the boundaries of the nation – intensified. If the state governs on the basis that there's not as much to go around and that failing to get spending under control is a matter of national survival, then there are going to be effects. These effects interact with existing patterns of power and privilege. Those with resources – ranging from the tangible, such as wealth, to the intangible, such as whiteness – worry that they will lose out, either by falling down a rung in social status or by losing out to others. People wonder where the money went, and which people – or what types of people, more accurately – took the money. Simmering resentment about (re)distribution from the good times now becomes urgent.

Those groups were deemed a problem. As the sociologist Imogen Tyler has analysed so clearly, the age of austerity was initially characterised by scapegoating and stigmatising imaginary figures such as 'the scrounger', 'the rioter', 'the asylum seeker', 'the Muslim'.[59] This invited increased scrutiny and state intervention for those not deemed 'us', and/or those deemed at fault for Britain's decline or deemed a risk to national renewal; and so the boundaries of 'us' draw in to protect those deemed most worthy of it. Taken together, this was a nationalising move because it legitimised narrowing the formal boundaries of state (re)distribution to those deemed more British, as Chapters 2, 3, and 4 show.

The conflict also developed a populist angle. In addition to making a problem out of, say, 'the immigrant' or 'the troubled family', some elite and privileged groups were also made into a problem through a series of scandals. As Chapter 4 shows, the most important of these were the MPs' expenses scandal, which made a problem of 'the politicians'; the financial crash, which made a problem of 'the bankers'; and tax evasion scandals, which made a problem of 'the wealthy'. These scandals coalesced in public discourse to make a wider problem of 'the elite': a group who are deemed a collective because they interact with one another, play by different rules, and, to an extent, inhabit an alien world. This resonated especially in the context of austerity (because it was evident that the pain was being shared unevenly) and inequality (because disparities in the distribution of income and wealth continued to rise, despite the crash). This gave rise to the political heroes of the initial austerity era: the 'hardworking family', 'squeezed middle', or 'just about managing'. This moral majority were positioned as the groups in need of, and deserving of, protection.

This set the scene for nationalising moves. In the framework introduced above, and unpacked further throughout the book, the goal of nationalism is nationalisation: that is, taking power of a state and moulding its boundaries around a national peoples. This requires mobilisation, in this case, of voters. The most tried-and-tested method of mobilising for nationalisation is by narrating the relatively lowly position or status of the national peoples as the fault of an oppressor – who must be overthrown to restore the rightful power of the national peoples. This sort of situation requires inequality. If the national peoples have no case for being oppressed or powerless, mobilisation is unlikely to work. And so here lies the significance of these post-crash developments, of which austerity was central.

Three nationalisation projects

From this post-crash situation, two or possibly three viable nationalisation projects emerged. Although only one of these projects has been successful, a significant bulk of the decade's political energy has been invested in them. The first project and single success is obvious enough: Brexit. It is evidently nationalising because leaving the European Union ended up redrawing the formal boundaries of economic authority. There are many reasons for its success, but the one the book focuses on is how Eurosceptic elites developed a nationalising narrative that mobilised a unique coalition of voters through concerns over inequalities, including with immigration. By claiming to speak up for the 'left behind', those elites could tell a compelling nationalist story about how leaving the EU would take control back from the so-called metropolitan elite. By betraying the left behind through their pro-immigration and out-of-touch metropolitan values, this metropolitan elite also betrayed whiteness and its links to the British, and especially English, nation. Leaving the

EU was thereby justified as a way of reasserting the status and dignity of hardworking, ordinary, (and white) working classes.[60]

The second is less discussed because it did not work out (yet): Scottish independence – which is a nationalisation project to make a Scottish state for the Scottish people. The book shows that there is a lot to be learned from comparing Scottish independence and Brexit, especially when situated as post-crash nationalisation projects. As with Brexit, Scottish independence depends on inequality to mobilise voters. The inequalities these two projects mobilise, however, as Chapter 5 demonstrates, are very different. The modern Scottish National Party owes its successes first to the dislocation Thatcherism caused to Scotland and the promise of nationalising North Sea oil, and then latterly built on the successes of devolution and the failure of Westminster parties to represent their interests, including support for austerity. Through this period the lure of independence is a promise that life will be better if 'we' are in charge. So although Scotland is hardly a cosmopolitan utopia, Scottish nationalists can politically mobilise masses without recourse to racism. As the book shows, the same cannot be said for Brexit.

There is a potential third nationalising project of this era too: Jeremy Corbyn's Labour Party. Corbyn was able to mobilise through the sense that stagnating growth, low wages, and years of austerity meant that some parts of society were losing out and staying poor as a feature of the system. Labour's job was to rebuild Britain 'for the many, not the few'. The most high-profile policies that were mooted to do this invoked post-war and post-imperial nationalisation, especially in public ownership of key industries such as railways and increased progressive taxes. Although the Corbyn project shifted the terms of political discourse leftwards and provided the left with hope, the project was in hindsight some way away from taking power.

The period between the referendum and leaving the EU was, in turn, sustained through the further morphing of dividing lines. The most important and obvious of these is the line between Remain and Leave, which has given rise to so-called 'culture wars', which are intensified conflict over what the nation should be and who it should represent (see Chapters 5 and 6). The Johnson administration has governed through these divisions to develop a clunky and uneven nationalising agenda: getting Brexit done; 'levelling up' poorer regions, especially those who voted Tory; ending austerity and fiscal discipline; claiming to be governing for 'the awesome foursome' of the UK's constitutive nations; stoking culture wars issues over the moral character of the nation; and, in keeping with Britain's outward-facing traditions, unleashing Britain's potential through policies such as reformed immigration policy and creating freeports. The pandemic continues this story. As Chapter 7 shows, lockdown was full of patriotic gestures and nationalising moves, but is likely to accelerate Britain's break-up.

The approach of the book

We can now finally return to my experience with the automated holographic assistants in Birmingham New Street station. The anecdote serves as both a metaphor and example of social conflict. As an example, it is admittedly pretty trivial. The holograms, it turned out, were removed within weeks, never to be seen again. As a metaphor, however, it shows both how social conflict works or operates – and especially how it feels: that is, to be disenchanted, or even outraged, in a politically meaningful way. In that short experience with the holograms, a lot happened: I identified myself, implicitly or otherwise, with 'the taxpayers', who naturally guard against supposed wasteful use of public money, especially so because of austerity and scarcity; I made contact with a Network Rail employee, something I have never done before or since; in conversation we united against the holograms and whoever put them there; I googled Network Rail and learned about arcane statistical disputes; and then afterwards I told friends and families about it all. In short, the experience made me relate to myself, others, and the nation-state in a different way. But that was dependent on the context.

Imagine a different context, such as 2004 rather than 2014. Had I seen the holograms in 2004, I don't think I would have reacted in the same way. Sure, I may have been frustrated at the possible waste of money, but it would not have been as meaningful, or as *political*. Yet, in both 2004 and 2014, the hologram is the same thing in essence – that is, a three-dimensional image formed by the interference of light beams from a laser. But the experience, the interaction, the *social meaning*, is different. In 2014, we lived in a world defined by a scarcity of resources, both public and private. Writing in 2021, we live a world shaped by 2014, even if those conflicts have evolved.

Experiences – both the hologram and the narrative of the book – cannot be reduced to either economic or cultural factors. Let us consider an alternative starting point for thinking about human experience that does not need a divide between economics and culture: everyone needs to feed, clothe, and shelter themselves and those they care for, and everyone wants to live as full a life as they can, defined in their terms. There are a series of relationships replicated across society (or 'social relations', to use a more conceptual term) that potentially enable those needs. Some of these are interpersonal relations, such as with family or a local community. Some of these are more abstract and distant, but nonetheless made real through flows and processes such as paying tax and other formal nation-state boundaries. And some of these are entirely imaginary, but nonetheless made to feel real through affective ties and hypothetical scenarios, such as the informal boundaries of the nation-state. In that experience with the holograms, I was disgruntled with a distributional outcome. This disgruntlement cannot be understood as either cultural (identity, values, and so on) or economic (such as my material interest in saving money as a taxpayer). This refusal to separate out economic and cultural factors is a spirit that runs through the book.

Likewise, there is nothing intrinsically nationalising or protectionist about this kind of social conflict. Any outcome like that requires politics and, in a democracy like the UK, the mobilisation of voters. This book looks to trace this – and it looks to do so without explaining outcomes through the swing of the pendulum from market to state. The book focuses on state-nation rather than state-market configurations. When doing so, it avoids wherever possible suggesting that there is anything automatic or preordained to changes or evolution in these relations.

This informs the approach taken by the book, of which there are two strands. The first strand could be described as taking an 'everyday' approach.[61] Much of the social conflict relevant to this book takes place over those informal boundaries of the nation: who should be valued and protected, and who is deemed less deserving and therefore more expendable. However, as many examples from the book will show, this conflict is not always participated in knowingly, in an explicitly political manner, or with purposeful deliberation. Conflict over these kind of values can therefore be found in various sources. This includes scandals, which help reveal what a society finds acceptable or not at any particular moment.[62] It also includes political narratives, collective nostalgia, and pop culture, all of which need to resonate with an audience and their values to make sense, including the use of stereotypes. Rather than analyse these as factually misleading or different from the underlying economic reality, the book assumes (and often shows how) they must be meaningful and coherent to work in the context of lived experiences. In doing so, the book analyses parts of everyday life that many may not find intuitively political, but always are, to greater or lesser extent.

The second strand is historical. Much of the conflict of this decade was latent. These battle lines did not just spring out of nowhere during the fallout of the global financial crisis. They typically evolved slowly and dynamically over time, and then accelerated and sometimes twisted in the post-crash era. Being aware of and tracing the historical development of these conflicts is therefore essential to the book's account. Different distributional and/or constitutional settlements will make more sense – and seem more justifiable or urgent – in one period than another. So one needs to trace the context to see what is meaningful at any one time, to see what kind of politics is legitimated. This Introduction has already given a potted history of Britain's state-nation configurations, including its shift from an empire-state-nation to a nation-state. This is expanded throughout the book. So although the book's chapters follow a rough chronology from 2010 to 2020, the questions posed in some of those chapters cannot be satisfactorily addressed without studying the historical development of conflicts.

The structure of the book

The book consists of seven chapters. Taken together, they tell the story of Britain's post-crash nationalisation.

Chapter 1 starts with the initial post-crash austerity era. Although austerity was justified through an economically dubious story of Labour's fiscal irresponsibility, it was also justified through a lesser-told narrative of national renewal. To 'live within means' was also an implicit promise to restore the nation after a debt-fuelled moral decline. This was framed as restoring some of the values associated with Britain's supposed historical glories and national values, thereby making the state more congruent with the nation.

Chapter 2 asks why the glories and values around the Second World War were such a prominent source of inspiration in the initial austerity period. The chapter shows how the nation was mobilised – as in, the informal boundaries of Britishness were made clear, and then people were compelled into policing those boundaries – around a nostalgic and disciplined vision of Britain. This entailed political conflict: rounding on those who refuse to commit to that vision and living within one's means by adequately suppressing their appetites for food, sex, and shopping.

Chapter 3 uses the recent 'hostile environment' changes to the NHS as an exemplar of nationalisation to explore how and why the formal and informal boundaries of British nationhood have been drawn inward. In doing so, the chapter tells the story of post-imperial and post-war British nationhood, its relationship to race and immigration, and the role of the NHS – and how these became problematised in the context of austerity and scarcity.

Chapter 4 shows how a particular meaning of inequality became salient in the post-crash years. Scandals over undeserving poor and rich groups, coupled with new evidence of increasing income and wealth inequality, gave the sense that a majority 'squeezed middle' were suffering and losing out from a rigged system. This imagined hierarchy created the conditions for the racialising 'left behind' representation that helped justify the Brexit project and coalesce its unusual coalition of support – an essential move in the nationalisation process studied in this book.

Chapter 5 compares the two most significant nationalisation projects to emerge from this context: the referendums on Scottish independence and Britain's EU membership. The chapter shows that it is not simply a coincidence that these two key questions of Britain's constitution – Scotland and the EU – became urgent enough for referendums within eighteen months of each other. Both projects were nationalist backlashes against the British state, one from England, the other from Scotland. The chapter explores what an English revolt against the EU through nationalising Britain means.

Chapter 6 analyses the Johnson government's nationalising vision for post-Brexit Britain. By 'unleashing Britain's potential' and 'getting Brexit done', the Johnson government promised national renewal. The chapter shows how post-EU nationalisation differs from post-imperial nationalisation: not as inward-looking in terms of global capitalism as policies such as freeports show, and more divisive through stoking culture wars issues over the moral character of the nation.

Chapter 7 explores how the lockdown in response to the coronavirus interacted with these nationalising moves. The key debate of the initial lockdown period saw the health of the nation pitted against the wealth of the nation, which ended up in unprecedented interventions, such as furloughing, that brought together nation and state. Coupled with displays of patriotism – clapping for carers, and rallying around that classic symbol of post-imperial Britishness, the NHS – one might expect this to be nationalising. Yet the response also further exposed the tensions in Britain's constitutional set-up, pushing it further towards break-up.

1

A nation in debt

*How can you stand there and say you didn't overspend, and didn't
end up bankrupting this country? That is absolutely ludicrous. You're
frankly just lying.*
Audience member, BBC *Question Time* Election Leaders Special,
30 April 2015[1]

Following this angry accusation and telling subsequent applause,
the then Labour leader Ed Miliband nodded, smiled, and hesitated:
'I guess I'm not going to convince you'.

He had a record to defend. Before becoming leader, Miliband
was central to the previous Labour government as a special advisor
and then Cabinet minister. During the *Question Time* special, he
had already tried to persuade the audience over the Labour government's fiscal performance.

In response to an earlier question – 'I've just got a really simple
question: do you accept that when Labour was last in power, they
overspent?' – Miliband stuck to his lines. Schools and hospitals have
been rebuilt. There *was* a financial crisis, and the *real* reason the
UK has a deficit is because of its relatively large financial sector. He
also mentioned that, despite all this, spending *has* got to fall, and
'that's why we will reduce spending'. Given the impassioned response
from the audience member – 'bankrupting this country … absolutely
ludicrous … you're frankly just lying' – it seems Miliband was not
very convincing. Labour, it seemed, had 'overspent'. This may have
just been one moment, one interaction, but it was also the culmination
of a half-decade of political manoeuvres to trap Miliband, Labour,
and, to some extent, the nation. All three ended up ensnared by a
story from which they could not easily escape.

What was this trap? And how was it set? Or, in other words, why was austerity so compelling to so many? And why did people get so upset, angry, and emotional at the prospect of their nation being indebted? Answering these questions is key to understanding the social and political conflict that created the conditions for nationalisation. Doing so, however, requires some significant re-evaluation of the austerity period associated with the Coalition government. The common answer to these questions lies in what many critics have called 'the austerity myth' or 'austerity delusion'.[2] This refers to how the Conservative Party, both in opposition and in coalition government with the Liberal Democrats, consistently reiterated a story that at its most basic went: Labour overspent; the UK is thus indebted and in danger; and so the Conservatives will spend less to reduce the debt, thereby further retrenching the power of the market over the state. Although critics have consistently noted the flaws in the economics of this story, it worked by positioning fiscal consolidation as the only possible path. The myth thereby closed down debate over the issue and misled people into thinking austerity is right and proper. Why this would lead to people investing so much, emotionally, into the issue is, however, not addressed.

By looking back with the benefit of hindsight, I will show that this is a limited way of interpreting this narrative and its impact. To 'live within means' was also presented as way of reversing a national *moral decline*. In rediscovering and repurposing the nation's past, austerity can somewhat surprisingly be a virtue by restoring some of the values associated with supposed historical, national glories. By reconstructing and unpicking the austerity narrative in this way, we can start to understand why austerity was so affecting – as a coherent, meaningful, and powerful narrative that mobilised the nation. In doing so, we can see how a kind of nationalist mobilisation has been bubbling away for the whole of the post-crash period, thereby creating the conditions for nationalisation.

The making of austerity

Before we get to that austerity myth, let us first recall how the Conservatives could position their opponents as fiscally irresponsible because of New Labour's legacy. New Labour's approach to economic policy was, to use political economist Scott Lavery's phrasing, a 'hybrid': it was a composite of Thatcherite economics and social democratic redistribution.[3] With regards to the former, they granted the Bank of England operational independence; introduced fiscal rules to promote sound finances; remained committed to being Europe's flexible labour market; introduced more disciplinary welfare delivery; and promoted the City of London and liberalised finance.[4] With regards to the latter, however, they significantly increased public expenditure, especially on the NHS; developed a range of redistributive social policies, from various tax credits to Sure Start centres; used the public sector to drive job creation in deindustrialised regions; and introduced a minimum wage for the first time.[5] This hybrid model, Lavery argues with the emphasis added, 'was crucial to stabilising British capitalism throughout *this* period'.[6]

In the long run, beyond this period, it proved to be unsustainable. New Labour's electoral success was built on speaking to a coalition of middle-income voters, global capital, and their traditional working-class base. For the first two groups, Labour maintained low inflation (except for house prices), low interest rates, and low (direct) taxes.[7] To reach their base, they boosted public services, especially education and healthcare.[8] To fund those increases in public services without raising the equivalent revenue, Labour started to run a fiscal deficit. Confident that boom and bust was over, and producing optimistic economic forecasts to justify it, this did not pose an immediate problem. In other words, when their presumption of never-ending growth was combined with a commitment to redistribution without headline tax rises, New Labour gave themselves little room for manoeuvre if the economy crashed. To some extent, they trapped themselves.

This came to fruition in the economic downturn caused by the 2008 global financial crisis. The fiscal situation deteriorated. Spotting a once-in-a-generation opportunity, the Conservative Party abandoned their commitment to match Labour's spending, and rebuilt their political strategy around restoring 'fiscal responsibility'. The path was made for austerity. In June 2010, newly installed Chancellor of the Exchequer George Osborne enacted an 'emergency budget'. It combined moderate tax rises with the largest cuts to public spending since the Second World War. 'Fiscal consolidation' is, however, generally considered a risky move. Many economists see it as counterproductive to generating economic growth. In the words of former International Monetary Fund (IMF) Chief Economist Olivier Blanchard, the UK was 'playing with fire'.[9] Why pursue it?

Austerity was a once-in-a-generation chance to strip Labour of their reputation for economic competence. It was classic Conservative statecraft.[10] But it was still 'playing with fire'. And not just with economic growth, but with the livelihoods of people and the Conservatives' own electoral chances. Enact spending cuts too quickly and they risk social breakdown. Phase in spending cuts too slowly to minimise the effect on society and electoral support, and they risk undermining their own argument against the emergency of 'fiscal irresponsibility'.[11] The Coalition government used a number of well-documented techniques to resolve these dilemmas. These included concentrating cuts on unpopular and politically electorally apathetic social groups, delegating cuts to local government, and frontloading cuts to the beginning of the five-year 2010 and 2015 parliamentary cycles. Official economic forecasts in 2010 predicted a swift return to business as usual.[12] Growth would eat away at the budget deficit (since it is measured in relation to GDP) and reduce the need for further spending cuts. With the deficit on the slide and growth restored, the Conservatives would reinforce their reputation on running the economy, dent Labour's record further, and ensure that spending cuts did not dent the social fabric (or their electoral chances) too severely.

This strategy depended on making austerity a necessity. There are very few economic policy choices that are truly necessary. Yet, as many critics have pointed out, austerity was just that: a choice. To make it necessary, austerity was justified as a responsible course of action to avert national catastrophe. The Conservative leadership did this through an ingenious narrative, which is what critics refer to as the myth of austerity. We can reconstruct this using excerpts from key speeches of the period.

This story starts with how the previous Labour government 'bankrupted our country, [and] left a legacy of debts and cuts'.[13] Consequently, 'everybody knows that Labour's Debt Crisis means public spending cuts'.[14] Blaming Labour was aided through a folksy analogy between state and household. Austerity makes sense, in these terms, because we should always fix the roof even if the sun is shining. Since Labour in effect 'borrowed and borrowed and borrowed on our nation's credit card',[15] the Conservatives will make sure Britain starts 'living within our means'. Because:

> This is what households up and down the country do. When people get a pay rise, they don't go and spend it all at once and then go to the bank manager asking for more money. They spend some – and put some aside in the kitty. We should expect the same from government.[16]

Fiscal stimulus – one of the key Keynesian policy tools during a recession – is presented as 'merely extending an overdraft'.[17] The risks of not dealing with these debts is clear:

> Today, the British state is borrowing one pound for every four it spends. Our Budget deficit is set to overtake Greece. If we don't deal with this, there will be no growth, there will be no recovery.[18]

To avoid being like an indebted household, and to avoid the disorder seen in Greece, austerity is made the only solution. To accept the terms of the narrative is to accept the terms of the solution.

This narrative was hugely influential. Research has demonstrated that almost every newspaper endorsed austerity.[19] Other research, meanwhile, has highlighted how this kind of narrative is influential in making austerity popular.[20] This is reflected in public opinion polling. YouGov tracked public opinion on austerity from 2010 to 2015 through asking a monthly panel of respondents a variation on the question 'Thinking about the way the government is cutting spending to reduce the government's deficit, do you think this is …'.[21] The survey shows that Labour were the most blamed during the first five years of fiscal consolidation (with 30–50 per cent of respondents blaming Labour over the five-year period). Only around 30 per cent of people blamed the Conservative government – *the government that explicitly introduced and implemented spending cuts* – for the spending cuts in question. A second question, meanwhile, shows that a majority of the British population believed that spending cuts to reduce the government's deficit was 'necessary' (50–60 per cent of respondents answered 'necessary' over the five-year period). One may believe that a policy is unfair and harmful, but the political force of these feelings will likely be negated if one also believes the policy is necessary.

The Labour government had nowhere to go. Given that their electoral success was built on promising no direct tax increases, their position inevitably became austerity-lite. The final Labour government Budget of March 2010 set out proposals to reduce the structural budget deficit over a five-year horizon through cuts worth £11 billion (which was ironically less than was actually cut by the Coalition government).[22] Austerity-lite remained Labour's approach until Miliband stepped down as leader after the general election defeat in 2015. A 2010 memo by Miliband pollster James Morris, later leaked in 2015, claimed that: 'A Labour leader who argues that we should keep spending to secure growth is flying in the face of common sense and would need a *volte face* by the entire media to have a chance of success.'[23] And in Labour Party focus groups during the 2015 election campaign, participants were highly critical of Labour's perceived overspending, with some participants demanding an official apology.[24] The narrative worked.

The meaning of overspending

It is no wonder, then, that so many austerity critiques have focused on busting the austerity myth. Critiques at that time demonstrated how austerity is a flawed idea: it severely misdiagnoses the problem to be fixed, has no substantive theoretical underpinning, and has never worked in the global conditions of the time.[25] While these critiques were and are essential – voters require information and know-how in order to make choices, scholars have an obligation to ensure that this information is not misleading – one can see, with the benefit of hindsight, that they were also technocratic. Reading back through these criticisms of the austerity myth, there is sometimes a sense that once the battle over ideas was inevitably won, everyone would come to see the truth that fiscal consolidation is flawed. The political change in direction away from austerity would thus organically follow. In hindsight it was somewhat more complex than that.

The simplest reminder of this is to return to the accusation thrown at Miliband at the beginning of the chapter: 'How can you stand there and say you didn't overspend, and didn't end up bankrupting this country? That is absolutely ludicrous. You're frankly just lying.' The key claim from the audience member is that the Labour government *overspent*. This is not a technical macroeconomic argument; rather the claim that Labour 'overspent' is also a simple and moral one. *You overspent.* You do not get more simple than spending more than you can afford. Or so it seems. Because 'more than you can afford' already muddies this simple message. It is contextual; it depends. To accuse someone of *overspending* is not just an economic claim that can be empirically adjudicated or not.[26] It is closer to an accusation of bad behaviour.

To see how, imagine two households: one that is poorer and one that is wealthier. Both usually stick to a monthly budget. Take the poorer household. They do not have the capacity to save each month. So, when their boiler breaks down and they must replace it to ensure continued hot water and heating, they must pay for the replacement and associated labour using their credit card – thereby borrowing money that they cannot afford to repay and disrupting their carefully planned budgeting. Now imagine the wealthier household. They usually save a significant portion of their monthly ingoings, but who, this month, impulsively buy an unbudgeted luxury item. They can easily afford the item, but as a result they do not save as much as they intended to that month, thereby failing to meet their targets for saving. Both of these households have exceeded their budgets. But which of those two households would you feel more comfortable accusing – because it is an accusation – of *overspending* that month?

To say 'you have overspent' is not *just* an economic statement about the imbalance of expenditure over income in a particular period. It is also a moral and political statement about the *rightfulness* of that imbalance, in the context of who gets what, when, and how. We are often tempted to make a distinction between an underlying economic reality of numbers and money, and then a cultural discourse full of meaning that sits on top of that. Yet this relationship between economy and culture, material or meaning, or however we wish to put it, does not operate like that. In the abstract the distinction may seem clear, but they cannot be meaningfully separated in real life.

Overspending is seen as bad because living beyond one's means leads to debt. And debt is be avoided. For formal debt, there is an infrastructure made up of financial institutions, enforcement agencies, and the legal system that enforces repayment.[27] Yet debt is central to our ideas of right and wrong – and vice versa, right and wrong is central to our ideas of debt – because of its wider meaning and history. Understood as something broader than formal credit instruments, debt is navigated through popular wisdom that highlights the importance of always living within one's means and to always honour one's debts: if you borrow the money, you have to pay it back. Consider, for example, the criminal who is prosecuted and imprisoned on the basis of 'paying their debt back to society'. Anthropologists have shown that these relations of debt – and with it, the notion that debt is bad – have an 'astonishing consistency' across time and space.[28]

Debt is essentially a relationship of inequality. Debt is defined by a situation in which two parties are made unequal in some way, whether that inequality is in material means (such as lending money) or moral standing (such as the stigma generated by committing an unjust or harmful act). Yet within this inequality always lies the possibility for equality being restored, because a debt must be in principle payable or forgivable. At the point of repayment, the relationship is ended and the debtor is freed. As David Graeber put it, '[i]f there was no conceivable way to salvage the situation, we wouldn't be calling it a "debt"'.[29] For example, many religions imagine that human life is indebted to ancestors and deities – the ultimate favour, perhaps – which must be repaid through leading a good life or through performing special rituals. On this basis, it is unsurprising that being indebted is seen as a situation to avoid. For it is to enter a fundamentally hierarchical relationship in which the power of the debtor is diminished in some way, and violence on behalf of the creditor can and has been justified in lieu of repayment.[30]

Some scholars have even argued that debt is a foundation to our most basic moral thinking. For linguist George Lakoff, morality often takes place through a metaphor of accounting: if you do something good for me, then I owe you something because I am in your debt, and vice versa.[31] This morality manifests itself in language. Famously, the German word *schuld* means both 'debt' and 'guilt'.[32] And in English we speak of 'forgiving' a debt or 'making good' by fulfilling a promise or repaying a debt. To be moral is to be responsible. This kind of morality is reflected in popular wisdom about debt: avoid accruing debts one cannot payback, to live within means is the right way to act, and that to needlessly go into debt is a moral failing.

To argue 'you have overspent' is both a moral and economic statement. Busting the austerity myth, which incorporates this kind of argument, was an urgent political task in showing how austerity was politically constructed as a necessity. However, a decade down the line, with this period of austerity all but over, this task is less important. We push further, and continue to look back and look to deepen our understanding of how this narrative worked – why Miliband got trapped, and how, in turn, this created the conditions for nationalisation.

When one thinks about it, it is rather obvious that myths are not supposed to be true or scientifically robust. After all, myths often serve a purpose. They can, for instance, tie together otherwise unconnected people across space and time, thereby providing sense and coherence to the experience of daily life. To understand *how* myths work therefore requires analysing them not just at something rational and technical, but also as emotional and social in character. The way in which we interact with people, environments, and objects often *does* something to us, stirs something in us, gives a feeling or experience that 'sticks' (like the holograms discussed in the Introduction).[33] This helps explain those feelings of togetherness that one might experience when getting carried away in the crowd at a football match, or the feeling when everyone goes quiet and looks at you if you accidentally break a glass in a pub.[34] These feelings of togetherness operate at a national level, whereby complete strangers can feel united through the imagined community of nationhood.

By approaching the austerity myth in these terms, we can build further on our observations about debt and morality to interpret and reconstruct the austerity myth differently. To do so requires starting our chronology a little before the move to austerity with the subprime crash. As we will see, the popular narratives of the subprime crisis and austerity share a number of key features that add up into an arc larger than both. They are both stories of excess and piling up of debt in the good times, and then coming to terms with shame over indebtedness and its effects when the good times end. They are both stories about the past, present, and future of the nation, but in contrasting ways. By participating and buying into these stories, the national peoples are invited to unite together, whereby austerity is justified, arresting a sense of moral national decline and shame. By living within our means, the nation could rediscover itself.

Subprime bastards

Our starting point is the subprime crash. One of the popular narratives of that time can be unpicked via the following excerpt from a televised comedy stand-up from 2009, by entertainer Patrick Kielty:

> At least we know, folks, that it's not our fault. No, no. It's these subprime bastards. I was trying to think who they were the other night, as I sat on my DFS sofa that I haven't paid off for three years, looking at my 54-inch plasma television on interest-free credit, [etc.] and I thought, 'Who are these subprime bastards?' It's us! We are subprime. It's like Spartacus meets Ocean Finance. Nobody wants to admit, do we? 'I'm not subprime', 'I'm not subprime!', 'I'm not subprime'. You are, IT'S US![35]

This is an ironic take on popular responses to the subprime crash. The excerpt's tension reflects the public atmosphere at the time: between the instinct to look for scapegoats to blame for the subprime crisis (and for resulting falling house prices and the associated potential loss of wealth) with the acknowledgement that this was a game that many people played and benefited from. During the boom years, many Britons used unsecured credit and the promise of ever-rising house prices to build wealth or otherwise meet living standards in the context of stagnating wages. This fostered the expectation that homeownership was the route to the good life.[36]

This expansion of finance and homeownership was explicitly built into the political economy of New Labour. New Labour pursued so-called 'asset-based welfare' as part of their wider regime of low inflation, low interest rates, and low (direct) taxes.[37] Asset-based welfare involves reducing the costs of the welfare state by delegating some of its 'piggy bank' function to the individual by encouraging them to develop future flows of income and wealth through personal investment (e.g. in housing, especially via owner-occupation).[38] Politically, this entailed support for the housing markets and the financial system that underpins it, and a series of schemes designed to help the public with their financial and saving goals.[39] At its best, this policy is win–win for states *and* households: a responsible household that lives within its means to invest in property for an asset-based 'pension' help themselves, but also relieve state financing of pensions and elderly care pressures.[40]

A number of socio-economic conditions made this expansion possible. So-called financial innovations such as 'collaterised debt obligations' transformed household lending. These processes allowed banks to pass on the risks of mortgage lending by taking vast pools of securities and selling shares of the mortgage and interest payment streams to investors around the world, while simultaneously refreshing capital for more loans.[41] This transformation famously underpinned the US subprime mortgage market. It also made possible 125 per cent mortgages in the UK, which were emblematic of Britain's own housing boom.[42] With the housing market seemingly only going up, many people's life chances became intertwined with it. That home-ownership became more like an investment opportunity had political implications. The greater number of homeowners, the greater the potential constituency of voters whose interests became aligned with policies that promised low inflation (except for housing), low interest rates, and low taxes.[43] In a world in which there would supposedly be 'no return to the old boom and bust', this all made a lot of sense.

This world was shocked by the 'credit crunch' in 2008. The credit crunch itself had two elements: the seizing up of the interbank lending system caused by a panic and then crash in subprime financial products that spread through global finance; and the subsequent impact upon the credit conditions for households and businesses and therefore 'the economy' itself. This process was reported by the media in melodramatic and personalised ways. This was typified by one of Jeremy Paxman's introductions to *Newsnight*: 'Today, stock markets *across* the world *tumbled – imploded* – continued to *collapse* like deflated *dirigibles*' – a genre of sensationalised reporting that was satirised by comedian Charlie Brooker as 'moneygeddon'.[44] In a world in which the problem of boom and bust had been proclaimed by the Chancellor and then prime minister to be solved, this was a shock.

The crash deflated house prices, thereby threatening the wealth of many. In making sense of this and any shock, we tell stories to recreate stability and apportion blame.[45] During the fallout from subprime, one key kind of story focused on personal responsibility for the immoral behaviour in lending and borrowing. These focused on the individuals involved: the lenders and the borrowers. Many stories of that time focused on how mis-sold mortgages had led to more debt and increasing difficulties in making ends meet, thus, as political economist Matthew Watson puts it, 'shattering illusions of the wealth that was to be unlocked by trading up on the housing market'.[46] The figures of the 'greedy banker' and 'irresponsible borrower' were contrasted with the helpless homeowner victims of the crash, who were presented as being swept up in a financial tsunami.[47]

This sense of shock was reflected in some research I conducted in 2012. I was interested in how members of the public discussed austerity, so conducted a series of group interviews to find out.[48] Many participants identified 2008 as a turning point; the nation was turning away from a period of credit-fuelled profligacy.[49] Memorably, one discussion made a distinction between the pre-crisis era in which the UK was caught on a 'hamster wheel', consuming beyond its means through 'finance up to our eyeballs'. In this past, there was a 'feeling that anything you wanted you could go out and buy', but now that it was 'much better to go back to the way I was brought up which was you don't buy anything until you could afford to buy it within reason'.[50] Finance-and-credit-fuelled consumption – what could be called *overspending* in the terms outlined above – was a game that nearly everyone played, especially homeowners. It was normal. The crash upset those appearances.

This is the wider affective atmosphere in which Kielty tells his audience that we are all 'subprime bastards'. However, the 'us' in the sketch is ambiguous. Beyond the immediate audience in the theatre, there are two versions of 'us' that we can tease out. The first 'us' is the 'we' of the responsible borrowers, who were positioned as the hapless victims of a financial tsunami triggered by some bad borrowers and unscrupulous lenders. This 'us' is generally invited to feel anger at the bad apples who have wrecked the game through their immoral behaviour, thereby ruining it for those who played by the rules and in the right spirit. The second 'us', however, is a larger group still, and incorporates everyone who played that game. Kielty's skit questions the hypocrisy of making a boundary between 'responsible' (or 'good') borrowers and 'irresponsible' (or 'bad') borrowers, thereby implying an unease with that first conception of 'us'. When he tells his audience that 'We are subprime bastards', they respond with laughter rather than hostility and quizzical looks; he captures the atmosphere. Rather than inviting 'us' to feel anger, this 'us' invites us to feel shame.

Shame is a feeling made through interaction. As feminist theorist Sara Ahmed puts so clearly, shame is a feeling of distress or humiliation regarding foolish actions – 'an intense and painful sensation that is bound up with how the self feels about itself'.[51] Although shame can refer to a secretive act that no one else knows about, it is a feeling that is typically produced by the potential for that act to be revealed to others. Shame is not necessarily a feeling that emerges from direct interaction or accusation ('I shame you!'); rather, it is a feeling that works in part on the *potential* of such an interaction, based on a mark of disgrace or stigma from failing to meet up to expectations.[52] In the context of the subprime crash, everyone is exposed, being looked at – we are all subprime bastards. This shame is related to a sense that now that the tide has gone out, we can see that almost everyone, ourselves included, was swimming naked. This is where the humour of the sketch lies. To be collectively exposed is a release, the laughter perhaps emerging from recognition.

The 'subprime bastards' sketch invites an ironic and collective shame. By claiming that we are all subprime bastards, we are invited to face up to the fact that 'we' – the nation – all face shame, and that the people should in some sense repent for pre-crisis excesses. As one group of scholars put it, the UK 'found a new affective register with the financial crisis: the invocation of public and personal shame'.[53] One of my research participants memorably shared a similar sentiment:

> The whole thing just exploded from nothing really. We're just reaping what we sowed before, and everyone benefitted because they've all bought the conservatories, the car, they've all had a new settee … Everything just exploded and now we're back to how it should have been in the first place. We're back to where we should have been ten years ago.[54]

The participant is invoking the finance-as-the-route-to-the-good-life game discussed above. The shame surrounding that game is not necessarily found in revealing how certain individuals cheated in one way or another. Nor is it that the entire game is crooked. Rather, in the case of pre-crash excess, it can also be found in the sense that there was something wrong in the relationship between the game and its players. If almost *all* the recent players of a game have been playing it in an immoral fashion then the problem perhaps lies in a waning of the spirit or morality of the game. And so that game – the game that nearly all in the nation plays – should lose its *loose* and *excessive* qualities, and instead become *stricter* and *restrained*. Part of this is changing the culture to ensure that individuals take more personal responsibility for their actions. This way of 'assuming personal responsibility for the proper operation of economic order' is what political economist Martijn Konings has named 'the spirit of austerity'.[55]

Mobilising the nation

By 2010, stories of state indebtedness had supplemented subprime. Enter the austerity myth. The way this myth resonated with the atmosphere of subprime is evident in hindsight. Consider this excerpt from the David Cameron speech that marked the Coalition governing agreement, where he is outlining his vision for Britain:

> [A] people that believe in themselves. A Britain that believes in itself. [...] At this time of great national challenge, two parties have come together to help make it happen. [...] Your country needs you. And it takes two. It takes two to build that strong economy. We'll balance the budget, we'll boost enterprise, but you start those businesses that lead us to growth. It takes two to build that big society. We'll reform those public services, we'll devolve power, but you step forward and seize that opportunity. I know the British people and they are not passengers – they are drivers. [...] So come on: let's pull together. Let's come together. Let's work, together, in the national interest.

There is a lot going on here. Cameron is reassuring Conservative voters who may be worried that they are working with another party. Perhaps he is trying to give a sense of occasion to the first coalition British government in decades. However, it is the part about needing to 'work, together, in the national interest' that I would like to pick up.

Cameron draws parallels between opposing political parties forming a coalition and the need for the nation to do something similar. The coalition agreement can be taken as a model of the kind of benevolent action required 'at this time of great national challenge'. Cameron talks of the British people as drivers and not passengers, and so implores the nation to 'come on: let's pull together' in order to 'build that strong economy ... balance the budget'. In doing so, Cameron invites us to make a link between a balanced budget and the British national character. It is implied that to have an unbalanced budget is linked to a decline in national character.

Viewed through this lens, the austerity narrative has a similar arc to the subprime narrative looked at above. The basic narrative arc is like this: *Before 2008, we lived in a world of excess fuelled by credit; but the bubble has burst and that game is over; so we must hold those that are to blame to account; while we must now start to live within our means.* Crucially, when put in these terms, *the basic narrative works for both the subprime and austerity.* Like the subprime narrative, the austerity narrative invokes a twin 'us' in relation to feelings of shame. The first 'us', like in the subprime story, are the responsible ones, who are hapless victims. Instead of borrowers, however, this is a hardworking and taxpaying 'us', who are invited to feel anger at the New Labour government that overspent, the local councils that wasted money, and the undeserving others (both rich and poor) who received handouts. As Chapters 2, 3, and 4 show, we are invited to expose and shame these others. The second 'us', as before, is also a larger group that possibly incorporates everyone. The indebted nation is in some senses something that all of the nation is responsible for.

This equivalence between the stories – and the way they both invoke the nation in different ways – is central to the cultural politics of the period. And it was something that Cameron himself invoked, even as far back as 2008 when referring to Gordon Brown's economic record:

> Who was it who presided over a debt-fuelled boom and never called time on it? Who was it who spent and spent and borrowed and borrowed and gave us that massive budget deficit? And who was it who said that he and he alone had rewritten the laws of economics to end boom and bust?

The equivalence between the subprime crash and austerity is clear: treating the finances of states and households as equivalent is typically criticised as misleading, economically invalid, and therefore problematic. Rather than just mythbust this 'household analogy', we can also offer a supplementary analysis that highlights what is hiding in plain view: an affecting narrative that is coherent and consistent in *moral* – and *nationalising* – terms.

While the equivalence between household and state finances is nonsense in a macroeconomic way, the equivalence makes sense in a moral way. The equivalence is part of a consistent story about how the nation – represented by both the state and by households – bought into a feeling of optimism and thus partly lived through credit, and so must now relearn how to live within its means now the good times are over. Taken together, the subprime and austerity narratives give sense to an atmosphere of ambiguous moral decline: we were all irresponsible and spendthrift, and now we must all pay the price. This was typified by Conservative MP Caroline Spelman who, in a BBC *Question Time* appearance, claimed that 'thrift' is an appropriate economic policy for both the state and households: 'lets call it thrift then because thrift is a virtue and thrift needs to be part of the solution to our nation's problems [...] thrift is living within your means'.[56] Living within means therefore becomes a way of restoring national pride, of arresting a morale decline. Austerity becomes restorative. This is, in part, what austerity means. This captures the atmosphere of the times.

Within Cameron's comments a national ideal is invoked. Britons are 'not passengers', they are 'drivers', who will 'seize the opportunity' to 'balance the books'. This kind of idealisation is a central part of shame, whether that is on a personal or national level.[57] Shame is always related to something more 'positive' – as in an ideal to be striven for, even if those expectations of good behaviour have not been lived up to.[58] As Ahmed puts it in general terms:

> By witnessing what is shameful about the past, the nation can 'live up to' the ideals that secure its identity or being in the present. In other words, our shame means that we mean well, and can work to reproduce the nation as an ideal.

Shame thus becomes a moment for rediscovering and reinventing the national ideal, in a way that can be 'positive'. By tackling this shame, by living within our means, Britain can reassert its identity as a nation. Austerity becomes the story of national recovery – not necessarily just economic recovery, but also moral recovery from a spoiled national identity; spoiled following the debt-fuelled excesses being exposed. To rediscover those lost ideals, the nation can look to the past.

The equivalence between households and states can be interpreted in this context. As the Introduction touched on, the post-war and post-imperial nationalisation project involved a turn inward, especially economically. This was matched with what David Edgerton characterises as the rise of the British nation – the boundaries of the British state and of the British nation were made more congruent. The British state governed a national economy for a national community. Thatcher and then New Labour oriented more outwardly. The national economy was increasingly displaced by an imagined global economy; and the community of national peoples were governed instead as a population of economic actors and their families.[59] Although the trope of the national household that needs to balance its book is hardly new, in this case it came with a nationalising logic. Global competitiveness was still important in this post-2008 age of austerity, but it was now accompanied with – if not superseded by – a fiscal conservativism and the ideal of the prudent public household. The prudent public household in need of balancing the books invites the nation to work together in the national interest in response to the debt emergency. The austerity narrative therefore mobilises the nation.

We often make analogies with the past to make sense of the present, to twist history and make it into something new. The key historical analogy in this period was the Second World War and the five-or-so-year period after it that is typically referred to as 'austerity Britain'.[60] This was when post-imperial Britain was born and made. It was also when Britain made collective sacrifices to live within its means. As we will see in Chapter 2, this ideal of living within means was made sense of and reproduced through the collective memory of wartime Britain – including the rise of so-called 'austerity chic', the trend for thrifty pastimes such as baking and allotments, and the cult of the Keep Calm and Carry On poster.[61] These histories provided an ideal for a shamed nation to return to. To live within one's means is to commit to this recovery of the British identity, to show one's love for one's country. In this light, we can start to see a different side to Cameron's speech that may be controversial or uncomfortable: it is about goodness, about hope, and possibly even about a *love* for and of the nation – to start living within means after a period of excess is a way that Britain can rediscover and remake itself.

We must not overstate the good feelings, as there were many bad feelings too. For this kind of mobilisation also produces conflict. This ideal to strive for is, in Konings's words, simultaneously 'a demand for a particular kind of moral order'.[62] It compels the population to see who is with or against the nation, who is willing to reap what they've sowed, and who is willing to make sacrifices. This process tends to generate bad feelings of anger and disgust at those deemed against the people. The practical past of post-war austerity Britain also has a dark side as an ideal, or something to strive for. For that imagined nation of the past is one organised along particular gendered and racialised lines: a nuclear, heterosexual family; and a whiter national community, before it got 'swamped' by Asian and Black people, whose very presence and practices are said to fray the social ties that make Britain what it is.

Conclusion

To conclude, we can return to the BBC *Question Time* Election Leaders Special in April 2015. Before Miliband got grilled on his party's overspending, Cameron was still rocking his classics. At that debate, and at many other campaigning events during that election, Cameron routinely reached into his jacket pocket to reveal audiences his favourite prop: the letter left by Labour MP and the then Chief Secretary to the Treasury, Liam Byrne, to his successor in 2010. The letter reads: 'Dear Chief Secretary, I am afraid there is no money. Kind regards – and good luck!' Even in 2015 the letter remained an artefact in the battle over austerity. For some, it represents the flippant and reckless character of the New Labour government, and even their lack of love for their country.

The way in which the note continued to resurface – especially during the 2015 election, where many had wrongly predicted that austerity would not be relevant – appeared to be genuinely traumatic to Byrne. In an article for the *Guardian* in the lead up to 2015 general election, he issued an astonishingly contrite and emotional apology. Below is an excerpt, to which I have emphasised the affecting language:

> I am *so sorry*. David Cameron's daily flourish of my leaving note at the Treasury helped hurt the party I *love*. And offered sheer *offence* to so many of the people we want the chance to serve. [...] [M]embers of the public ask: 'How could you do something so *crass*? And so bloody *offensive*?' [...] I've asked myself that question every day for five years and believe me, every day I have *burnt* with the *shame* of it. Yet 'the note' was not just *stupid*. It was *offensive*. That's why it has made so many people so *angry*. And that is why it was so wrong to write. People's *anger* – and my party's *anger* – at me, will never ever match my *anger with myself* or my *remorse* at such a *crass* mistake. I made it easy for our opponents to *bash* our economic record by *bashing me*. And for millions of people and businesses who have had to make such *sacrifices* over the last five years, there was *nothing funny* about the national debt when the national task of cutting it has brought them such *pain* in their everyday life.[63]

The austerity narrative is affecting and powerful. As Byrne's note and Miliband's struggle indicate, this narrative affected how people related to themselves, to others, and to the nation-state.

Yet seeing the narrative in this way – including its nationalising effects – has required a retelling of the post-crash austerity era. The dominant accounts of that period analyse the narrative through a technical, macroeconomic lens. The result is those critiques that unpick the austerity 'delusion' or 'myth' so effectively. Instead, this chapter has looked at this narrative through an emotional and moral lens, analysing how the narrative was able to capture the atmosphere and give sense to the shock of disturbed normal appearances. The retold narrative is simple enough. It told a story of renewal following moral national decline: the nation should be shameful for becoming so indebted through living excessively; and so the nation should restore its ideal self by looking back to the past when 'we' lived within our means. This shows how a kind of nationalist mobilisation has been bubbling away for the whole of the post-crash period, thereby creating the conditions for nationalisation.

This created a trap for the Labour Party, including Miliband and Byrne. It also trapped the nation. This enforced scarcity and austerity – including the constant public iteration of there not being enough, of living within means – leads to intensified, twisted, and new conflict over resource distribution. Austerity invites all to take an emotional investment in the fiscal health of the country. Since all politics is fiscal – there is no political phenomena that is not touched by state regulation or redistribution – this investment reaches into all aspects of life, stoking conflict over who gets what, when, and how. As we will see in Chapters 2, 3, and 4, this includes the formal and informal boundaries of the nation.

2

Nostalgic visions

Philip Hollobone, the Conservative backbench MP for Kettering, is noted for making a high number of short and sometimes irrelevant speeches in Parliament. This is apparently to improve his parliamentary participation stats on websites such as theyworkforyou. com, where even the briefest comment is classified as a 'speech'.[1]

His contribution, in January 2017, when the House of Commons met for Question Time with the Department for Environment, Food & Rural Affairs, is best situated in this oeuvre. Before MPs had the chance to debate flood defence schemes and hill farmers, a Labour MP asked minister George Eustice a question about how the state measures household food insecurity. Up steps Hollobone. His contribution, which had no direct relevance to the question, pondered whether poor families experiencing food insecurity can learn from the Second World War:

> Food insecurity is a terrible thing, and it is exacerbated by low-income households spending too much on food that is not good for them. During the war, the wartime generation knew how to manage on a very tight budget, and nutrition actually improved for most households, including the very poorest. Could we learn some lessons from the wartime generation about how best to feed our people?

The 'speech' was picked up by the press. Left-wing tabloid newspaper the *Mirror* reported the comments as emblematic of the way in which the Conservative Party fails to take food insecurity seriously – which, for the paper, is ironic, given the government's 'punitive welfare reform policies'.[2]

I am interested in a different aspect of these comments: analysing how it is coherent to respond to the problem of poverty and food insecurity by referencing war. Hollobone is not alone in looking back to the Second World War fondly. Yet let us not take this coherence for granted. Consider for a moment if Hollobone had instead drawn on, say, the history of the Anglo–Turkish War of 1807–09 to imply a new scheme for how pensioners can stay adequately warm in the cold winter months. Instead of sticking like the Second World War comparison, those comments would likely fly past its audience, detached and meaningless, and disappear into the ether. But the Second World War analogies stick. Why is that? What makes those analogies and wider nostalgia for that period an intelligible response to this issue? In this chapter, I unpick the web of meaning that not only catches these analogies, but makes them stick. The purpose of this is to build on the analysis in the previous chapter to show how the austerity narrative and wider scarcity of resources intensified social conflict, thereby creating the conditions for nationalisation. In Chapter 1, we saw that austerity is made compelling and desirable through positioning it as a national good, with living within one's means as a way of reversing a moral decline.

This chapter develops this analysis in several ways. It shows how that conflict can be quite subtle and insidious, reaching into many aspects of life (such as food and eating) and with unwitting participation. For the nation to live within its means requires greater discipline, especially when individual consumption poses risks to the prudent public household. This invites the nation to shame those who don't live within their means. Conflict therefore includes moves to show that one's desires – for food, sex, shopping – are the right kind (thrifty and safe) rather than the wrong kind (greedy and dangerous), thereby including oneself in the informal boundaries of Britain and thus able to benefit from its wealth. One explanation for the meaning of war analogies, therefore, is that it provides a fantasy about a past when discipline was enforced and appetites were suppressed for the national good. The Second World War not only takes Britain back to when it was great, but also to its birth in its modern, post-imperial form. Even though this conflict centres on desire, morality, and national nostalgia (ostensibly 'culture'), these battles are shifting the wider values on which decisions and outcomes over resource distribution (ostensibly 'economic') are justified and made intelligible. This process is nationalising, insofar as the British state should regulate and distribute resources in a more British, warlike way.

Scandals of the appetite

In this chapter, I look at three types of desire: for sex, for food, and for shopping. This analysis is inspired by queer theorist Lauren Berlant's work on 'scandals of the appetite'.[3] Berlant observes how food, sex, and shopping have been made into 'sites of moral disapprobation, social policy, and self-medication'. In other words, in the disillusionment and hardship of modern capitalism, the promised good life of wealth and happiness is (apparently) just around the corner – until then, people do what they can with their freedom to get by and live some sort of good life.

These excessive appetites can become a problem for the state, to the extent that the population's health is at risk, at great cost, meaning that state intervention is deemed necessary. This problem becomes more severe in times of austerity and scarcity, when the prudent public household needs everyone to live within their means so that it can, itself, live within its means – shorn of the high health costs for treating the medical issues of the obese, or providing resources for those who step outside the norms of the heteronormative family, or supporting those who 'decide' to have children without the resources to do so. By not living within their means, these imagined figures become the target of conflict over scarce resources and, to apply a term retrospectively, a kind of proto-culture war over who the nation should be for and who should have access to its wealth.

Following Hollobone, we start with food. Food is a key resource: everyone needs access to it. In the UK, most food is allocated through markets. This is an efficient system – most people do not even think of accessing food as an issue. However, the system is dependent upon people having the prior resources (i.e. money) to meet those needs. Even so, it is unusual for the British state to directly feed its population unless formally institutionalised (e.g. in a hospital). As we will see, what to eat and access to food was a key site of conflict in the initial austerity years. Yet, before the crash, there was as much concern over the problem of *over*consumption.

Unsurprisingly, obesity has been interpreted as a failing of choice and therefore of personal responsibility and control – and governed as such.[4] This has meant that, come austerity, those who are overweight have been targeted by spending cuts or discipline, including withholding NHS treatment and welfare payments. For example, research by the Royal College of Surgeons (RCS) found that over one in three Clinical Commissioning Groups in England are denying routine surgery – including hip and knee replacements – to patients who exceed a certain body mass index, until they lose weight.[5] The RCS concluded that overweight patients are becoming soft targets for enforced NHS savings. In 2015, David Cameron proposed plans to withhold sickness benefits from overweight people if they refuse to participate in weight-reduction programmes: 'It is not fair to ask hardworking taxpayers to fund the benefits of people who refuse to accept the support and treatment that could help them get back to a life of work.'[6] Similarly, the then Work and Pensions Secretary Iain Duncan Smith asked his department to investigate the possibility of putting obese benefit claimants on the Cambridge Weight Plan – a liquids-only all-encompassing Total Diet Replacement scheme that costs from around £2.40 per meal.[7]

However, in the age of austerity, the problem of overconsumption was supplanted by the problem of underconsumption. While it would not be accurate to say that there was a scarcity of food, many more people have gone hungry since the global financial crisis due to not being able to afford adequately nutritious food. Thus the rise of food aid. Food banks, especially those organised through The Trussell Trust, have become standardised on a national scale and embedded within evolving patterns of welfare provision.[8] In March 2010, The Trussell Trust organised 54 food banks; by April 2012 there were 201; and by April 2018 there were 428.[9] Between 1 April 2017 and 31 March 2018, their foodbank network distributed 1,332,952 three-day emergency food packages, compared to 128,697 in 2011–12.[10]

Food banks are supposed to be for 'emergencies'.[11] The Trussel Trust only provide recipients with up to three food parcels for the duration of a 'crisis situation'; those recipients must be referred through frontline service providers in the local community to receive a parcel. This is seen as crucial in maintaining the sustainability and legitimacy of the scheme.[12] By ensuring the mechanisms of eligibility are controlled by long-term service providers, food bank operators avoid having to make decisions about the deservingness of potential recipients; and by only providing food in emergency situations, they avoid creating long-term and permanent relationships with recipients and so can still credibly hold public service providers to account.[13]

Food bank users are often positioned as having made poor choices, or otherwise having failed. For example, the then Minster of State in the Department for Work and Pensions, Esther McVey, rode into a rowdy parliamentary debate on food banks with the following:

> Labour left the UK with the highest structural deficit of any major advanced country. That whirl of living beyond our means – that increase in prices, debt and unaffordability – had to come to a stop. It came to a stop suddenly and, sadly, we are all paying the price. The Government are paying the price, charities are paying the price, businesses are paying the price and individuals are paying the price as we try to balance not only our household budgets, but the budget of the country ... Let us be honest. The Trussell Trust saw what was happening in 2000. It looked at the evolving problem that was caused by personal debt, overspending and people living beyond their means.[14]

Similarly, outrage erupted over comments by Baroness Anne Jenkin, a member of the inquiry team at the all-party parliamentary group on hunger and food poverty. At the launch of a report entitled *Feeding Britain*, Jenkin claimed that some people in Britain were going hungry because they don't know how to cook: 'We have lost a lot of our cooking skills, and poor people don't know how to cook. I had a large bowl of porridge today. It cost 4p. A large bowl of sugary cereal will cost 25p'.[15]

This emphasis on poor choices reproduces the stigma that food bank users already face, and the shame that some users have been recorded as feeling. In response to this, some food banks have a policy of giving out food in supermarket-branded carrier bags to allow users 'dignity when they walk around the street'.[16] Other researchers note users who travel significant distances to food banks outside their community to avoid being recognised.[17] Meanwhile, there is extensive evidence that problematises the focus on consumer choice. In-depth research with food bank users found two triggers for seeking food aid: extreme housing vulnerability, which is often linked to rising costs of living, especially in the rental sector; and extreme financial vulnerability, which is often linked to benefit sanctions, changes, or errors.[18] There is also strong evidence about the effect of fiscal consolidation and welfare retrenchment on food bank usage.[19]

Scarcity and austerity intensified food insecurity to crisis point. And for a nation thinking about how it has or has not lived beyond its means, what one eats and how much is a key site of conflict. The way in which the population consumes is key to how people relate to the claim that the nation lives beyond its means. For there is a double meaning at play: excessive consumption creates a problem (whether obesity from overconsumption, hunger from household mismanagement, or a fiscal deficit from the previous government), so now one must make do and relearn the forgotten craft of thrift and living within one's means (which entails state intervention to enforce better nutrition, food aid for those still mismanaging, and austerity for the nation). State and households are linked together by a sense of moral decline entangled with budgetary excess, as outlined in Chapter 1. This equivalence reached new absurdities in 2014 when the media reported on how the then Chancellor George Osborne had lost weight through a new diet and fitness regime, making direct links between his ability to discipline his body and the prudent public household: 'Chancellor tackles surplus with an austerity diet'.[20]

Wartime Britain

By proposing that Britain can 'learn some lessons from the wartime generation', Hollobone is referring to one of the major myths of modern Britishness. During 'the People's War', the nation came together and made sacrifices – including over food – to help the war effort and ultimately defeat the Nazis. With regards to wartime lessons over 'how to best feed our people', Hollobone is presumably referring to a combination of state interventions that included rationing, 'dig for victory', and communal feeding (we will say more on each in a moment). Together, these wartime efforts to 'feed our people' were about enforcing different, thriftier production and consumption as a collective sacrifice for the future of the nation. In this way, they were nationalising in both design and effect. By claiming that Britain should return to this ethos, Hollobone is implying a return to British values.

Hollobone is far from alone in turning to the past in general and military successes in particular to make sense of the present. Wartime is often considered Britain's finest hour: that Blitz spirit, that Keep Calm and Carry On, that stiff upper lip; the country buckled up, got fit, for the common good; a heroic and self-sacrificing fight to save Europe from fascism. As the Introductory chapter highlights and Chapter 3 develops, this is how post-imperial Britishness was forged.

As Hollobone correctly indicates, controlling food and consumption was crucial to the British war effort. Rationing is perhaps the key reference point in the collective memory of wartime and post-war Britain, and is presumed to be a major way in which non-combatants made a sacrifice for the nation. Although only a limited range of food was truly 'rationed', the state enacted emergency legislation and created a bureaucracy to regulate and control consumption.[21] The state deemed rationing necessary to ensure that productive capacity was filtered into war, to secure an affordable and equitable food supply to the population by anticipating shortages, and to maintain social and public order that could be vulnerable in a context of mass queuing or food shortages.[22]

Rationing made the state and nation congruent in a number of ways. For instance, rationing mobilised women for this national effort, albeit in uneven and gendered ways. Due to the gendered division of labour, in which women tended to take on feminised unpaid work to do with the social reproduction of life and labour, the burden of implementing rationing fell disproportionately on housewives. At the height of military mobilisation in 1943, around 50 per cent of women of working age were full-time housewives – and their socially reproductive work was intense.[23] The state was very much aware of this division of labour. A Ministry of Food leaflet entitled *Wise Housekeeping in War-Time* starts with: 'The line of Food Defence runs through all our homes ... It may seem so simple, this urgent duty, that we may tend to overlook its full meaning' – the full meaning being: win the war, save the nation. It goes on: 'True economy begins with careful buying. *The woman with the basket* has a vital part to play in home defence. By saving food you may be saving lives.'[24] In this way, rationing incorporated a particular kind of domesticated femininity into the boundaries of Britishness.

It is important to note that the idea of the people coming together in collective sacrifice to the nation is, unsurprisingly, far more complex than British collective memory might imply. The state consistently prosecuted people for breaking the emergency laws surrounding rationing. At its height, the Ministry of Food had 1,370 enforcement officers who sought to prevent food crime, detect black market dealings, and secure compliance through routine inspections.[25] Between 1939 and 1951, the Ministry of Food made around 250,000 prosecutions (although few people were imprisoned).[26]

Interventions went beyond rationing and related controls, and extended into areas that we might today call social policy. For example, the wartime British state embarked on a 'communal feeding' project of heavily subsidised canteens. These canteens were originally going to be named 'Communal Feeding Centres' until Winston Churchill intervened and suggested 'British Restaurants' instead because it conjured images of 'a good meal' rather than 'communism and the workhouse'.[27] At their peak, there were 2,160 British Restaurants, and by 1942 about one in five Britons had eaten at one.[28] There were other feeding schemes too, including a 'rural pie scheme' whereby pies made by British Restaurants were transported to feed farm workers unable to reach the city.[29] Reviewing the Mass Observation collection on British Restaurants makes for interesting reading.[30] A housewife reports her displeasure because a table of youths were 'making a noise and eating with their hats on'. 'Snobby?!', she asks of herself: 'Perhaps'. Another diner reflects on the 'different atmosphere' because people are willing to talk to one another: 'I had a curious feeling that I was at the start of a new and wonderful experiment.' The contrast to the post-crash rise of food banks discussed above could hardly be starker.

While nation-building and militarism have a natural fit, the history of British militarism is especially nationalist, even putting the Second World War aside. Unlike most other European nation-states, British troops must swear allegiance to the monarch. This may seem archaic, but, as military scholar Victoria Basham argues, it is symbolic of a unique, nationalist configuration of the British citizen-soldier.[31] In other European nation-states, citizen-soldiers are incentivised and rewarded through, for example, the exchange of political and social rights or through the expectation to fulfil one's civic duties. In Britain, however, military service bestows, if anything, a degree of political status earned through national service. As the 'military covenant' agreed by the British state puts it: soldiers must 'make personal sacrifices – including the ultimate sacrifice – in the service of the Nation'.[32] For those of already considerable means, the status gained can be significant and life-changing (although less so today). But for those from poorer backgrounds, this often translates into inadequate care and abandonment.

Following British military operations in Afghanistan and Iraq at the turn of the century, these concerns fuelled the high-profile rise of charities such as Help for Heroes.[33] There are even charitable projects that explicitly link the military with food and consumption. Recently launched militarised, charity-appeal food brands include Eggs for Soldiers, Forces Sauces, and Rare Tea Company's Battle of Britain Tea.[34] Although charity appeals for the British military emerge from the historical lack of state support provided to veterans, it has also taken on a nationalist edge in recent years. Remembrance Day – held on the Sunday nearest to 11 November each year, to commemorate those who were killed in the First and Second World Wars – is, as the political scientist Mick Moran puts it, 'the one enduring, and still successful, civic ritual created by the British state in the 20th century'.[35]

Austerity chic

Hollobone's comments are a call to deal with the problem of how the population eats by returning to the discipline of wartime. This is nationalising insofar as it is calling for the state to regulate and redistribute resources in a more 'British' way – that is, by rediscovering British values of thrift. This might make this political conflict over who gets what, when and how – the 'what' in this case being access to food – as mainly taking place between those facing food insecurity and those that rule them. Yet this is not the case. Since austerity invites the whole nation to live within its means to solve an emergency and secure its future, conflict pops up in unlikely places. For if those who make poor consumption choices and eat the wrong things are stigmatised and pushed towards the boundaries of Britishness, then those who make the right consumption choices and eat the right things are logically going to be celebrated, valued, and possibly even offered greater protection in the face of austerity. Committing to living within one's means by adequately suppressing one's appetite for food, but also, as we will see, sex and shopping, becomes nationalist: a way of signalling one's inclusion within the informal boundaries of Britishness.

This is what happened. As analysed so clearly by Rebecca Bramall, Owen Hatherley, and others, the age of austerity coincided with a middle-class rediscovery of wartime Britain as a period ripe with wisdom and trends for the times.[36] Wartime and post-war nostalgia allowed middle-class consumers to rediscover and repackage the self-sufficiency and pride of the past into, in Bramall's words, a 'self-conscious performance of thriftiness in a bid to further one's cultural capital'.[37] The increasing popularity of allotments is one key example. Growing one's own fruit and vegetables allows people to explore a degree of self-sufficiency, which can be practised as environmentalist or anticapitalist, but also as nostalgia for a previous time, such as the 'Dig for Victory' spirit of wartime rationing.[38] Allotments have proven so popular that demand now significantly outweighs the supply.[39] This middle-class shift in how to relate to food is reflected in *The Kitchen Diaries* of Nigel Slater, a food writer for the *Observer*. While much of the 2005 volume is dedicated to discussing the virtues of trendy North London eateries, the 2012 sequel sees Slater retreat into his home to discover the humble benefits of thrifty cooking – making particular use of carefully selected special ingredients alongside leftovers.[40] Meanwhile, cupcakes were identified as 'the definitive food item of 2012', in part because they symbolised an ironic and kitsch kind of thriftiness.[41]

This kind of appropriation of wartime working-class culture extended beyond just food. Certain aesthetic and lifestyle trends have boomed in the post-crisis years: knitting and other craft-consumption activities; thriftiness and other downsizing-as-good-life ideals; and Keep Calm and Carry On and other modernist wartime aesthetics. These trends have been characterised as *austerity chic*.[42] Austerity chic fuses a strange sort of kitsch nostalgia with a sense of historical national wisdom into something new altogether.[43] To be a thrifty household has long meant saving and balancing the books. Yet, in the post-crash years, to be a thrifty household also came to mean reorienting one's consumption practices and lifestyle in ethical and conscientious ways – even if those consumption choices do not lower overall consumption or save money.[44] Austerity chic is therefore distinct from frugality whereby the purpose is to genuinely reduce consumption.[45]

The ultimate symbol of austerity chic is the Keep Calm and Carry On poster. Designed in wartime modernist aesthetic, the poster is simple: a red background, with the slogan in block capital white text, topped with an insignia of a crown. The poster was originally a motivational poster created by the British government to raise morale at the beginning of the Second World War, although it was never used or mass-produced at the time. It only came to prominence when it was unearthed in the 2000s and transformed for consumption via posters, mugs, postcards, and just about anything else.

'Keep Calm' is now an internationally recognised brand that can seemingly be applied to anything. It is used by authorities to issue instructions in a passive aggressive way (Keep Calm and Wash Your Hands; Keep Calm and Keep Shopping) or to signal one's willingness to consume in the right way (Keep Calm and Eat a Cupcake; Keep Calm, You're a Yummy Mummy). It has also been adapted for (somewhat misplaced) attempts at subversion (Don't Keep Calm; Get Angry), as well as ways that do not necessarily make much sense (Keep Calm There's A Royal Baby; Keep Calm and Play Squash).[46] The design taps into British national pride about stiff-upper-lip stoicism, the importance of muddling through adversity, Britain's wartime 'finest hour', and a desire for thrift and sacrifice in the name of the nation.[47] In an age of austerity it found new life as a way of committing to living within means – i.e. to continue consumption as normal, albeit, to quote Hatherley, 'with a less garish aesthetic than was customary during the boom'.[48]

One way this new thrift entered mainstream culture was through a post-crash genre of television that provides expertise on living within one's means. TV programme *SuperScrimpers*, a Channel 4 show that regularly had ratings in the millions, is exemplary of this trend.[49] The TV programme and its associated media (including a website and books) are essentially primers on how to consume cleverly. They are literally instructions on how to be a responsible, thrifty and good household – often bound up in the aesthetic of wartime Britain. The self-declared mission of the show is to turn so-called 'superspenders' into 'superscrimpers', by teaching thrifty tips and tricks in the spirit of discipline, sacrifice, and self-help.[50] 'Now Britain is in financial meltdown, and nearly half of all adults in the UK are worried about their finances ... But never fear', the introduction to series four of *SuperScrimpers* announces, 'Mrs M. [the presenter] and her superscrimper army are back to show us how to survive the slump'.

There is a cruel irony to these trends and lifestyle changes: this romanticisation of austerity is only available to people with sufficient resources to choose them, those who are probably some way away from experiencing the rise of food insecurity or facing the brunt of spending cuts. These class dimensions were made clear enough by a contribution to a 2009 BBC Radio 4 documentary on thrift, whereby this new trend means:

> almost being embarrassed of over consumption. Sitting at a dinner party and people apologising to others that they're taking their family on holiday to Bali and kind of bemoaning the fact that the cancellation fees are too high and that their children would far prefer to go to Cornwall this year. This idea of sort of conspicuous austerity is becoming very fashionable.[51]

This is the context in which it was possible to speak of Kate Middleton as the 'thrifty royal'. Her version of superscrimping – shopping at high-street store Mothercare and being noted to wear the same dress twice – was celebrated in the British press.[52]

Chapter 1 showed how austerity was positioned as an implicit promise to address a moral decline typified by pre-crash excess by restoring British values. Austerity chic and new thrift emerged in this context. To live within one's means provides a means to rediscover the moral code of thrift and prudence in a context of pre-crisis guilty excess. Rather than a response to scarcity per se, however, austerity chic is better understood as a way of marking middle-class distinction: it is a way of saying that 'we' are not like the people who have bankrupted both themselves and the country, who are now are failing to be in it all together, who are failing to pull their weight in the national interest. By being wary of overconsumption, by appropriating wartime working-class culture, and by celebrating wartime aesthetics and values, those practices are a way of confirming the boundary of proper Britishness. As Bramall puts it, it shows 'we are all entangled and implicated in austerity in complex and contradictory ways'.[53] This demonstrates how austerity changes how the British public relate to themselves, to others, and to the nation-state – sometimes in strange, subtle forms.

Responsible households

Hollobone also speaks of 'low-income households spending too much on food that is not good for them'. Within that lies the ideal of a responsible household which manages its desires responsibly in the context of raising a family. The prudent public household of the austerity narrative seen in the previous chapter was positioned by the architects of austerity as having similar responsibilities, through appeals to avoid 'saddling' the next generation with debt. In 2008, George Osborne spoke of how 'it is not fair to live beyond our means and leave the next generation to clear up the mess'.[54] During the 2010 election campaign, one of the Conservative adverts was a photo of a new born baby with the heading 'Dad's Nose. Mum's Eyes. Gordon Brown's Debt.' Underneath, it said 'Labour's Debt Crisis: Every child in Britain is born owing £17,000. They deserve better.' In 2014, Cameron made a speech on 'The values that underpin our long-term economic plan' which asked the public whether they could look 'your children in the eye' to 'explain why we crippled their future with our debt'.[55] ('I couldn't do that. And I'm sure you couldn't either.')

Before the advent of contraception, choosing to have children was limited – and when it was chosen it was often because one needed an heir or more labour. It is increasingly expected that deciding to have a child or not is a personal choice in which parental (but especially motherly) responsibility is played against future expectations of life chances, happiness, and self-actualisation.[56] This is reflected in the evolving politics of the family household. Rather than treat it as part of private life, the New Labour government consistently treated the family as a site of state intervention. New Labour discovered that the family household could be used alongside other institutions, such as schools, as a mechanism for delivering outcomes for children (relating to nutrition, educational attainment, and so on) to encourage the right kind of citizens.[57] Such interventions, including the Troubled

Families programme, continued under the Coalition government.[58] Taken together, these trends have fed into contemporary expectations about how and when to start a family, which increasingly centre on careful deliberation about how to best enhance the life of both parents and their kin. To do otherwise is deemed irresponsible for future generations. This loops into the austerity narrative insofar as that it is not just the previous Labour government who are blamed for excess state spending: it is also parents, and, in particular, single mothers, who are often framed as the epitome of Britain's declining moral fibre.

In August 2011, riots sprung up across cities and towns in England. The riots followed a protest in Tottenham on 6 August against the police killing of a young Black man, Mark Duggan, two days previously. Looting became the central story of these events. The focus on the seeming self-indulgence of looting high-end consumer goods in tandem with destructive acts meant that more structural or political counter-narratives did not seem to resonate, even among some left-wing commentators. In this analysis, the riots were characterised by a lack of politics and an abundance of desire (or, perhaps, the wrong kinds of desire).

Parenting became one of, if not *the*, leading discourse around the riot. Cameron consistently made these connections in his responses to the riots:

> The question people asked over and over again last week was 'where are the parents? Why aren't they keeping the rioting kids indoors?' [...] Well, join the dots and you have a clear idea about why some of these people were behaving so terribly. [...] So if we want to have any hope of mending our broken society, family and parenting is where we've got to start.[59]

A *Guardian*/ICM poll found that 86 per cent of the public cited 'poor parenting' as the main cause of the riots.[60] It was often related to a wider disgust at a 'feral underclass' and sense of moral decline – or, in Cameron's words, a 'slow-motion moral collapse'.[61] The sense of moral decline was difficult to disentangle from anxieties over race and multiculturalism (a topic expanded on in Chapter 3). One high-profile explanation for the riots was the rise of a 'black gangsta culture'.[62] Exemplary of this were historian David Starkey's infamous comments on *Newsnight*.[63] Noting that Enoch Powell's

'Rivers of Blood' speech was 'absolutely right in one sense', Starkey argued:

> The Tiber didn't foam with blood, but flames lambent wrapped round Tottenham and wrapped round Clapham, but it wasn't intercommunal violence, this is where he was completely wrong. What's happened is that a substantial section of the chavs have become black. The whites have become black.

He went on to say that 'so many of us have this sense of literally a foreign country'. Starkey's comments reflect concerns over the decline of a white, British or English culture as it gets mixed up with other cultures.

Cameron's question of 'where are the parents?' became gendered and racialised. Gendered because the vast majority of the rioters were male, which led to speculation that young men with absent fathers lack masculine role models and therefore have an underdeveloped sense of discipline and responsibility.[64] Due to the concerns over race, this was often 'where are the black fathers?' David Lammy, a Labour MP whose Tottenham constituency was where the rioting began, rose to prominence as one of the central commentators on the riots. Lammy consistently claimed that the riots were caused by absent fathers – using anecdotes and his own experiences as extra authority for his claims.[65] It was consequently implied that one solution to the crisis is for more men to take part in family life and show the right kind of masculinity – and to support and protect the heteronormative nuclear family.

The riots reinforced the Coalition government's commitment to family support and turning around Troubled Families, including freeing up millions of pounds to fund relationship support.[66] This decision seems odd in the context of fiscal consolidation in general, and one that provides insight into the kind of household and family the state wishes to encourage and why. As Cameron put it in 2013, 'the character of love, which marriage reflects: [is] faithful, stable, tough, unselfish and unconditional'.[67] This came at a time where LGBTQ+ services, like almost all services that are highly dependent on public sector and local government funding, were especially vulnerable due to spending cuts.[68] LGBTQ+ volunteers and service users reported being treated as problematic because 'their needs differed from the norm in times of scarce resources'. There is a sense that LGBTQ+ needs were beginning to be seen as a 'luxury'.[69] When the boundaries of the nation are narrowed because of scarcity, everyone is affected; those with desires deemed 'luxurious' are seen as less valuable.

The three themes of this chapter – sex, shopping, food – are all present in the rise of the 'austerity cook', Jack Monroe. Monroe rose to prominence in 2012: while getting by and supporting their child without work, they started a blog that shared precisely costed and very cheap budget recipes, along with reflections on the daily life and wider politics of poverty as a single parent. Their carrot, cumin and kidney bean burgers are emblematic of 'austerity cooking': the recipe can make '4 generous burgers at 15p each or 6 good sized ones at 10p each'.[70] The most expensive ingredient is a standard size can of kidney beans at 30p. Although Monroe was explicitly speaking to those impoverished parents, they proved just as popular among the thrift-conscious middle classes. Monroe went on to have a recipe column in the *Guardian*, featured in adverts for supermarket chain Sainsbury's, and released a series of cookbooks. The backlash was inevitable. One tabloid article called Monroe 'the pesto kid of welfare Britain' which focused on their recipe for kale pesto ('it is beyond parody').[71]

The backlash seemed to get worse when Monroe spoke about their sexuality and gender. Already known as gay, in 2015 Monroe came out as non-binary, and, in the process, changed the name of their blog from 'A Girl Called Jack' to 'Cooking on a Bootstrap'. There is little doubt that Monroe has a less sympathetic public profile after coming out as non-binary and raising the profile of sexuality politics in the UK. Monroe has reported an increase in social media abuse, has been subject to coordinated attacks, and their queerness has been used as political ammunition against them. For example, Sarah Vine, a right-wing newspaper columnist known for her proximity to the Conservative Party leadership, argued that Monroe should have *decided* against having a child due to the economic and sexual situation that they were in at the time.[72]

The backlash is illustrative. In many ways, Monroe is precisely what Hollobone is asking for. Monroe represents the exactly the right kind of thrifty and responsible household: cheap, nutritious, on trend even. Their recipes and wider approach to cooking could surely be taken as an example of learning 'some lessons from the wartime generation about how best to feed our people'. However, while Monroe is deemed to have disciplined their desires when it comes to food, in many other ways they pose a threat to those who wish to restore British values following moral decline: queer, single mother, politically rebellious – the kind of person the nostalgia for a wartime Britain does not include.

Conclusion

This chapter asked why the Second World War seemed such a compelling source of inspiration for living in the initial austerity period. The chapter has shown how this nostalgia can and did work to police the boundaries of Britishness as a site of disciplined desires, even if that discipline is performed ironically by those under no pressure to adapt to scarcity. Those who refuse or cannot commit to a vision of living within means are deemed increasingly expendable when it comes to inevitable 'difficult decisions' about resource regulation and redistribution – whether that is through high-profile welfare interventions that force some to use food banks, or less noticed cuts to LGBTQ+ support or refusal of routine healthcare to those deemed obese. The conflict is not just over resource distribution and regulation, but over the meaning of Britain and who is included within it. In this way, the initial austerity period was a kind of proto-culture war over who the nation should be for and who should have access to its wealth. As the next two chapters will show, this created the conditions for competing nationalising projects.

And what about Philip Hollobone? As a concluding note, let us to return to him, because in addition to giving an inordinate amount of speeches to the House, Hollobone was also once noted as being 'Westminster's cheapest MP'.[73] Unlike most MPs, Hollobone does not have a PA, a research assistant, or a diary secretary. He never takes first-class trains. As a newspaper feature on him reports, '[w]hilst most MPs have a small army of helpers, paid for by the taxpayer, Mr Hollobone takes the view that he should work a bit harder himself and save the taxpayer some money'. The photo accompanying the article shows Hollobone in his office, which is adorned with a framed Keep Calm and Carry On poster and a Union Jack erected over his desk. From Tuesday to Thursday he's apparently at his desk from 6.15 am to 10 pm.

An uncomfortable truth could lurk in this: Hollobone lives what he preaches. For if everyone was this dedicated to the public good, if everyone was this thrifty with public money, if everyone worked this hard, if everyone loved their country this much – if every household fed themselves efficiently and responsibly – then austerity would not have been necessary. In the moment of the country's need, in which the future of the country is at stake, the population should come together in collective sacrifice for the greater good of the nation, just like in the war. Rather than something to suffer, austerity becomes virtuous, something to celebrate, something to desire. A way of uniting the nation.

However, the article also notes that Hollobone has tried to avoid claiming the additional costs allowance. This is a benefit for MPs that reimburses those with constituencies outside of London for housing inside the capital so that they can easily attend Parliament without incurring personal expense. As the article notes (with my emphasis added): 'Mr Hollobone tried commuting from Kettering every day but found he was not getting home until the small hours. He was too tired to keep it up so he now claims for a house in Blackheath, south east London. He admits this *one weakness with obvious disappointment.*' Most people faced with the problem of a draining commute would face three options: stump up the costs of accommodation near the workplace, presumably at the expense of something else; start looking for a new job nearer to home; or move permanently closer to work. For someone who enjoys their job, and who doesn't want to or cannot spend hundreds of pounds a month on a hotel room, or who is rooted and connected to their local area, this is not a pleasant trilemma. Hollobone did not face this trilemma in any meaningful sense, because he has access to a significant expenses account, which most people do not. There could hardly be a better illustration of what austerity means.

3

White Britain

In November 2017, Sylvester Marshall arrived at the Royal Marsden hospital expecting cancer treatment. Instead, he was presented with a potentially life-threatening dilemma.[1] Before his treatment could begin, he was asked for his passport, or at least otherwise prove his immigration status and therefore his eligibility for NHS care.

Marshall was born in Jamaica and moved to the UK in 1973 with his NHS-employed mother. He lived and worked in the UK for the following forty-four years. When he was unable to provide documentation to prove his status, Marshall was given a stark choice: either arrange to pay the £55,000 cancer treatment *upfront*, or forego the treatment. Given that he had no savings, he only really had one option. Some years before, the NHS had treated Marshall for blood cancer lymphoma, and that was legitimate. His immigration status had remained consistent since then. So what had changed?

The difference is that the British state had stopped providing free healthcare to 'overseas patients'. A 'health surcharge' for immigrants was introduced in 2014, and upfront charges for overseas patients was introduced in 2017. Despite living his entire adult life in the UK, Marshall was formally classified by the state as 'foreign', and therefore ineligible for NHS treatment. It was only thanks to a media storm around his situation – driven by activists, and then reported by the *Guardian* – that Marshall eventually got his treatment and recovered.[2] Many were not as fortunate. Thousands of people who legally moved to the UK – some of whom are seen as part of the 'Windrush generation' – were detained, deported, and/or otherwise stripped of their rights to live and work in the UK thanks to this move: 164 people were wrongly held in immigration detention, and 83 were wrongly removed from the country.[3] The Home Office has searched for those wrongly deported to Caribbean Commonwealth countries to inform them that they can return to the UK, but, as of April 2020, they are still searching for fourteen people.[4] This became known as the Windrush scandal.

The scandal is connected to the 'hostile environment', which is the name for a set of anti-immigration policies introduced by the then Home Secretary Theresa May to lower immigration by making the (prospective) lives of migrants miserable, costly, and precarious. As well as a hostile environment, these changes to healthcare represent nationalisation of the NHS – not in terms of state ownership, but in the definition that this book focuses on: making the state more national, especially in its regulation and distribution of resources. To put the above in more conceptual language, the British state has narrowed the boundaries of resource distribution in response to austerity, thereby excluding people like Sylvester Marshall from benefitting from the nation's wealth in the same way as they could before. How and why has this happened?

This chapter shows how these changes have their origins in post-war and post-imperial conflict over Britishness, race, and citizenship. In other words, this recent NHS nationalisation was evidently sparked by the need to save money due to austerity. Yet the particular dynamics of these changes can only be explained through longer histories of welfare and immigration, relations of race and class, and post-imperial British nationhood. It is these histories that position different groups as closer to the core or closer to the periphery of Britishness, thereby gradating how valuable and worthy of national resources they are. These boundaries are not only made more visible when resources become scarcer, like objects revealed by a receding tide – but the conflict over them intensifies, in this case narrowing them further. In analysing these histories, this chapter therefore develops the book's argument by highlighting, first, how nationalisation is a process that cannot be reduced to Brexit and, second, how the kinds of conflicts that the Brexit project relied on for its referendum strategy did not spring from nowhere.

Nationalising healthcare

Sylvester Marshall's experience would have been completely different were it not for the NHS visitor and migrant cost recovery programme.

Introduced by the Department of the Health in 2014, it was launched in the midst of renewed anxieties about 'welfare tourism' in the context of austerity.[5] Its aim was clear: to recover an additional £500 million per year by 2017–18 by charging migrants and overseas visiting patients for using the NHS.[6] The two major policy changes were the Immigration Health Surcharge and NHS overseas patient upfront charges.

The Immigration Health Surcharge was introduced through the 2014 Immigration Act. Aside from humanitarian migrants and visitors, all individuals entering from outside the European Economic Area must pay in excess of £624 for healthcare, a tripling of fees since 2017. Aside from already hefty visa fees, a family of four coming to the UK will need to pay £12,480 just to be admitted.[7] Without the first year's payment upfront, a visa will not be issued. The surcharge brought in an estimated £164 million during the 2015/16 financial year, thereby contributing the majority of revenues to the cost recovery programme, which was otherwise still some way off its £500 million aim.[8]

The second major pillar of the cost recovery programme is the NHS overseas patient upfront charges, introduced in 2017. Overseas patients accessing secondary care – including cancer treatment and maternity care – are charged *upfront* at 150 per cent of NHS internal market value of that treatment or service. Those who cannot pay upfront are turned away. Those who cannot pay for urgent care, such as maternity services, are charged retrospectively. And so new mothers have been chased by their hospital or bailiffs to repay the debts to the NHS they accrued through giving birth (typically around £6,000 overall). In one example, one woman was billed the day after she gave birth and put on a repayment plan of £100 per month by a debt collection agency.[9] The woman was undocumented, and therefore barred from taking on paid employment or receiving benefits, thereby making repayment extremely unlikely.

Although this specific cost recovery programme launched in 2014 under austerity, the wider issues have been a tension in the NHS since its foundation. The NHS was established in 1948 with the aim of providing healthcare, free at the point of service, for everyone – with 'everyone' defined as 'ordinarily resident in the UK'. Free healthcare extended to anyone who has moved to the UK to live, work, or study. It also implied that (short-term) overseas visitors were liable to pay for secondary care, but this was never more than a theoretical principle.[10] Although regulations for charging overseas visitors were introduced (but never properly enforced) in 1982, 2004 was a major turning point. In April that year New Labour removed free NHS care from those whose applications for asylum were rejected, undocumented migrants, and those with expired visas.[11] This included the creation of Overseas Visitor Managers and a melange of bureaucracy.

The changes were not, however, cost effective. A review of the policy in 2011 by the new Conservative-Liberal Democrat Coalition government concluded that 'the overseas visitor charging system may not generate a net financial benefit to the NHS'.[12] The costs of administrating the system (including the creation of Overseas Visitor Managers and the use of NHS staff time) added up to at least £18 million, while hospitals were only recovering between £15–25 million per year for the NHS.[13] Although the changes were a fiscal failure, it created institutions – legislation, internal NHS bureaucracy, the Overseas Visitor Managers – that the later Coalition government could continue and intensify. One of their priorities was to extend this policy to fit with their aim of 'reducing pressure on the NHS budget and protecting resources for patients who are entitled to free NHS treatment'.[14]

This need for austerity fitted well with the Home Office hostile environment policy. As the cost recovery programme documents explain:

> The government has a clear objective to tighten up the immigration system, stop abuse and support only the most economically beneficial migrants ... The Home Office is concerned that the provision of high standards of healthcare may attract new migrants to enter the country unlawfully, or discourage them from leaving when their right to stay has expired.[15]

The programme was also justified in more abstract terms about fairness and benefit to society. A Department of Health impact assessment justifies the programme as a way to 'reduce the pool of individuals eligible to access highly sought after NHS funded acute care trusts ... and thereby *benefit UK society*'.[16] A similar document states that 'the Government believes that the NHS can no longer afford to be so open and generous to non-permanent residents and to make a reality of the belief that *everyone should make a fair contribution to the cost of their healthcare*.[17]

The meaning of 'fair contribution' and 'benefit UK society' is vague. To some extent, it is clearly about austerity and the political pressures that engenders. The changes are in effect extra and highly targeted new taxes aimed at raising extra revenues for a squeezed NHS. The logic of these changes cannot, however, just be fiscal and down to austerity alone. There are plenty of people in the UK who do not make much of a year-on-year fiscal contribution, such as children or pensioners. To levy extra charges on these potential patients is presumably not deemed fair or considered beneficial to the nation. But for people like Sylvester Marshall, the British state does deem it fair, at least implicitly. To understand why, we need to consider post-war Commonwealth arrivals into the British Isles – how this was racialised as 'immigration', how this forged post-imperial Britishness, and, ultimately, how immigration was consolidated in the post-crash era as one of the most significant political issues of the times.

The birth of immigration policy

The entanglement of immigration, race, and citizenship in post-war Britain has some clear patterns. The British state has an interest in maintaining its status as a supposedly tolerant global power in a post-colonial world. It did so initially though the Commonwealth, and then shifted its attention to Europe. Through both of these relationships, the UK instigated policy change aimed at ensuring British status and power (consolidating post-colonial citizenship and nationality in 1948, permitting the free movement of the Eastern European 'Accession 8' in 2004). These changes had unintended consequences for the movement of peoples (Black and Asian post-war immigration, Eastern European immigration in the new millennium) that the state could not easily undo without geopolitical and constitutional ramifications. In the context of capitalist crises (of the 1970s and the 2010s) and the evolution of British nationhood, this mobility was racialised and politicised for electoral gain. In doing so, the stage was set for political economic reorderings that reassert the status and dignity of 'ordinary people'. Let us unpack this.

The movement of people to Britain was shaped by empire, with its globe-spanning territory and associated subjects. Up to the Second World War, most of the movement was white British people emigrating to the Empire as administrators, traders, and missionaries.[18] At this stage, Britain had no 'immigration policy' per se, and large-scale Black and Asian movement from the so-called 'New Commonwealth' to the British Isles was not imagined, let alone discussed.[19] The notion of migration is a modern term, which only really makes sense in a world of nation-states and citizens. Before 'citizens and migrants' it was 'subjects and aliens', and subjects were demarcated by which sovereign they swore allegiance to rather than their legal status.[20] This helps explain why the policy that was the key turning point – the British Nationality Act 1948, which granted British citizenship to all Commonwealth subjects – was a citizenship policy rather than an immigration policy.[21] At no stage in parliamentary debates over the Act did anyone raise the possibility that colonised citizens might exercise their new legal status to permanently reside in Britain.[22] Yet this Act created the immediate conditions for the post-war movement of Black and Asian peoples from the Empire to the British Isles.

From the vantage point of today, this could seem a remarkably open and liberal approach. But it was an accident. It is better thought of as an unintended outcome of Britain's post-imperial retreat. The change to citizenship was intended to maintain the cohesion of empire and its subjects in an era of post-colonial national independence. Hence, the 1948 Act transformed subjects in an empire into citizens in a commonwealth.[23] Once the unintended consequences of this – i.e. the unexpected arrival of Black and Asian people, now with a new status as British citizens – had been noted, the British state looked to push back and limit it. However, it felt unable to do so formally. Placing explicit racial limits on immigration would severely damage relations with the Commonwealth and thus threaten British power.[24]

The state instead looked to informally limit Black and Asian immigration. It created incentives for New Commonwealth governments to limit the issue of passports and travel documents.[25] The Commonwealth Immigrants Act 1962 formalised some of these restrictions through measures such a labour-voucher scheme, but citizenship was not formally transformed until the Immigration Act 1971.[26] The 1971 Act removed citizenship rights from Commonwealth peoples (but did contain an exemption that those with a grandparent or parent born or naturalised in Britain could preserve citizenship, which was designed to aid the mobility of mostly white Australians, Canadians, and New Zealanders).[27] Further policy changes under the Thatcher government helped make the reputation of 1980s Britain as a country of near zero immigration.[28]

Although Britain has never been ethnically or racially homogenous, the post-war period of free movement nevertheless changed the nation. In 1951, the Black population of Britain was estimated to be 74,500; by 1959 it was 336,000; and it reached 500,000 by 1962.[29] With this movement of people also came the figure of 'the immigrant'. While the category of immigrant can be understood as a technical term to denote legal status, scholars have consistently demonstrated that when 'migrant' replaced 'alien' as the key category for distinguishing those outside or strange to the nation, it was racialised.[30] In this context, 'immigrant' came to denote a Black or Asian person, usually male. In contrast, white Australians and Canadians were typically seen as 'us', and their movement to the UK therefore as 'returning home'.[31]

European migrants were not problematised in the same way as Black and Asian migration, despite that movement being as large in scale in the post-war years. While the state was actively trying to find ways to limit Black and Asian immigration through ad hoc measures, it was also actively encouraging Irish and European migration to supply the labour market through the European Voluntary Worker (EVW) scheme.[32] EVWs were preferred because they were, to quote the 1949 Royal Commission on Population, deemed 'of good human stock and were not prevented by their religion or race from intermarrying with the host population and becoming merged in it'.[33] Not only did the scheme fit into a British story about saving Europe from fascism, but EVWs were attractive because, unlike Commonwealth migrants, they did not have citizenship, therefore giving them less labour rights.[34] Those arriving to Britain through the EVW scheme were not as problematised as Black and Asian 'immigrants', but they still faced discrimination and tended go into lower-paid and lower-status work.[35]

Many people arrived in Britain following the Second World War, but arrivals were racialised into a hierarchy. In principle, difference in physical appearance and cultural practice are meaningless; but in the context of power relations – including struggles over (de) colonisation and post-war Britain's interest in maintaining its status as a global power – those differences become meaningful and even naturalised as hierarchal markers of power, privilege, and status. Hence, the difference in ascribed status between 'Old' and 'New' Commonwealth movement, and the racialisation of the latter as 'immigrants'. This highlights how we would be mistaken to think that post-war anti-immigration sentiment arises just from conflict over resources, because the antagonist identities that make conflict possible in the first place needed to be made and institutionalised (thereby highlighting the indivisibility of economy and culture). As demonstrated by Robbie Shilliam, this was a process in which European heritage working-class Britons were provided with a white identity in opposition to Black and Asian others of empire through colonialism, (British) nation-building, and party politicisation for electoral gain.[36] We will look at these three features in turn.

A national whiteness

English and then British colonialism exploited the less powerful; reinforced and modified racialised hierarchies to further justify that; and then governed through those hierarchies. The process produced an entrenched and naturalised link between skin colour, status, and power. These links were lived through the everyday life of white Britons as a distinction between whiteness 'at home' and racialised others abroad.[37] British nationhood is odd, however: for the majority of its empire 'Britain' referred not just to the political boundaries of the United Kingdom but also incorporated colonial territories as the Empire.

The shift from empire-state-nation to nation-state happened alongside a shift in nationhood and whiteness. Historians have observed how narratives of British nationhood shifted in the 1930s and 1940s away from empire and supremacy towards the ordinary and everyday. Whereas whiteness was previously explicitly idealised and extraordinary, it started to 'cast as the identity of the ordinary; it connotes lack of exceptionality, the homely virtues of quietness, tidiness, cleanness and decency'.[38] This helped reimagine Britishness and Englishness in non-imperial terms. As British historian Wendy Webster puts it:

> Englishness is increasingly invoked as an intimate, private, exclusive identity that is white. The English spend a great deal of their time indoors and their major preoccupation is keeping themselves to themselves ... In keeping with the story of a quiet, private, domestic nation ... boundary-markers were often domestic: windows, doors, letter-boxes, back yards.[39]

This was a shift away from a heroic identity in which whiteness and Anglo-Britishness was outwardly facing, *extraordinary* in its supremacy and empire, and differentiated by class (in which workers were seen as less white and thereby less valuable as elites, for example);[40] and a shift towards a homely and domesticated identity in which whiteness and Anglo-Britishness was inwardly facing, *ordinary* in its privacy and respectability, and homogenous across class (in which elites and workers share a whiteness). The former was a whiteness made for an empire-state-nation, the latter a whiteness made for a nation-state.

This evolution provides context to those seemingly banal symbols of contemporary Britishness: fish and chips; cup of tea; Keep Calm, Carry On. The state too deliberately engineered this national identity, especially' during the Second World War when it collaborated with scientists from the emerging fields of psychology and public relations to develop moral-boosting and nation-building campaigns.[41] Keep Calm and Carry On, that epitome of ordinariness and Britishness which was analysed in Chapter 2, surely emerged in this context. By forging an 'ordinary people', these moves paved the way for a cohesive and homogenous post-colonial British (white) nationhood. While the formal boundaries of Britishness were being cast broad, the informal boundaries of Britishness were drawn narrower. Therein lay a tension that was there from the beginning of the post-war and post-imperial nationalising project.

Historical work has shown how post-war British elites worked with a definition of Britishness that was unwilling to include Black and Asian colonial subjects within its boundaries.[42] The nationalisation project of that time, then was conceived in terms of 'the British common people'. This is the origin of the famous myth of a 'People's War'; the sense that the sacrifices of the British nation-state – not the British Empire, especially its Black and Asian subjects, now citizens – should be rewarded with a welfare state that benefits and belongs to those people.[43] Historian Alastair Bonnett is surely right, then, when he says that these reforms 'came wrapped up in the Union Jack'.[44] The foundation of the NHS in 1948 was a central part of this nationalist project. On the surface, the NHS is a symbol of national pride and identity. Just look to the 2012 Olympics ceremony held in London, where the NHS was idolised as a modern marker of British collective unity, generosity, and tolerance. Yet the NHS is also wrapped in the Union Jack on a deeper level, through a complex tangle of fiscal, legal, and familial rights and responsibilities that give the sense that the NHS is 'ours' and not 'theirs'.[45]

Racialised anxieties about immigrants have existing from the very beginning of the NHS's inception. Even before the NHS was formed, Conservatives pushed back at Labour over concerns that Egyptians would abuse the service to claim and then sell NHS-sourced spectacles and prosthetics.[46] These anxieties only work if Britain is imagined as a nation rather than empire, thereby obscuring the colonial scale of Britain's economy, its transcontinental division of labour, and the role of Commonwealth workers in the NHS itself.[47] White, European arrivals were not seen as threatening.

Black and Asian Commonwealth settlement led to the politics of race relations in the 1950s and 1960s: a bipartisan consensus between Labour and the Conservatives to control Black/Asian immigration, to theoretically commit to integrating migrants, and to avoid politicising race in the context of national electoral competition.[48] This consensus was challenged most famously and publicly by the then Conservative Cabinet member Enoch Powell, and his infamous 'Rivers of Blood' speech. The race relations consensus became more difficult to maintain as the post-war welfare settlement came under strain through the waxing and waning of capitalist stability: to make the most of a slow-burning crisis, find the scapegoat that will strike a chord.[49] This was the context for the reaction to Powell's 'Rivers of Blood', in which he warned of how English identity and resources were under threat from Black and Asian immigration. His immediate dismissal from the Cabinet highlighted that consensus, but the consequences of the speech were far-reaching. As Shilliam puts it: 'Overwhelmingly, it was through Powell's rhetoric that Black and Asian Commonwealth settlement was rationalised in public fora as a fundamental threat'; a threat to the privileges provided by the post-war settlement including the NHS, and to the preservation of a prosaic and ordinary national identity.[50] It was a form of post-imperial nation-building.

Ordinariness was central to Powell's nationalism. In Rivers of Blood, Powell positions himself as the spokesperson for the people by sharing a series of (likely apocryphal) anecdotes. He shares the racist concerns of 'a middle-aged, quite ordinary working man employed in one of our nationalised industries', and reports on the hundreds of anti-immigration letters he received from a 'high proportion of ordinary, decent, sensible people'. Attached to this ordinariness is a respectability. Powell tells the story of a how a once 'respectable street in Wolverhampton' now only has one white person left, an elderly woman – who is turned down for state benefits after revealing her racial anxieties, and finds 'excreta pushed through her letter box'. This anecdote ties together the fiscal fears of welfare state access and the supposedly broken boundaries of ordinary respectability ('her letter box') that racialised Black and Asian immigration provoked. In doing so, it cemented 'ordinary people' into a trope that, as we will see, remains a central part of immigration and race discourse today.

The 'crisis' of multiculturalism

Immigration controls remained strict until New Labour. From 1997 onwards, the UK's immigration policy went from restrictive to one of the most liberal in Europe. Two and a half million foreign-born workers were added to the population between 1997 and 2010, with over half of Britain's foreign-born population arriving between 2001 and 2011.[51] New Labour introduced a dizzying array of changes to immigration policy: relaxing work permits and limits on over-seas students; work programmes for specific jobs; a points-based system with tiers. These were implemented alongside authoritarian treatment of 'failed' asylum seekers; tough welfare conditions for non-citizens; and investment visas for the mega-wealthy. This may appear a hodgepodge, but there was a coherence to this system: a hierarchy based on what migrants could contribute to GDP and the public purse. This move to mass economic migration was part of the wider political economy of New Labour: maintaining stability and enhancing competitiveness through labour market flexibility, as justified through grand and abstract claims about globalisation as a necessary and modernising force for good. This approach was a break from the past: in the 1970s, the British government discussed whether to reshape immigration on the basis of economic needs, but concluded that 'justification by GNP is a pitfall ridden approach', and so remained committed to restrictive policy.[52]

This competitiveness approach was therefore uneven in the freedoms and rights it produced for different kinds of mobility: detention centres for rejected asylum seekers, complex and ongoing bureaucracy for migrant workers, and a relative wave-through for overseas investors. This approach could be justified in principle as a kind of technocratic race-blindness, since the most important factor was one's potential contribution to the national economy, like an entry in a spreadsheet.[53] In practice, however, the approach was racialised, inasmuch that wealth and human capital are not distributed evenly across the global economy for historical reasons.

The exception to this approach was Europe. Freedom of movement is one of the core principles of the European Union, meaning that the UK could not control arrivals from other member states. This might reasonably represent a tension in New Labour's 'managed migration' approach. Yet, curiously, it was a decision taken by the New Labour government that undermined their own approach: the accession of eight new member states from the former Eastern bloc, including Poland and Hungary (known collectively as the Accession 8, or the A8). The UK was one of the only states that permitted the immediate free movement of A8 nationals with no transitional arrangements. Like with the post-war changes to British citizenship, this decision was motivated by geopolitics rather than immigration per se.

By favouring the A8, the British state hoped to strengthen trading ties and shared interests with Central and Eastern European states to forge alliances and increase British power in the EU. As the then Home Secretary David Blunkett put it in an interview: 'because of our [Britain's] links with Poland, the Polish diaspora in Britain offer quite a good counterweight to the German/French axis without making it aggressive'.[54] The decision was then rushed through so that Prime Minister Tony Blair could announce it at the Copenhagen Council in December 2002.[55] Meanwhile, the forecasts for A8 migration were wildly inaccurate. Official forecasts legitimated this decision by predicting 5,000–13,000 A8 migrants in the first year of accession. In reality, 293,000 A8 migrants entered the UK between May 2004 and September 2005, and over a million entered in the next decade or so).[56] As in the post-war years, an attempt to manage the UK's global power and status had unintended consequences for migration. And like before, as we will see below, this movement was racialised, which stoked conflict and a backlash, thereby legitimating stricter policies. To make clear these connections, we need to look at multiculturalism.

In narrow and descriptive terms, 'multiculturalism' refers to the presence of different distinct cultural or ethnic groups within a space. In practice, it is a slippery and ambiguous term that can be put to work in a number of ways: from liberal celebrations of tolerance to dog-whistle fascist cries of its ongoing 'crisis'.[57] However, it is perhaps best defined simply as 'the widespread recognition that we can no longer be in any doubt as to whether or not cultural difference is here to stay'.[58] Multiculturalism can thus be seen as the modern incarnation of the liberal race relations consensus: it characterises the state's approach to integration of Black and Asian migrants, but for a new era. And as that post-war consensus went together with a particular racism, so too does multicultural Britain.

Grasping how multiculturalism fits together with the evolving meaning of race and racism is complex, but crucial to the argument of this chapter. As post-colonial scholar Paul Gilroy put it in 2002:

> Thus today's British racism, anchored in national decline rather than imperial expansion overseas, does not necessarily proceed through readily apparent notions of superiority and inferiority ... The order of racial power relations has become more subtle and elusive than that.[59]

Gilroy's identification of a new subtle and elusive racism corresponds with what other scholars have termed the 'culturalisation' of race or, more simply, 'post-racism' or 'neo-racism'.[60] This is a way of bringing attention to how, from the 1980s onwards, racial prejudice became increasingly justified through cultural difference. The simplest way to think about this is to accept that the discursive shift from the 'multiracial Britain' of the 1960s to the 'multicultural Britain' of the 2000s is not simply a neutral shift in vocabulary – it also represents an evolution in the meaning of race and racism.

The more complex way to think about this connection is through discourses of 'crises' or 'failures' of multiculturalism – which attempted to problematise the tensions of uneven social and cultural integration of non-British peoples – that gained momentum in the 2000s. When multiculturalism was at its height in the 1990s and early 2000s, it became difficult to openly discuss race – with two critical race theorists going so far as to say that it had become 'taboo'[61] – because of the supposed triumph of tolerance and living with difference.

In the current climate of Black Lives Matters, it is strange to think that if you go back a decade or two ago, it was common to hear the argument that racism no longer exists (and that when it occasionally does still exist, it is in the form of extremism and irrationally unsustainable explicit race hate).[62] Within this narrative of failure or crisis is a kind of cultural relativism whereby the refusal of immigrants to adopt to British national values is seen itself as racist, because it's implied that immigrants think that their culture is superior.[63] Sometimes this culturalisation of racism is still rooted in biology, with some conservatives turning to evolutionary biology to argue that it is natural – our evolutionary instincts – to cling to our culture (and therefore giving reason to avoid the artificial and contrived hope of multiculturalism).[64] More commonly, however, actions are simply essentialised as cultural difference. When this critique is turned to the state, it is to argue that elites prioritise race over class, and that the state is not doing enough to encourage migrants and their families to integrate.[65]

'Secure borders, safe haven'

The rise of multiculturalism as discourse and policy approach can be traced to at least the 1980s, but 2001 was a turning point. The combination of supposed 'race riots' in Northern English towns, and the UK's role in the 'War on Terror' following the September 11 terrorist attacks in the US, problematised multicultural Britain. The state consequently started to intervene in the name of 'community cohesion' and 'safe haven'. In response to the riots, Home Secretary Blunkett launched the Community Cohesion Review Team. The resulting report explained the riots through a lack of shared values, and so prescribed a healthy dose of civic nationalism.[66] Meanwhile, the War on Terror further transformed Islam – and the mobility of Muslims – into a national security issue. This was the context for a shift in how the state related to immigration. Prior to this, the state saw immigration in relatively positive terms due to an emphasis on the economic and fiscal advantages of migrants.

The tone clearly shifted in the infamous 2002 White Paper, *Secure Borders, Safe Haven*, where immigration was now presented as a threat to British values, especially tolerance.[67] Bringing these two threads together, the Nationality, Immigration and Asylum Act 2002 introduced many changes, including: the requirement that citizenship applicants have sufficient knowledge of the UK, meet (strengthened) language requirements, and can demonstrate 'good character';[68] and the creation of 'citizenship ceremonies'. Original citizenship ceremonies invited those who gain citizenship a 'rite of passage' into 'full membership of the British Family', including swearing allegiance to a large portrait of the Queen.[69] Labour also created detention centres for asylum seekers, and new powers to detain and deport foreign nationals.[70]

If multiculturalism has some sort of equivalence to the post-war liberal race relations consensus, then one key difference is the permission to politicise immigration. Post-war immigration was explicitly racialised as Black and Asian. Yet, as outlined above, the racism of multicultural Britain was more subtle with an emphasis on cultural difference. Islamophobia highlights this. The War on Terror prompted the British state and media to problematise Muslims as a threat to national security and to British values. This was not new (consider Salman Rushdie's fatwa in 1989, for example), but it was intensified and twisted.

The political and media responses to the terror attacks of the 2000s onwards helped produce the Muslim as a category distinct from the racialised post-war immigrant.[71] Until the 1980s, Muslims were generally imagined through ethnic categories such as Black, Asian, Pakistani, or Arab.[72] With cultural (and religious) difference core to race and racism, British Muslims, so historian Humayun Ansari shows, 'have increasingly come to represent the ultimate stranger in the British imaginary'.[73] A constant stream of media scandals over the last two decades have positioned Islam as a cultural threat to Britishness: child sexual exploitation is posed as a threat to the safety of white girls, halal meat is posed as a threat to freedom of choice, and Muslim-controlled state schools are posed as a threat to tolerance.[74] Islamophobia can be characterised as the view that Islam is incompatible with Western culture due to behaviours that are seen as breaking with Western cultural norms.

Along with Muslims, Eastern European migrants associated with the A8 in 2004 – as well as Romanian and Bulgarian accession in 2007 – are the key figures that make up the contemporary popular image of the immigrant. However, Eastern European migrants are not problematised by the state in a way equivalent to post-war Commonwealth settlers or 'community cohesion'-era British Muslims. If anything, the presence of Eastern European migrants was cautiously welcomed by some businesses as providing high-quality (European and white) labour.[75] The media, however, was different. Newspaper headlines framed the accession as 'floods' and 'invasions'.[76] Studies into how Romanian migrants are reported on and in the British media found that they were often depicted as criminals.[77] The repetition of 'Romanian' with 'criminal' often implies that Romanian culture is the cause and problem – thereby framing crime as an essential characteristic of Romanian culture, and implying its incompatibility with Britain and British values. So although this treatment may not fit with racism narrowly defined as prejudice based on skin colour, it does fit with the culturalisation of race. This racialisation of Eastern European immigrants in tandem with the unexpectedly large movement of people strengthened the link between anti-immigrant sentiment and the EU, and provided Eurosceptics with something to work with.[78] Political economist Helen Thompson argues, not unreasonably but perhaps with a hint of perfect hindsight, that the A8 decision made Brexit 'an eventual inevitability'.[79] But this required politicising the issue.

As we have seen, 2001 was a turning point for state intervention; it was also a turning point for public opinion on immigration, and the start of its explicit (re)politicisation.[80] Although public opinion data on immigration needs to be handled with care, there are nevertheless important trends. While public opinion has consistently agreed for decades with the proposition that there are 'too many immigrants' in the country, this has not always been identified as an important political issue or priority – that started to change from around 2001 onwards.[81] These changes in politics and public opinion at the very least correlate with one another.

This rising anti-immigration sentiment posed a problem for the New Labour government. Both the centre and the left of the Labour Party was to some extent committed to pro-immigration rhetoric – if not necessarily in policy and practice – through its respective liberal-cosmopolitan and socialist-internationalist traditions.[82] The opposition Conservative Party had no equivalent tradition to uphold. Accordingly, while the Conservative Party manifesto for the 2001 general election contained a single paragraph on immigration, by 2005 it was front and centre, including an entire chapter on dealing with the 'out-of-control immigration system'.[83] These proposals were backed by 97 per cent of the readers of populist tabloid, and Britain's most-read newspaper, the *Sun*.[84] Nevertheless, New Labour won the 2005 election comfortably; but back in office they got tougher on immigration.

Recent political science research has found that the British public definition of 'immigrant' is significantly different from the formal definition. When the public think of 'immigration' they tend to think of asylum seekers and permanent arrivals, yet the most common form of immigration to the UK is people coming to study.[85] One implication is that public opinion is connected to a perception of immigration rather than a direct experience. It seems that the post-2005 Labour government had a similar realisation: the appearance of controlling immigration can be as politically important as controlling immigration itself.[86] So physical manifestations of borders, such as in airports, were rebranded to look tougher, along with militarised border police.[87] The media started getting invited along to report on immigration raids.[88] The Home Office even funded a now popular TV programme called *UK Border Force* (although their funding was later withdrawn under pressure from the Taxpayers Alliance).[89]

This tougher approach was not simply show, as it had policy implications too. The 2005 Labour government withdrew some migration schemes, placed transitional controls on Bulgaria and Romania on their accession to the EU, and tightened the criteria of the points-based system.[90] The Labour government had already taken steps towards NHS nationalisation. In April 2004, the government removed access to free NHS care from unsuccessful asylum seekers, undocumented migrants, and those with expired visas; doing so included the creation of the aforementioned Overseas Visitor Managers and related bureaucracy. During the following years, the fascist British National Party (BNP) sprung from the wilderness into a potential political force, thanks in part to their shift to Islamophobia: votes for the BNP in local elections went from close to zero in 2000 to over 300,000 in 2010.[91] Although the 'hostile environment' was a specific Conservative policy, it built on and extended what was already happening.[92]

'That bigoted woman'

Immigration was not meant to play a big part in the 2010 general election. As part of the self-styled modernisation of the Conservative Party under new leader David Cameron, their hard stance on immigration was diluted to detoxify their 'nasty party' brand.[93] Immigration was barely mentioned in their 2010 general election manifesto.[94] Meanwhile, under Prime Minister Gordon Brown the Labour Party intensified and modified its defensive position: civic nationalism with a defence of the British Empire; the BNP-endorsed 'British jobs for British workers' line with a tightened points-based system.[95] Immigration was nevertheless a key part of the 2010 general election, largely thanks to 'Bigotgate'.

On the campaign trail in the Northern town of Rochdale, Brown had a televised conversation with Labour-voting pensioner Gillian Duffy, who asked what Brown would do about the number of East European immigrants in the town (in a surprisingly wide-ranging conversation, she also asked about the national debt, taxes, and university tuition fees). Brown responded fairly and firmly, albeit in a politician's way (he noted that as many Britons have moved to Europe as vice versa). But, back in his car, he forgot to switch off his microphone and was inadvertently recorded asking his advisors in exasperation why he was being asked to engage with that 'bigoted woman'. *Sky News* recorded the clip, played it back to a visibly upset Duffy, and packaged the whole drama into a story – including an apology from Brown – that captured the news cycle for at least the next twenty-four hours.[96]

At the time, Bigotgate was framed as a 'gaffe'; but it was more than that. As with the deficit, Labour found themselves trapped on immigration in 2010 and 2015. This reflected the strange and damaging race politics of the multicultural era: racism is defined only as explicit race hate, which is totally illegitimate and has no role in politics; any other concerns about immigration or cultures are therefore legitimate so long as they avoid *that*; and to call someone with those 'legitimate concerns' racist is considered in practice worse and more insulting than addressing 'the concerns' (and their racist forms) themselves. With Bigotgate, Brown was clearly worried about the electoral implications of his leaked comments, but he was also clearly shaken by the sense that he might have insulted someone by calling their anti-immigrant concerns 'bigoted'. Brown later described it as his worst day in politics.[97] Duffy became a short-lived feature of the political circuit as informal spokesperson for working-class anti-immigrant sentiment – the *Observer* interviewed her in December that year as one of the 'Faces of 2010' (alongside Labour politician David Miliband, celebrity physicist Brian Cox, and seven others).[98] Although Duffy's fame waned, the impact of Bigotgate went beyond the election. It became seen as an exemplar of how the political 'metropolitan elite' secretly dismiss 'ordinary' concerns about immigration as prejudice.

Bigotgate helped the concept of the 'metropolitan elite' to catch on. It has since become a regular feature of British politics. For instance, in a lower-profile rerun of Bigotgate four years later in 2014, Shadow Attorney General Emily Thornberry resigned after tweeting a photo of a house that was flying three England flags with a white van parked in the driveway. A *Daily Mail* headline read: 'Emily is so at home in Islington luvvie-land, a metropolitan liberal allergic to the ideals of patriotism and the self-reliant family'.[99] These kinds of identity, as we will see in Chapter 5, were essential in building a pro-Brexit coalition. This was likely connected to Conservative opposition leader William Hague's response to the Macpherson report, the result of an inquiry into police mishandling of the murder of Black teenager Stephen Lawrence that condemned the institutional racism of the police. In response to the report, Hague made headlines criticising the 'condescending liberal elite' for enforcing a political correctness that allowed crime to flourish (i.e. stopped the police from targeting Black youths).[100] He went on to say that: 'The Macpherson report has been used to brand every officer and every branch of the force as racist, it's contributed directly to the collapse of police morale and recruitment and has led to a growing crisis on our streets.' That this usage of liberal or metropolitan elite came from the political fallout over a racial scandal involving the police is likely no coincidence. But who this metropolitan elite consists of, exactly, is not necessarily clear.

The metropolitan elite are imagined as a group of establishment figures who use their decision-making power and positions of cultural authority (especially in universities and the BBC) to promote immoral and dangerous social practices – multiculturalism, feminism, queer rights – instead of ensuring 'law and order' and the sanctity of the British family. To do so, the metropolitan elite supposedly enforce 'political correctness', which is a lay account of how public discourse has been captured and bounded by a multicultural left to ensure that some viewpoints (e.g. anti-immigration) can never be aired, less so addressed. In ensuring political correctness through capturing universities and the BBC, this analysis continues, the metropolitan elite in effect puts the interests of Britain's Black and Asian population (i.e. race) above the interests of poor people who need help (i.e. class, and typically white, if the logic is taken seriously). The 'metropolitan' part suggests that this group inhabit cities and 'urban' (i.e. Black and Asian) spaces and culture. The 'elite' part, meanwhile, also suggests a crude class analysis; that this elite do not face to the same day-to-day material struggles as ordinary people.[101] The term 'metropolitan elite' is used consistently to identify how an out-of-touch and un-British cadre are enabling Black and Asian people (as well as sexual minorities and some feminists) to threaten Britain. It may appear as a neutral term, but if this analysis is taken seriously then one must conclude that it is a profoundly racialised (as well as gendered and sexualised) term. This set the scene for the Brexit era culture wars analysed in Chapter 6.

'Ordinary people' are pitched in contrast to the metropolitan elite and the supposedly dangerous minorities they serve. As we have seen, 'ordinary people' is a trope that was popularised by Enoch Powell. It cemented a post-colonial British nationhood that marked out whiteness through the boundary of ordinariness: Anglo-British whiteness is ordinary and respectable; racialised others are extraordinary and unruly. The letter box and respectable street of Powell's anecdotes come to mind. A quote from conservative philosopher Roger Scruton can help us further tease this out:

> disquiet over immigration was the result, it seems to me, not of racism, but of the disruption of an old experience of home, and a loss of enchantment which made home a place of safety and consolation.[102]

Although Scruton does not explicitly write of 'ordinary people', his analysis here is an exemplar of its underlying logic. While 'disquiet over immigration' may not be an example of explicit race hatred, it is still racialised. Those who are deemed to 'disrupt an old experience of home' are immigrants. And so it is not a person who threatens that place of safety, but rather a 'Muslim' or 'Eastern European', with the perceived threat they pose essentialised to a seemingly incompatible culture. So the analysis goes: multiculturalism (and its perceived failings) has therefore *left behind* 'ordinary people' because of the supposed priority of ethnic minorities. It is a flexible analysis that can be put to work for different political ends: some socialists are attracted to this analysis because it gives them the basis to claim race has been placed above (the white working) class; many conservatives are attracted to this analysis because it gives them the basis to claim that race has been placed above (the white) nation. To speak of or seek to defend 'ordinary people' with 'legitimate concerns' is to make an implicit claim about who the nation – and its wealth and services – should belong to and benefit. 'Ordinary people' with 'legitimate concerns' are almost exclusively imagined as white. In times of scarcity and conflict, the boundaries of the nation are contested, policed, and, in this case, narrowed.

This is the key context for the hostile environment policies associated with Theresa May's Home Office during the Coalition government. In a study of the hostile environment, the approach was often justified in the name of ordinary people.[103] For example, the study highlights a speech by the then Immigration Minister James Brokenshire:

> For too long, the benefits of immigration went to employers who wanted an easy supply of cheap labour; or to the wealthy metropolitan elite who wanted cheap tradesmen and services – but not to the ordinary, hard-working people of this country[104]

The hostile environment was a strategy to bring down immigration numbers through deterring migration. This included a wide range of policies such as increasing processing fees, upping deportations, and extending the border into everyday life – for example, by asking doctors, teachers, and high-street bank workers to surveil and report on radicalisation and illegal status.[105] It also includes the nationalisation of the NHS.

Conclusion

As prime minister, David Cameron liked to say how immigration and welfare were 'two sides of the same coin'.[106] Sylvester Marshall's story from the beginning of this chapter highlights this too, although probably not in the way that Cameron meant. Immigration and welfare – and race and class – are interrelated, as scholars such as Shilliam and Bhambra encourage us to see. When seen like this, we can see that Britain has always been hostile to providing welfare for 'strangers', the meaning of which has shifted with the scale of the help and home. In the eighteenth century, vagrants from neighbouring parishes were routinely expelled back home; in the nineteenth century, English and Welsh parishes deported thousands of Irish paupers (including 50,000 between 1824 and 1831); and, as we have seen, this pattern continued in the racial discrimination of post-war Britain.[107] This process has almost always been racialised, whether the socially inscribed biological difference took the form of blood, stock, and/or skin colour. The conflicts that have emerged from these histories – including the recent nationalisation of the NHS studied here – are neither just economic *or* cultural, nor just fiscal *or* racial, but all of those things together. Austerity and scarcity intensifies this.

NHS nationalisation was governed to 'benefit UK society' and to ensure that everyone makes a 'fair contribution to the cost of their healthcare'. It involves systematically taking away resources from people who previously had access down the lines of the citizenship which, as we have seen, intersects strongly with race and Britain's post-colonial struggles and power plays. This nationalisation was done partly for 'ordinary people', as was the Brexit battle bus's infamous NHS promise, and as was the Johnson government's pledge to increase NHS spending – all part of plans to 'level up' the so-called 'left behind', which is the focus of the next chapter.

4

From exclusion to inequality

Is white working-class Britain becoming invisible?
BBC *White* series website, 2008[1]

In metropolitan circles, where sneering at any minority ethnic group would be regarded as an outrage, this white working-class opinion is all too often treated with suspicion or contempt.
Richard Klein, the commissioning editor for the *White* series, 2008[2]

In March 2008, the TV channel BBC Two launched its flagship series for its spring programme: *White*, which focused on the 'white working class'. Episodes included 'Last Orders' ('The members of a Working Men's Club in Bradford speak out'), 'Rivers of Blood' ('Exploring the legacy of Enoch Powell's controversial speech', described as 'sympathetic' by the Financial Times),[3] 'White Girl' ('Drama about a white working-class family who move into a Muslim area' and whose daughter converts to Islam), and 'The Poles Are Coming!' ('What effect does a million Eastern European workers have on the British economy?').

As the commissioning editor explained, the aim of the series was 'in part an attempt to revolt' by giving voice to the white working classes, who had been marginalised by the political correctness of the political and media classes.[4] The accompanying BBC press release implied that this constituency was ignored by stating that the motivation for the season was to get the country talking about the 'white working class'.[5] The advertising campaign, however, came under criticism. It showed a close-up of white man's face being scrawled on with a black marker pen held by a brown hand to the point until the face disappeared – in effect, erased.[6] If the aim of *White* was to get the country talking about the 'white working classes' and their concerns, then it can be considered an especially prescient commission. Talk of the white working classes has been a feature of the post-crash years, most notably through the discourse of how the 'white working classes' have been 'left behind'.

What do these categories mean? And where do they come from? The left behind are most associated with the 2016 referendum on EU membership. In making sense of the shock result, the major narrative focused on how Northern white working-class voters used the referendum to voice their displeasure and anger at the cultural and economic changes associated with globalisation. This 'left behind' narrative was complex and amorphous, and could at different times include the following strands: deindustrialisation and austerity had left them behind from British economic development; multiculturalism (and its perceived failings) had left them behind because of the supposed priority of ethnic minorities; and cultural change left them behind in terms of liberal and cosmopolitan progress on gender, race, and sexual values.

This chapter builds on the work of Gurminder Bhambra and Robbie Shilliam to show how the 'left behind' discourse emerged from the shifting meaning of inequality.[7] In the pre-crash years of never-ending boom, income and wealth inequality could be justified as the legitimate outcome of meritocratic competition. The austerity period was legitimated by a more extreme of this, whereby hardworking families were pitted against the undeserving poor. In these periods, those at the bottom end of income and wealth distribution were treated as 'socially excluded' – as in, they have excluded themselves from the positive forces of globalisation because of poor choices or upbringing, and so are to blame for their position.

As the post-crash era unfolded, blaming people for their poverty became increasingly untenable – because in a world defined by scarcity, some people will inevitably be 'left behind'. While the socially excluded low-income white Briton of the pre-crash and austerity period were seen as undeserving of help, the left-behind low-income white Britons of later years were seen in the opposite light. The rehabilitation of low-income white Britons as 'left behind' therefore created the image of a relatively powerless national peoples – racialised as white – whose interests a nationalist wildcat elite could represent because the metropolitan elite will not. As highlighted in the Introduction and detailed further below, a sense that a national peoples are suffering unequal treatment and therefore in need of lifting up is the classic mode of nationalist mobilisation, and thus also a clear path towards nationalisation. It was, in the conceptual terms laid out in the Introduction, a way of drawing the implicit boundaries of Britishness to mobilise a nationalising project.

Nationalist mobilisation

Nationalisation is the process in which the boundaries of the state are made more congruent with the boundaries of the nation. To purposely make the state more national, one needs considerable authority and power. This poses a problem for nationalists: how to take or consolidate power? The answer is to mobilise.

Nationalism requires a nation, of course: a homogenous set of people who are tied through a shared culture. To mobilise, however, nationalism also requires a kind of *inequality*. It is when the relative lowly status of a national peoples can be narrated as the fault of an oppressor – mythical or otherwise – that is outside of or against the nation that we have a situation ripe for nationalist mobilisation. The link to the analysis of previous chapters – austerity, scarcity, conflict – should be self-evident. However, The kind of inequality needed for nationalist mobilisation is not necessarily what the term has come to mean in post-crash political discourse. As we will see below, in the post-crash era 'inequality' has taken on a particular meaning as 'disparities in the distribution of income and wealth', based in part on the pioneering research of economists such as Thomas Piketty.

To simplify, the kind of inequality required for nationalist mobilisation entails both 'objective' and 'subjective' components. Objective because it depends on the uneven distribution of resources; but also subjective because it requires those uneven patterns to be interpreted through some sort of entrenched difference (such as class or race) to be made political. Most people do not evaluate their lives in abstract terms of wealth or income quintiles. Rather, we tend to place ourselves into imagined groups (such as hardworking, middle class, or Scottish) and evaluate our position in society according to fairness in relation to other groups.[8] *Uneven* distribution requires a comparison point; it is relative to something else. If that uneven distribution can be compellingly shown to be drawn down ethnic lines – especially in contrast to down class lines – then the times may be ripe for nationalist mobilisation.

Ernest Gellner shows in his classic text, *Nations and Nationalism*, how the kind of inequality required for nationalism is inherent to capitalist development.[9] The starting premise is simple: that capitalist growth systematically benefits distinct regions, ethnicities, or other units over others. The early machinations of industrialisation created ideal conditions for nationalism. Industrialisation typically requires the vast movement – displacement, even – of otherwise locally tied people from their communities to urban centres, where they are left little option but to sell their labour in exchange for a wage to survive. This pattern is replicated among different communities across a national territory. This loosening of community, combined with vast inequality and a sense of shared experience, provides the perfect conditions for someone to identify those who toil together as united by a community – imagined across a national territory, rather than a literal community anchored through the ties of place.

Forms of 'inequality' existed and continue to exist in feudal and pre-feudal economies. However, in European historical terms, those disparities could be justified by hierarchies rooted in absolute difference (e.g. 'blue blooded'). In those worlds, a man born a peasant is very likely to die a peasant. Capitalist development introduces the conditions for the kind of inequality needed for nationalism through two processes. First, capitalist development accelerates the formation of imagined communities through mass education, a national press, and the creation of 'national' markets, including that for labour. Second, capitalism tends to bring with it a promise of meritocracy: that with mass, standardised education anyone can in principle achieve and do anything, so long as they work hard enough (a process explored by Gellner through the idea of 'social entropy and equality'). When uneven distribution can no longer be accounted for by randomness or through just deserts, then we have the makings of mobilisation. And when that uneven distribution is narrated down ethnic lines, then we have the makings of nationalist mobilisation in particular.

Nationalist mobilisation requires the sense that the national peoples are systematically losing out to another group *because* that group have control or patronage of political decision-making, which they use to reward themselves and their supporters. This provides the purpose of taking or consolidating formal political power. Nationalism may well 'punch down' in terms of stigmatising those who are supposedly a threat to the status of the national peoples, who may have less power, and are likely to be narrated as outside the boundaries of the nation and/or undeserving of a share in the nation's wealth (e.g. 'immigrants'). But it must also 'punch up', to remove or keep out of power those who are outside of, or against, the nation (e.g. 'the metropolitan elite'), otherwise it has no purpose in seeking power. Taken together, nationalist mobilisation works on the basis of a shared observation that the 'rightful' peoples are kept out of power, and that in doing so they do not have a 'fair' proportion of resources; by gaining power, those peoples can redistribute resources to the nation. Or at least that's the promise.

If there is no oppressor to punch up towards, then one can be exaggerated or made up (such as the European Union or the metropolitan elite). This is perhaps why nationalism often manifests in anti-elite, populist forms in otherwise non-oppressed nation-states. Think, for example, of far-right anti-Semitic conspiracy theories, the supposed hegemony of 'cultural Marxism', or Trump's attacks on global governance and international organisations. In each of these examples, it is alleged that there is some sort of elite who support the interests of those outside of the nation at the expense of the nation. By reducing the power of those groups, replacing it with a new elite that is closer aligned to the interests of the nation, the boundaries of nation and politics can be realigned.

Nationalism thrives when a relative low status produced by capitalist growth provides a basis to mobilise an ethnically homogenous group to take power away from (supposed) oppressors, gain self-determination, and redistribute resources accordingly. This requires a kind of imagined community – a homogenous, ethnic identity – that can cut across class divisions to unite the interests of a nationalist elite vanguard with the national peoples. In the conceptual terms outlined in the Introduction, this requires placing both nationalist elites and the national peoples within the core of the informal boundaries of national identity. As we will see, the left behind did this by creating a homogenous sense of race (whiteness) and ethnicity (Englishness) that cut across class division and placed lower-income white Britons as the most deserving of national wealth.

From poverty to exclusion

The practice of distinguishing between poor people who deserve help via the nation's wealth and those who do not has a long history. The Poor Laws family distinguished between the 'able-bodied poor' and the 'idle poor'. Both groups were considered poor because they were out of work, but the latter were considered undeserving of help and so were denied relief.[10] Although the post-war welfare state with its culture of universal entitlement was a temporary exception to this rule, these sorts of deserving/undeserving distinctions have been institutionalised into British culture. The Thatcherite project turned back to these 'Victorian values' in justifying welfare state retrenchment during the 1980s. This retrenchment was backed by a discourse of self-reliance and personal responsibility in which overtaxed individuals were being cheated out of their income by, in Stuart Hall's analysis of Thatcherite discourse, 'the emotive image of the "scrounger": the new folk-devil'.[11] The idea that the state should help only those who deserve it lives on today. Recent political science research demonstrates that contemporary public opinion on welfare is driven by perceptions of recipient deservingness.[12]

A distinction between a deserving and undeserving poor was implicit to New Labour's welfare reforms, especially around unemployment benefits. The kind of means-tested benefits instigated by New Labour institutionalised a deserving/undeserving distinction because benefits were dependent upon claimants fulfilling a criteria (e.g. active and supervised job-seeking and associated 'behavioural changes' such as training courses on how to write CVs). The New Labour approach was typical of how they navigated Britain's relationship to the global economy.[13] They justified more means testing through a distinction between those who are integrated into the globalised labour market and those who exclude themselves as a moral underclass.[14] Let us unpack this further.

Competitiveness was key to the political economy of New Labour. Under New Labour, the national economy as an imagined space and community was further displaced by a narrative of globalisation; and the national peoples of the post-war era were further displaced by a population of human capital.[15] Welfare in the form of unemployment insurance shifted further away from a safety net and towards a tool to ensure that all parts of the potential workforce are geared towards the labour market, to ensure global competitiveness. The main barrier to this was deemed to be 'social exclusion'.[16] The New Labour era was governed as a time of perpetual economic growth, of beyond boom and bust, of optimum global and European integration, and therefore of steadily rising living standards for everyone in society. To be out of work is to be excluded from this and, to some extent, from society altogether.[17] 'Social exclusion' is more a temporary and contingent problem compared to poverty, and so presents itself as an issue that can apparently be overcome, intervened into, fixed.[18]

An institutionalised culture of responsibility which leads to exclusion in turn poses a risk to long-term fiscal pressures and national competitiveness. Welfare policy was therefore increasingly geared towards delivering an equality of opportunity by looking to 'include' the unemployed in the globalised workforce through boosting their human capital.[19] As with the shift from 'multiracial Britain' to 'multicultural Britain' in the previous chapter, this reconfiguration of the poor as a problem of exclusion rather than poverty entailed treating unemployment as a cultural problem. By realigning poverty with social exclusion and a culture of passivity, the poor were essentially divided into those who earned their relief through active behavioural change and those who were deemed undeserving for foregoing such activities. In doing so, they were deemed to be excluding themselves from the pool of human capital available for the nation's integration into, and competitiveness within, the global economy, and so undeserving of help.

In this world, income and wealth inequality is not justified but necessary and even encouraged. If competitiveness requires a competitive labour market – and the whole point of competition is to distinguish between winners and losers – then this regime requires and justifies inequality.[20] The remaking of the poor as a problem of exclusion and deficient human capital means that the signs of systemic inequality can be justified as a failure for the 'losers' from competitive struggle to rationally and efficiently invest in themselves.

Personal irresponsibility provided both state and society with a cultural explanation as to why some parts of the population were so detached from the labour market.[21] Unemployment was therefore the individual's fault and responsibility, because those who worked hard got what they deserved. Unsurprisingly, then, the political heroes of this world were the 'hardworking families', that favoured constituency of austerity-era centrist politicians. Ed Miliband always spoke of helping 'the squeezed middle', which shifted to the 'just about managing' – or JAMs – in Theresa May's short-lived one-nation rhetoric.

This way of imagining society carved up into different groups of people – a class system, in other words – is not especially amenable to nationalist mobilisation. This can be highlighted through one of the key cultural figures of these times that paralleled New Labour's 'social exclusion' approach: the 'chav'. This figure emerged in the 2000s and peaked in popularity and fascination in the middle of that decade.[22] The chav was marked out by excessive consumption of vulgar and luxury goods (e.g. ostentatious gold jewellery and Burberry attire), the adoption of Black American mannerisms (e.g. slang and patois), and a culture of irresponsibility (e.g. workshy, welfare dependency, and large state-supported families).[23] Chavs were distinguished by irrational economic choices and (reminiscent of Chapter 2) vulgar consumption habits. The chav was represented in the media, on TV, and on the internet as simultaneously a figure of fun (e.g. a stereotype for comedy characters) and a figure of disgust (e.g. the internet forum *Chavscum*, with its tagline: 'Chav Scum: Britain's peasant underclass that is taking over our towns and cities'. The figure was a way of stigmatising young, poor, white people – especially women and mothers – which also amplified long-standing anxieties about the cultural and ethnic implications of interracial coupling. [24] Above all, the figure of the chav played on anxieties and curiosities about this supposed underclass who excluded themselves from the labour market.[25]

Chavs also highlight the racialised underbelly of the 'moral underclass' discourse. Representations of chavs were almost exclusively white-skinned, to the point that a media representation of a black-skinned chav is barely conceivable (try a Google image search of 'chav'). A Black or Asian poor person who acts in 'chavvy' ways does not require the extra distinction or stigma of 'chav' because race already provides that; and lower-income or 'underclass' white people taking on the characteristics of already stigmatised Black and (to a lesser extent) Asian culture provides a racialised script for class stigma. (Think back to David Starkey's comments about 'the whites have become black' from Chapter 2, for an example). The racialised aspect of chavs also suggests another way to think about the boundaries of national exclusion: as not just outside competitive labour markets but also as outside the national boundaries of whiteness.

Any discourse of the 'left behind' in the first decade or so of this century would likely conjure the image of the 'underclass' or 'chav'. These groups were stigmatised by all because of their apparent non-commitment to hard work, thereby depriving those who were deserving of resources. In the forward march of globalisation and never-ending boom, inequalities must be the fault of the individual. The underclass or chavs were deserving of their lowly position in the distribution of resources and their lowly status in British culture. Research has shown how some of the most impoverished people in Britain have internalised this idea of an undeserving poor.[26] One study interviewed residents of a council estate in the Northern post-industrial town of Middlesbrough between 2008 and 2010. They asked those stuck on a low-pay-no-pay cycle – the 'long-term churning between insecure, low-paid jobs, and unemployment' – about their experiences of poverty. Their findings present something of a paradox: interviewees typically denied their own poverty and the category of 'poor' despite living in evident material hardship. 'Poor people' were other people who were judged for their irresponsible consumption and their failure to resiliently manage the situation they'd been dealt.[27] Other research has reported similar findings.[28]

Throughout this period, attitudes towards welfare hardened, with most people less likely to support redistribution or tackling poverty with the use of public money than they were before. While support for higher spending on the poor peaked in 1989, the general trend since then has been clearly downwards. The percentage of respondents agreeing that government should 'spend more ... on the poor, even if it leads to higher taxes' has also declined from over half in 1993 to around a quarter in 2009.[29] This was the context in which the

Conservative-led Coalition government came to power with the promise of austerity.

Undeserving others

The Coalition came to power in 2010 with the promise of fixing 'Broken Britain'. This extended the moral underclass narrative that New Labour governed through.[30] Their most infamous reforms were Universal Credit, which repackaged different benefits and tax credits into a single instrument to encourage work; the 'Bedroom Tax', whereby housing benefits were reduced by 14 per cent for one 'spare bedroom' and 25 per cent for two or more 'spare bedrooms'; and their changes to Work Capability Assessment (WCA), which is a test to assess the extent of illness or disability of those claiming Employment and Support Allowance (ESA). Each of these reforms had been introduced with the purpose of saving money, in the context of austerity. And each has faced significant criticism for increased bureaucracy and harm.

For example, the Coalition government contracted out the administration of Work Capability Assessments to private companies in 2011. WCAs are run via a rigid, computer-based points system and semi-structured interviews, and are consistently criticised for being mechanistic and inhumane[31]. The purpose of the intensified WCA is to lower the number of welfare claimants, which many have interpreted as an attack on disability in which all claimants are under suspicion of being fraudulent. Survey evidence shows that suicides among out-of-work disability benefit claimants have more than doubled since the WCA was introduced, and nearly half of people surveyed on ESA said that they had attempted suicide.[32] Taken together, these welfare reforms were regressive overall, with average losses of around 10 per cent of net income for the poorest 20 per cent of households.[33] Single mothers, the disabled, and Pakistani and Bangladeshi adults especially lost out.[34]

Benefit sanctions have evolved into a central part of the UK's welfare system, with the amount of sanctions doubling from around 2010 onwards.[35] Despite there being little evidence that sanctions are effective in changing behaviour, claimants being punished for a first offence – e.g. failing to accept a job offer, or applying for insufficient jobs – could lose up to 100 per cent of their benefit for three months.[36] Although there are no official figures, estimates for 2013–14 suggest that the average duration of a Jobseeker's Allowance sanction is eight weeks long, with an average loss of income of £530 – which would suggest an overall saving of around £280 million.[37] There is little evidence, however, that these welfare reforms were fiscally beneficial in the short term.[38] As both large-scale quantitative and small-scale qualitative research has shown, the intensification of sanctions and other changes have adversely impacted lives – sometimes even cutting off lines to subsistence and survival.[39]

As with 'chavs' in the preceding period, this politics was accompanied with cultural phenomena that legitimated the changes. In Chapter 2, we saw how the ways in which the poor lived, ate, consumed, coupled, and parented became a kind of national obsession. We can extend that analysis here through *Benefits Street*. When it first aired in 2014, *Benefits Street* was a television phenomenon. The five-episode long first series followed the ups and downs of a select group of residents from James Turner Street in Birmingham, which is depicted in the show as 'one of Britain's most benefit-dependent streets'. At the beginning of the first episode, a resident walks down the road identifying each house as 'unemployed … unemployed … unemployed … unemployed …'. *Benefits Street* was a national moment: the first episode achieved a national audience share of 17.2 per cent and was watched by 4.3 million people, which provided Channel 4's highest viewing figures over the preceding twelve-month period.[40] The show was controversial: it was criticised for exploiting its participants and for promoting anti-welfare attitudes. Although it is evidently a narrative-based quasi-documentary, its creators defended it as unmediated and honest[41]. Research has indicated that programmes such as *Benefits Street* are 'heavily edited, scripted and actively cast for in order to generate commercially successful content'.[42]

Benefits Street was just one example of so-called 'poverty porn' that was popular in the austerity era. Other programmes included: *On Benefits and Proud* (Channel 5, 2013), *We All Pay Your Benefits* (BBC One, 2013), *Benefits Britain 1949* (Channel 4, 2013), *Don't Cap My Benefits* (BBC, 2014), *Britain's Benefit Tenants* (Channel

4, 2015), *Celebs on Benefits: Claims to Fame* (Channel 5, 2015), *Battling with Benefits* (BBC One Wales, 2016), *The Great British Benefits Handout* (Channel 5, 2016–17).[43] The audience of these shows is implicitly invited to decide for themselves whether these people deserve their state benefits. *Benefits Street* was indeed explicitly framed in terms of austerity. The opening sequence of the programme notes that 'times are getting tougher … They're having to get by on less … And rely on each other more'. In the first episode, the increasingly stringent character of welfare benefits plays a role in the storyline, as residents on the street struggle with their lines of sustenance being cut off or reduced.

Given that austerity was governed as a national emergency that asked the population to act together to live within means, this obsession with the poor should not be surprising. If the state tells society that there's not as much to go around because the previous government wasted it, and that failing to get spending under control is a matter of national survival, then there are going to be effects – especially in the context of a prolonged recession. People wonder where the money went, and which people – or, more accurately, what *types* of people – took 'their' money. Those who are not being thrifty or living within their means are not just undeserving of help but are also letting the country down. Taking an interest in the poor, in the lives of welfare recipients – and, in particular, the ways in which they do or do not meet the fiscal-moral imperative to live within means – becomes consistent with acting in the national interest. It is also a way of confirming one's own status as hardworking, and therefore core to the nation.

Up until the Brexit referendum, hardworking taxpayers and their families continued as the key imaginary constituency in the rhetoric of British politicians. This was linked to a particular way of understanding inequality: that inequality is the necessary result of competitive struggle over resources, and those who are at the bottom are there because they have not worked hard enough. A world where inequality is justifiable in line with the dominant norms of the day is a world that is not especially amenable to nationalist mobilisation. That is especially so when people at the lower end of the income and wealth distribution are seen as outside or peripheral to the nation. However, as we will see later, the idea that the poor are to blame for being poor – at a time of significant scarcity and austerity

– became less and less credible, and with that the boundaries of nationhood shifted towards homogenisation across class.

Scandals of meritocracy

In addition to homogeneity across class, nationalist mobilisation also needs to 'punch up'. That is, it requires a compelling narrative that promises that the relatively lowly status of the national peoples can be restored or consolidated by taking power away from those who are outside of, or working against, the nation. The previous chapter started the account of where this punching up may be directed: the 'metropolitan elite', who secretly dismiss the legitimate concerns of the ordinary people. Just now, we saw how the undeserving poor became a national obsession. The financial crash and its aftermath also led to those at the other end of the wealth and income distribution being scandalised for their morally dubious ways. Three scandals were crucial here: the bank bailouts in 2008; the MP expenses scandal in 2009; and celebrity offshore tax abuse scandals in 2012 and 2013. These scandals challenged the idea of meritocracy that underpinned the supposedly pre-crash meritocratic order.

The first scandal was the bank bailouts. Bankers were already blamed for the subprime crash and subsequent recession. And since then other scandals such as LIBOR rate-fixing have hit the City. Yet the bailouts remain pivotal in problematising the rich elite. The government bailout was announced in October 2008. Through recapitalisation, credit guarantees, and short-term loans the government promised at least £500 billion to the finance industry.[44] This led to the de facto nationalisation of Royal Bank of Scotland and Lloyds TSB, two of the UK's largest banks. The UK bailouts were the second biggest in Europe, only surpassed by Ireland – and at least twice as large as the Organisation for Economic Co-operation and Development (OECD) average.[45] These measures were not Keynesian-style stimulus, but instead emergency measures to make safe the finance-dependent British economy, its housing market, and therefore the wealth of many middle-class and rich households.[46]

The bailouts publicly brought rich elites into the fiscal politics of help and assistance, with its deserving and undeserving distinction. And it's safe to say that the finance industry was not considered deserving of help. A piece of satirical songwriting entitled 'Bugger the Bankers' seemed to capture the spirit of the time, if not the Top 100 chart.[47] A typical response at the time was to ask why help the very people who caused the mess in the first place? As they sing in 'Bugger the Bankers': 'the workers get taxed while the wealthy relax'. 'Greedy bankers' is one of the cliches of recent British politics.

The second scandal was the MPs' expenses scandal that consumed British politics in 2009. Following a revelation by a major newspaper, detailed information from leaked documents demonstrated how some MPs had abused their parliamentary expenses, especially over allowances for second homes. The initial revelations involved some of the top politicians in the country such as Gordon Brown, John Prescott, Peter Mandelson, and Alistair Darling; but it was the wider revelations that proved truly damaging.[48] Two Cabinet members, several ministers, and the Speaker of the House of Commons eventually resigned; and three MPs were successfully prosecuted for fraud.[49]

The scandal was seen as symbolising everything that is wrong with the current political system: politicians who don't care about the average person and are just in it for their own personal gain. While the sense that politicians are by nature self-interested and self-serving is not especially new, this view was intensified during the scandal.[50] It took place alongside widespread concerns about political apathy, declining trust in politicians, and wavering faith in the democratic system – and there was a sense that this could be a tipping point into something darker. A poll conducted around a month after the major revelations found that 95 per cent of respondents had heard of the expenses scandal; that 91 per cent reported it had made them 'very angry'; and that 60 per cent now agreed that most MPs were corrupt.[51]

The third scandal is offshore tax abuse. Rather than one big reveal, this scandal has taken the form of a steady drip of revelations from around 2012 onwards, including the Paradise Papers, the Panama Papers, the Luxembourg Leaks, and the HSBC files. Although these leaks have revealed the structural and widespread character of offshore tax abuse – and raised some challenging questions for powerful individuals – it is the celebrity tax scandals that have resonated most with the British public. The scandal that kicked it all off in June 2012 is still the most memorable: when well-known comedian and entertainer Jimmy Carr was revealed to be funnelling

£3.3 million per year through the legal, but morally dubious, K2 Jersey-based tax avoidance scheme.[52] *The Times* ran the story on their front page with the headline 'The tax avoiders' that placed Carr and others within the wider K2 scheme. The story continued the next day, when the then prime minister David Cameron said that the K2 scheme is 'not fair, and it's not right', and that Carr's behaviour was 'not morally acceptable'.[53]

These comments came back to bite Cameron. Four years later the Panama Papers uncovered how Cameron and his family had benefitted themselves from offshore tax abuse. Cameron's comments on Carr were brought back up to demonstrate his hypocrisy. Although Jimmy Carr was the most high profile, this was part of a wider trend of celebrity and corporate tax shaming that campaigners used to deter would-be tax abusers in lieu of proper change from the state.[54] Together with the continued leaks, it gives a sense of how we are not all in it together, because rich elites can play by different rules. The rich may work for their wealth or not, but they keep it by cheating, from which hardworking, ordinary people lose out.

These three scandals are linked by a sense of outrage that there is an elite who are disconnected from the rest of society, an amorphous group that includes the Banker, the Politician, and the Celebrity. This elite are presumed to be held to different legal standards, with their rule-breaking or failures unpunished, and so they benefit from special treatment.[55] This was especially the case with bank bailouts, which fed into a populist narrative that explained those actions as the inevitable outcome of a corrupt elite that uses its economic might and privileged networks to secure its position of power while the people suffer the consequences. Scandals that reveal the distributional inequities of who gets what, when, and how are especially meaningful to a nation that has been told to make sacrifices because 'we're all in this together'. Recent research has shown how most of the British population believe the economy works unfairly and has become more unfair over the last ten years[56]. Notions of 'the 1 per cent' and the 'rigged system' have become core features of British politics. The idea of meritocracy is more difficult to sustain in this world, and so wealth and income inequality becomes a problem.

The idea of meritocracy was further challenged by social science research on income and wealth inequality. In the British context, a book called *The Spirit Level: Why Equality is Better for Everyone* started this off in 2009 with a slow burn. But it was Thomas Piketty's 2014 *Capital in the Twenty-First Century* when interest really took off.[57] It was an unlikely publishing sensation, selling over 2.5 million copies. Drawing on extensive data, Piketty demonstrates that capital and wealth have outstripped wages and economic growth over recent decades, thereby suggesting that inequality will continue to increase unless capitalism is reformed. The book was timed perfectly, and orthodox economists and the global commentariat felt unable to ignore its findings. As a group of top political economy scholars put it:

> However well written, it is safe to say that a massive tome sprinkled with graphs of economic growth rates would not have been a best-seller without the financial crisis ... [its] implicit moral economy, focused on the unequal (or even unearned) distribution of rewards, resonated with popular debates concerning the responsibility for the crisis and its social costs.[58]

Interest in wealth inequality exploded in the years following the publication of Piketty's book. Wealth and income inequality became a legitimate category of mainstream political debate in Britain and on the global stage, in a way unthinkable a decade earlier.

Inequality can be justified if it is generated by a system that makes everyone a bit richer in the long run. In a world where boom and bust had returned, the combination of scandals and Piketty challenged those terms, the latter through rigorous demonstration, the former through inviting the public to associate those wealth disparities with a class of failing, corrupt, and tax-cheating elites. When also considered as a 'metropolitan elite' who fail to consider the supposedly legitimate concerns of ordinary people, the conditions for nationalist mobilisation start to crystallise.

Alongside this, the idea that being poor is a moral, individual failing became increasingly untenable. For instance, the Coalition welfare reforms were accompanied by a continual stream of stories and research highlighting the life-altering and sometimes life-ending effects of these changes. Various researchers have used statistical methods to demonstrate how cuts to services like this explain excess deaths of people who depend on these services, or attempted to make a link between welfare reforms and increased suicide. Different estimates of the former have been produced, but a high-profile and recent research paper puts it at 120,000 between 2010 and 2017.[59] Within some sections of the British left, that 'austerity kills' has thus become a stylised fact. Consequently, it is becoming less and less tenable – and sometimes even just plain crass – to blame the poor for lacking competitiveness. Although welfare reforms have not got any more generous or less disciplining, the national obsession with the poor has dissipated.

Nationalising projects

This kind of inequality was ripe for nationalist mobilisation. This situation had, thinking back to Gellner's analysis above, both 'objective' and 'subjective' qualities. The objective qualities can be found in the relative scarcity of the slow growth post-crash period, in the hardship and violence caused by austerity measures, and in the rigorous evidence of an increasing gap between the rich and poor. The subjective qualities can be found in the quasi-populist fallout from the global financial crisis, where it became common and even compelling to speak of a corrupt, incompetent, and out-of-touch metropolitan elite who inhabit a different world. Unlike in the New Labour world of enhancing global competitiveness and sharing the proceeds of growth to enrich those who deserve it, the meritocratic justification for inequality was no longer holding so strong. This provided ample opportunity for nationalising projects – if they could convincingly speak on behalf of a national peoples by promising to restore their status and dignity by installing new rulers with a new kind of rule *for* the nation and *by* the nation.

Those national peoples must be mobilised, both electorally and rhetorically. There were three nationalising projects of note: Corbyn's Labour Party, Brexit, and Scottish independence. While the national peoples mobilised by the Scottish Independence Movement is obvious enough, the other two are less so.

Corbyn was never supposed to be leader. In effect an accidental candidate from the socialist wing of the party who no one thought would win (his odds were 100–1), he was able to win the leadership due to new rules that gave Labour Party members increased power over the election process.[60] A key symbolic moment in the leadership election campaign was when Labour MPs were whipped to vote with the government on further stringent welfare reforms. The other three leadership candidates from the centre of the party went along with the whip so as not to appear soft on welfare or economic credibility, but Corbyn rebelled, and his profile among the membership exploded.[61] The moment was of the times.

The Corbyn project was ideologically driven by a critique of neoliberal globalisation, which erodes popular sovereignty through neo-imperialist US wars, the power of global finance and corporations, and one-size-fits-all market-led reforms. Intellectually, the movement consisted of a unique combination of Bennite economic nationalism and post-capitalist techno-utopian accelerationism.[62] From this basis, Corbyn's Labour was able to mobilise the sense that with stagnating growth, wages, and jobs in the context of austerity, some parts of society will lose out and stay poor as a feature of the system – and that Labour's job was to rebuild Britain 'for the many, not the few'. High-profile policies included state ownership, higher taxes, and increased workers' rights.

It may be controversial to its supporters to describe the Corbyn project as nationalising in the terms defined here (that is, as making state and nation more congruent). This is especially because it mobilised considerable grassroots support through its pursuit of social justice and anti-imperialist causes, which seem miles away from the supposedly inherent conservativism of flag-waving and exclusionary British nationalism. The nationalising impulse of Corbyn himself is apparent in his Bennite Euroscepticism. But the wider nationalising impulse of the project lies instead in the inspiration it takes from British post-war (and post-imperial) nationalisation. As the political economists Matt Bolton and F.H. Pitts put it (with my emphasis added), 'Corbynism is defined by a steadfast faith in the ability of the *nation*-state to eradicate inequality and poverty through a radical programme of intervention in the domestic economy.'[63] Yet it was never comfortable with the rhetorical mobilisation of the nation, even though some of its policies were literally 'nationalising'.

While the problems with the Corbyn project were multiple, this tension in its nationalising impulse is especially relevant for us. The project relied on a collective memory of post-war nationalisation in its faith in state intervention to improve lives. Yet it fell into one of the traps laid out in the Introduction: the 'pendulum' view of British capitalist development, which can only account for the state and not the nation part of the nation-state. Corbyn supporters were never comfortable even exploring the idea of nation-building, let alone considering it as an option (e.g. the furore caused by Corbyn's call for 'British jobs for British workers'). Yet class-based and justice-based mobilisation seemed like an electoral dead end. Despite dire predictions prior to the 2017 general election, Corbyn's Labour Party had a late surge thanks to their populist and anti-austerity campaign. Although the Conservatives won the 2017 election, they did so with a diminished majority against the expectation of polling. However, this relative optimism for socialists was destroyed by the 2019 election, after which the party returned to centrism under Keir Starmer.

Like the Corbyn Labour Party, the political project to leave the European Union fed off the inequalities of the post-crash period. Unlike it, however, Leavers were able to rhetorically mobilise a homogenous and class-crossing imagined community. The 'left behind' and 'white working class' was at the base of this. Although it came to prominence in explanations for the Brexit referendum result, the underlying idea that the white working class has been left behind was bubbling away for sometime, as the BBC's *White* series suggests.

Political scientist Matthew Goodwin and his various co-authors popularised the term in explaining the rise of the UKIP from 2009 onwards.[64] In this analysis, the left behind consist of 'older, working-class, white voters with few educational qualifications' who: have been marginalised by uneven economic development and global integration, and are out of kilter with progressive social values, including on immigration and patriotism. The left behind have therefore 'become increasingly regarded as parochial and intoler-ant by the younger, university-educated, more socially liberal and financially secure majority who define the political consensus in early twenty-first century Britain'.[65] Although the specific term 'metropolitan elite' was avoided, it was all but there in spirit. From this kind of analysis, then, Brexit can therefore be presented as the backlash of ordinary (white) people against the metropolitan elite, but without the race analysis required to grasp the parentheses and its politics. As Chapter 3 highlighted, the concept of the 'metropolitan elite' is unintelligible without a historical analysis of racism.

This initial 'left behind' analysis was simplified by nationalist thinker David Goodhart. Once firmly associated with a liberal Third

Way politics, Goodhart caused a splash with his 2004 *Prospect* article 'Too Diverse?', which discussed the threat of immigration and ethnic diversity for a universal welfare state.[66] The BBC interviewed him shortly afterwards, and headlined the article 'Is this man the left's Enoch Powell?' ('not at all' replied Goodhart).[67] Ten years later, Goodhart had firmly moved away from identifying with progressive politics with his 'Why I left my liberal London tribe' *FT* article.[68] His 2017 book, *The Road to Somewhere*, was based on dividing Britain into two tribes: 'the anywheres' and 'the somewheres'. While the somewheres are less educated and value security and home, the anywheres are typically university graduates who value autonomy and mobility – and Brexit can therefore be explained by the disregarded somewheres rebelling against the cosmopolitan anywheres after decades of disdain. Theresa May claimed to be governing on their behalf as prime minister.

If the core conflict of the austerity period was 'hardworking families' v. 'the undeserving', then a core conflict of the Brexit period became 'ordinary people' v. 'the metropolitan elite'. The latter evolved from the former: they are both conflicts over where the boundaries of the nation should be drawn, thereby demarcating who should benefit from the nation's wealth. While 'chavs' and welfare scroungers were seen as peripheral to or even outside of the informal boundaries, the left behind were seen as core. As for the rhetorical mobilisation of an imagined community, this meant that Eurosceptic elites could forge a coalition with the supposed left behind white working classes. This thereby legitimated their projects to leave the European Union as restoring the status of those groups and, in the terms of this book, making the state more national. Leaving the EU would strike at the heart of the metropolitan elite to 'Take back control' (more on this in the next chapter).

One of the other key differences between the undeserving conflicts of austerity and the left behind conflicts of Brexit relates to inequality. The left behind are seen as victims of forces beyond their control, whereas chavs and scroungers are seen as socially excluded. Although some left behind analyses may seem compatible with a metaphor of exclusion – how some sectors in some regions are excluded from the positive forces of globalisation, for example – this is not core to the meaning of 'left behind'. This can be seen in the metaphor of being 'left behind' itself. Development through capitalist growth is imagined as an escalator, whereby one is simply carried upward towards gradual enrichment by virtue of standing on it – except some individuals can only watch, necks craned upward, as other people progress while they are denied a place on it, left behind. These people have had something taken away, unfairly, their status diminished.

This is in stark contrast to social exclusion and its figures of the chav or scrounger, who exclude themselves through a culture of irresponsibility – thereby implying that being poor is a behavioural problem that can be overcome and fixed at that level, and that until otherwise they are not especially deserving of the nation's wealth. In contrast, the left behind have 'legitimate concerns' that should be listened to because their culture should be respected and contested; the inequality they face is not their fault because it is due to the metropolitan elite who place race above class and nation; and as a result they are very much deserving of the nation's wealth. The left behind are accepted as a feature of the system, while the socially excluded are considered a glitch. The former are deemed valuable enough to justify geopolitical and constitutional transformation to preserve them, while the latter ought to be fixed so they can be included.

There is a racial component to the 'left behind' rhetoric, as Shilliam and Bhambra have shown. It is after all, the *white* working class. Logically, it could be used to refer to other inequalities. But, in practice, it does not. The 'left behind' narrative only really holds when it references white Britons. From this we can learn who this nationalisation project is for. As Shilliam highlights so powerfully, the residents of Grenfell Tower – a tower block of apartments in London that was catastrophically engulfed by fire on 14 June 2017, killing at least seventy-one people with many others injured or displaced – could qualify as 'left behind'. By most measures, the residents of Grenfell were poor, but also surely deserving, despite being stigmatised through their race and council estate associations. The disaster came to symbolise many ills in British society, including inequality, housing, racial discrimination, and austerity. The Grenfell disaster was caused by a range of issues – managerial, political, economic – which 'led to a deterioration in accountability for the provision of public goods'.[69] But Grenfell residents were not presented as 'left behind', and that's the point. They cannot be made sense of as left behind, because they are not fully considered as part of the nation due to their race and citizenship. In the escalator metaphor buried in the 'left behind' narrative, the residents of Grenfell – and Britain's Black and Asian population more generally – do not feature, apart from as a threat. You cannot be left behind if you're not meant to be carried along in the first place.

Conclusion

The BBC's *White* series asked: 'Is white working-class Britain becoming invisible?' The answer to that must be: no. This is because the meaning of income and wealth inequality has evolved along with the scarcity and austerity of the post-crash era. Disparities in income and wealth can easily be justified as the result of meritocratic competition in a world of consistent and strong economic growth. This became less tenable in a world defined by resource scarcity. With the crash came a series of scandals that solidified an amorphous 'elite' as corrupt, untrustworthy, and self-interested. Combined with the narrative that the legitimate concerns of ordinary people – especially over race and immigration – are ignored by a metropolitan elite, then there is a sense of otherworldly rulers who require replacement. Taken together, Britain was in a situation ripe for nationalisation, with objective and subjective components of inequality coming together to give a sense of a system that does not work for the majority. Different paths were possible, but, as we know, it was the Brexit project that successfully mobilised.

The 'left behind' narrative is therefore an important part of nationalisation. In a world of social exclusion, low-income white Britons are imagined as peripheral to or outside of the nation: outside of the pool of human capital available for the nation's competitiveness, and at the edges of whiteness through the figures of chavs and welfare scroungers. In contrast, the left behind imagined low-income white Britons as if they are – or should be – within the nation: with whiteness unified across class once again, as it was also imagined in post-war and post-imperial nationalisation. The next chapter continues this analysis.

5

In or out

The referendum was a long time coming.

As Britain transitioned from an empire-state-nation to something approaching a nation-state, the exact configuration of nation and state has periodically opened up to debate and contestation. The terms and intensity of that debate ebbed and flowed with the times, but capitalist crises seem to bring dilemmas of Britain's constitution to the fore. It was unsurprising, then, less than a decade after the 2008 crash, that the dilemma was again becoming urgent: in or out? This question was considered so fundamental that it was agreed that only the electorate could decide. The British state wanted to maintain the status quo. Most early analysis predicted that they would comfortably see through their preferred result.

For many of the upstart nationalists looking to leave the union, this referendum was the culmination of a lifelong political battle. Although the lineage of these battles goes back centuries and weaves right through empire and out again, it took new and renewed form in the 1970s – when there was also a referendum amid capitalist crisis. Back then, the British state had successfully secured its favoured response. Four decades later, many expected a repeat. And yet as the upstart nationalists gained energy and momentum, a radical surprise seemed increasingly feasible. The UK's future could go either way.

What happened next depends on the constitutional dilemma in question. In the referendum on Scottish independence in Autumn 2014, the electorate voted to stay in the union, to keep the status quo, by 55 to 45 per cent. However, in a second referendum around eighteen months later – this time on whether to continue British membership of the European Union – the electorate did quash the status quo by 52 to 48 per cent. The Leave result promised to reconstitute Britain and its configuration of nation and state – and, wittingly or not, its integration into the global economy. Despite their proximity in British history, the Scottish independence and Brexit referendums are not often compared. After all, one result was in, the other out. One was national, the other subnational. One is criticised as a sad and irrational hark back to a lost imperial greatness, while the other is defended as a rational step into a social democratic future. Brexit is often analysed as part of a global populist revolt, from which Scottish nationalism is often left out. And, ultimately, Brexit is a project to restore and transform the (English-led) British state, while Scottish independence aims to break it. In that way, they couldn't be more different.

This chapter shows how there is much to be gained in insight by treating these two movements and their respective referendums as the same kind of phenomena – that is, prospective nationalisation projects, that arise from the same historical conditions, made urgent by the inequalities of post-crash Britain (as defined in Chapter 4). It is not a coincidence that the two most urgent questions of Britain's nation-state configuration – Scotland and the EU, its two unions – became urgent enough for generation-defining referendums within eighteen months of one another. Both movements saw their popularity and political feasibility increase rapidly because of the inequalities of post-crash politics, of which austerity and scarcity were a part. The referendums are the most striking manifestation of post-crash conflict, because the contestation is not just over the distribution and regulation of resources, but over who should be included or excluded in the first place – the boundary lines themselves. They are both, then, nationalisation projects in the sense defined in the Introduction: they are seeking formal authority to align political boundaries with national boundaries. It is just that their respective projects directly clash with one another. However, like lungs inhaling and exhaling, both projects are simultaneously inward and outward: inward because they are drawing the boundaries of formal authority inward, to be congruent with a respective nation; but outward because neither are parochial or protectionist in their plans for global economic integration. But, how, exactly, did each movement mobilise?

The prospect of overdevelopment

The previous chapter highlighted how nationalist mobilisation thrives when the relative low status of a national peoples can be narrated as the fault of an oppressor from whom power must be won. By taking power away from these (supposed) oppressors, the nation can gain self-determination in order to redistribute resources and tackle that inequality. Nationalism thus requires to 'punch up', even if it also 'punches down'. However, if there is no oppressor to punch up towards, then one can be exaggerated or made up (such as the European Union, the metropolitan elite, or, indeed, their combination).

Tom Nairn developed this approach to explain the rise of Scottish nationalism in the 1970s in his classic book *The Break-up of Britain*.[1] One puzzle among many posed by Nairn is why there was no substantial nationalist movement in Scotland until the 1970s, especially given that nationalism had already swept across Europe in the nineteenth century. Nairn argues that this has little to do with how patriotic Scottish nationals are, but rather with Scotland's historical capitalist development.

England and Scotland formed Great Britain with the Act of Union in 1707 because it was in their respective national interests. Scotland had recently failed in its imperial ambitions with a disastrous and costly aborted colony in Panama. Union with England offered a way out from national ruin.[2] England, meanwhile, wanted union with Scotland to stave off the threat of France (and any alliances with Scotland). England's parliament became Britain's, but Scotland retained key institutional features such as its own church and legal system, as well as its own culture.[3] It was a unique union, that perhaps could have only been feasible in the peculiar period between absolute monarchy and national democracy.[4] The concept of Scottish 'unionist-nationalism' captures this pragmatic and opportunist approach: retaining Scottish nationhood, but embracing the union so long as that was the best for Scotland (or at least their elites).[5]

This union-nationalism went alongside the peculiarities of British capitalist development. The British state was marked by its early industrialisation, which provided initial first-mover advantages, but left it with an archaic class structure (exemplified by the House of

Lords and constitutional monarchy) and a tendency to externalise economic weaknesses through empire and then, to a lesser extent, Europe. Whereas other European national states such as Germany had their nineteenth-century nationalist moments, which led to formal constitutions and rapid state-led development, the British Isles had the ultimately futile Chartist movement and the glories of Whig history. There was no significant nationalist movement in Britain until the rise of Scottish (and Welsh) nationalism in the 1970s.

Nationalism gained considerable momentum in the 1970s not because Scottish people start feeling more Scottish, but because of the kind of inequality outlined in Chapter 4. Three factors were key. The first was relative British decline from being the 'workshop of the world' and the major imperial power, with the capitalist crises of the 1970s strengthening this sense of decline. The second was Thatcherism.[6] Thatcher had been voted in mostly by England, and her reforms – which were especially felt in Scotland – popularised the concept of a democratic deficit in the union. By 1997, the Tories were all but wiped out in Scotland. The third was the discovery of North Sea oil, significant oil fields in the waters to the north and east of Scotland. The promise of a nationalised economy built around North Sea oil gives a real sense that the Scottish people can self-govern and progress on their own terms, without the union. The SNP campaigned in the 1970s with the campaign 'It's Scotland's Oil'; and during the 2014 referendum SNP deputy leader Jim Sillars warned that 'BP [British Petroleum], in an independent Scotland, will need to learn the meaning of nationalisation'.[7] If Scottish unionist-nationalist pragmatism suggests that Scotland should remain in the union so long as it is in Scotland's interest, then there should be little surprise in the timing of their nationalist movement's rise.

Scottish independence is the promise of nationalisation in both senses of the term. Being part of Britain made sense to Scotland while the union was an economic and political powerhouse, but it makes a lot less sense as Britain demonstrably declined. With the promise of North Sea oil to help fund a small-state social democracy away from the backwardness of Britain, independence can be feasibly presented as in the Scottish national interest. Decline and oil brought the promise of '*over*development' with self-determination – an unusual prospect for nationalist movements, but one that is shared most notably with Catalonia.[8] The rise of Scottish nationalism is therefore political-developmental rather than just ethnic – as linked together by institutions as they are blood. The promise is that by governing Scotland for Scotland, the Scottish people will be better off. By redrawing the political boundaries of sovereignty around the Scottish people, the relative status of Scottish residents will be improved.

Scottish nationalism does not therefore need to exaggerate or fabricate an oppressor. The British state is evidently a barrier to self-determination. British elites in London indeed deem it in their interest to maintain the union and Scotland's role in it. The state's approach since the 1970s has been to placate nationalists while seeking to maintain the status quo wherever possible. An initial referendum for Scottish devolution in 1979 returned a negative result. Even though 52 per cent voted for devolution, the state had inserted a clause that 40 per cent of those on the electoral list had to vote 'yes' for devolution to go ahead, possibly aimed at maintaining the constitution.[9] Scotland's devolved parliament was introduced in 1999, and was intended by the New Labour government to stymie Scottish nationalism by providing Scotland with some power. The Holyrood additional member voting system promised representativeness, but also made a majority government unlikely – again, possibly a ploy to avoid giving power to nationalists.[10] The SNP nevertheless managed a majority government in 2011 against all expectation, which provided the mandate and authority to push for an independence referendum.

There were no new oil discoveries this time, but there was post-crash politics. The British state was spluttering through a series of scandals, including bank bailouts and MPs' expenses. Meanwhile, the Conservative-led Coalition government – for which few Scottish voters had voted – seemed to promise a return to the Thatcherite era with their commitment to austerity and implied risk to the NHS. England suddenly did not look like such a good partner, and the SNP pivoted left to provide a genuine alternative. The promise of *over*development through independence once again seemed feasible. Prominent independence campaigner Stephen Maxwell put this promise of overdevelopment clearly in a noted speech entitled 'British Inequality and the Nordic Alternative', which was republished in 2013:

The most striking feature of Scotland's situation today is the size of the gap between the reality of life for many Scots and Scotland's potential. I can think of no other democracy of a comparable size and stage of economic development which suffers a similarly sized gap between its potential and the reality of life as experienced by a substantial portion of its population.[11]

This sense of a progressive, alternative development path for Scotland has been further strengthened by the COVID-19 lockdown and the different approaches taken by Westminster and Holyrood (a theme that is explored in Chapter 7).

The aim of Scottish nationalism is self-determination. That aim is meaningless without ethnic difference and a strong enough sense of what it means to be Scottish to facilitate political mobilisation. Yet the way in which parts of the London media discusses Scottish independence, one might be forgiven for thinking that the Yes campaign were fascists in disguise. As discussed in the Introduction, here nationalism is mistakenly collapsed into patriotism, racism, prejudice, and even fascism. Examples of referendum analysis from the *Guardian* and *New Statesman* include predictions of 'the death of the liberal enlightenment before the atavistic forces of nationalism and ethnicity'; warning of the 'disturbing' and 'divisive' 'dark side' of Yes; and worrying that 'the portents for the 21st century are dark indeed'.[12] Many Labour politicians seem to share this view, offering weak comparisons of the SNP to neo-fascism, Nazism, and the English Defence League; others have compared Salmond to Mussolini and Hitler.[13] That the London media cannot seem to imagine nationalism as anything other than 'backward' and 'dark' is in part down to defending their unionist interests and scaremongering. It is also a failure of analysis and a misunderstanding of nationalism, Scottish or otherwise. Scottish nationalism emerges out of a vision of *over*development. As we will see, Scottish nationalism does not need racism to mobilise, but that is not the case for English nationalism.

English nationalism

The Brexit referendum result generated reflection on the relationship between England and Britain. As one group of political scientists memorably put it, Brexit was 'made in England'.[14] This observation holds on three counts. The first is that any UK-wide electoral result is likely to be driven by England because it comprises around 85 per cent of the population of the country. The second is that England and Wales voted most in favour of Leave (53 per cent each), with Scotland (38 per cent) and Northern Ireland (44 per cent) voting clearly in favour of Remain.[15] Taking these first two points together offers us the idea that leaving the European Union was to some extent illegitimate in Scotland and Northern Ireland because their electorates did not sanction constitutional change through a refer-endum majority. (This is directly relevant for Scottish independence, given the movement's arguments about self-determination and hope for post-independence European Union membership). While these first two counts in support of Brexit as English are uncontroversial, the third is more contentious: that Brexit was driven by English nationalism.

It is especially complicated because it is not clear what England actually is, let alone the content of its nationalist ideology. This has led some to argue boldly that 'England does not exist'.[16] But that is a cop out, historically and conceptually. Scholars such as Andrew Gamble and Norman Davies have argued convincingly that England used the union with Scotland as a way to expand itself and further secure the British Isles for itself.[17] Looking back, 'union' does seem a curious concept to describe the process in which the Scottish parliament was formally dissolved and the English parliament became the British parliament. As Davies recounts in his history of the Isles, 'Britain' likely gained its initial popularity as an identity through Scottish elites whose interest lay in shared identity rather than dif-ference in the years following union. Meanwhile, '[t]he English, of course, continued to call everything "England" as if nothing had changed'.[18] This confusion, if it can be called that, has many mani-festations: the UK's central bank is called the Bank of England, Oxford University's exam on British history was once titled 'The History of England', the crowd in England's 1966 World Cup win were largely waving Union Jacks, and Princess Diana was nicknamed 'The English Rose'. Davies's book is full of examples of this apparent confusion: 'apparent confusion' because while treating England as synonymous with Britain is technically incorrect, its meaning in use reflects the reality of English superiority.

This relative power of England is one reason why Nairn famously called English nationalism an 'enigma'.[19] Part of the mystery is how it became intertwined with Britain. This is reflected in how public debate about England and Englishness intensified in the years following devolution. However, the strange asymmetric constitution produced by devolution did not especially propel a serious English nationalist movement. While there are minor campaigns for it, it is unclear what political moves or vision an English parliament could pursue that aren't better pursued through the existing British parliament in union with Scotland. Indeed, almost every English politician deems it in their interest to maintain the union with Scotland. Yet in naming English nationalism as an enigma, Nairn was getting at something foundational, which ought to be intelligible through this book's framework. If nationalism is about gaining power and self-determination to restore or consolidate the status of the national peoples, then it is not immediately clear how that would manifest for a nation like England that has always seemed to dominate and does not need freeing from an oppressor. In other words, what or who would England 'punch up' against?

One of the controversies about English nationalism is whether it is 'inherently regressive'.[20] With nothing to punch up against, English nationalism only punches down, so goes the argument: an imagined community that is united by a shared sense of superiority and small-mindedness – or, worse, by xenophobia and racism. Englishness has became associated with whiteness, more so than Britishness. As Chapter 3 highlighted, whiteness and Britishness once went together. But as 'multiculturalism' became the dominant frame for understanding race, the boundaries of Britishness became more inclusive for Black and Asian citizens. England, however, remained less so, and so became the identity through which whiteness and racism could be laundered. Britons who identify as white are nine times more likely to define themselves as 'English' compared to those who identify as Black and minority ethnic (BME), who are more likely to define themselves as 'British'.[21] Likewise, research indicates that four out of five of those who identify as 'English not British' voted for Brexit.[22] 'Multicultural Britain' is a phrase that resonates; less so 'multicultural England'.

This taints England and Englishness as a political force, and has generated some kickback. Alex Niven has speculated on a 'new model island' of renewed regionalism to bypass England.[23] Political scientist Michael Kenny, meanwhile, has argued that the idea of England need not be binned.[24] Englishness has many progressive sides, including some of its folk traditions and myths, such as Robin Hood's robbing from the rich to help the poor. It is possible, for example, to support the England football team without punching down against anyone. The case that English nation*hood* is not inherently regressive is a strong one.

How relevant this observation is for our purposes, however, is questionable. The Introduction made clear that nation*hood* and national*ism* are distinct. We are only interested in nationhood insofar as it makes possible nationalist mobilisation for the purposes of nationalisation. Robin Hood is a great story, and it is conceivable that it could form the basis of a nationalising project that promised to make the state more English by introducing greater redistribution from rich to poor. But how is that going to mobilise millions of voters with their varied interests and ideas of Englishness, some of which go against the Robin Hood myth? It is not clear. To repeat: a potentially progressive nation*hood* does not necessary make a progressive national*ism*. It is a mistake to focus too much on national myths and symbols to the detriment of realpolitik analysis of where power lies, which is what ultimately drives nationalist mobilisation. For this reason, English nationalism *is* regressive – albeit historically so rather than inherently.

That England is in a position of superiority poses something of a wider puzzle: how and why nationalist mobilisation can work, if at all, in nation-states where the state or its national peoples are evidently not oppressed. The simple answer is that if there is no oppressor to punch up towards, then one can be exaggerated or made up – such as the European Union, the metropolitan elite, or, indeed, their combination. This is why nationalism in otherwise non-oppressed nation-states often manifests in anti-elite, populist forms. Although many English nationhoods are possible, Brexit is the only successful English nationalist mobilisation. It was able to achieve this by fusing together Euroscepticism and anti-immigration politics into an English nationalist ideology – and give this meaning in the context of the inequalities of the post-crash period.

Nationalism scholar Ben Wellings goes as far as to say that Euroscepticism is *the* contemporary manifestation of English national-ism.[25] The simplest way to make this case is through the character of nationalism itself. Even if nationalism mostly punches down, to mobilise people politically it always needs to punch up: to self-determine, to escape the oppressors. English nationalism, however, has little to punch up to – except for the European Union with its 'pooled sovereignty'. Although claims that the UK was a 'vassal state' of the EU were absurd, it is undeniable that the EU is a constraint which weakens parliamentary sovereignty. Wellings identifies the core of English nationalism in the defence (and, in imperial terms perhaps, the extension) of parliamentary sovereignty. With that often comes a celebration of the unique and organic development of the (Anglo-)British state favoured by conservatives, and a related sense that the (Anglo-)British do it better; that *Great Britain* means something, for England's Magna Carta gifted the world liberty and democracy. Note the slippage between England and Britain: recent public attitudes research has shown how those who identify as *English* (rather than British) are most likely to agree (with emphasis added) that '*Britain's* best time was in the past'.[26] In this context, accession to the EEC and later EU membership was considered the 'ultimate institutional expression' of British decline.[27] It was the moment Britain lost its greatness.

English nationalism also has its roots in anti-immigration politics. Chapter 3 traced how Enoch Powell helped make immigration a key battlefield in British politics, whereby Black and Asian people were racialised as a problem and threat to the nation. As these politics developed, the 'legitimate concerns' of 'ordinary people' were seen as ignored by the so-called metropolitan elite, who were more likely to point to the economic and fiscal benefits of the immigration, à la Project Fear (see below). The populist celebration of an ordinary people, a white working class, who are losing out or 'left behind' to immigrants – but whose presence is advocated and authorised by an out-of-touch and scandalised metropolitan elite – is a way of adding upward-facing punches to those already facing downwards. This anti-immigration politics gave English nationalist Eurosceptics something to work with. Indeed, linking the two was central to UKIP's successful political strategy. Narratives around the A8 forged a stronger link between the EU and immigration flows, which the so-called migrant crisis in 2015 strengthened further. Nigel Farage's infamous 'breaking point' poster was the epitome of this.

Although English nationhood or national identity is not *inherently* regressive, English nationalism is a *historically* regressive force. It has only mobilised through a combination of anti-immigration Euroscepticism, which has resonated as a wider anti-elite populism. Scottish nationalism, in contrast, can mobilise without recourse to racism. This does not mean that England is a more racist place than Scotland or that Englishness is conservative while Scottishness is not. Rather, it is a feature of the historical development of their respective nationalisms.

Project Fear

Both English and Scottish nationalist movements were energised by the post-crash historical conditions. Both are nationalising projects, insofar as they aim to align a national peoples with a respective territory and associated formal authority. English nationalism aims to cement the (English-led) British state. Its elites look to mobilise its peoples through a populist anti-immigration Euroscepticism, with the hope of using renewed sovereign powers to pursue free trade and low regulation. Scottish nationalism aims to undo the (English-led) British state. Its elites look to mobilise its peoples through a populist anti-Westminster and anti-austerity politics, with the hope of using renewed sovereign powers to pursue European small-state social democracy with the help of North Sea oil revenue. Both of these nationalisation projects are products of their post-crash time. Both found a barrier in the form of the British state, through which a counter-mobilisation – Project Fear – was launched. This counter-mobilisation stressed the economic dangers and risks of breaking from the constitutional status quo that enmeshed those national economies into larger markets through union. Let us unpack this further, starting with independence.

The SNP has hovered around the centre-left ground since its initial electoral success in the 1970s. However, pre-crash, their strategy was to ape New Labour's Third Way mix of progressive social policy, law and order, and economic growth.[28] As recently as August 2008, the then leader Alex Salmond claimed that he was bringing the SNP into 'the mainstream of Scotland' with 'a very competitive economic agenda' which 'many business people have warmed towards'. On Thatcherism, Salmond argued that Scotland 'didn't mind the economic side so much ... but we didn't like the social side at all'.[29] In 2007, SNP literature argued that an independent Scotland could join a Northern European 'arc of prosperity' that included Norway, as well as Iceland and Ireland. The 2008 crash – along with the crises of Iceland and Ireland's globalised economic strategies – made this approach untenable.[30] But it also opened up radical potential for independence that was visible during the referendum.

As with the Brexit referendum, the independence referendum was mandated through a surprise majority government. Very few predicted the SNP majority in the Scottish parliamentary election in 2011. After governing through a minority government in 2007, the SNP won the first majority in 2011 by promising something different to Westminster scandals and austerity. Research has shown how Scottish voters are more likely to trust Holyrood over Westminster: when health, education, and other services are perceived to improve, the Scottish electorate are likely to credit Holyrood (even when evidently not true) and vice versa (blaming Westminster for when things get worse).[31] Promising to end austerity and avoid NHS privatisation were pivotal campaign messages in 2011, and so the SNP offered something genuinely different to the status quo, by an administration that was trusted.

The SNP are able to blend governing competence with a radical edge.[32] Their two most recent leaders and First Ministers, Alex Salmond and Nicola Sturgeon, have a radical history that has given way to compromise and meticulous budgeting. They are joined in the party by a radical intergenerational coalition of socialist oldies and young millennials who operate more like a social movement. The promise of future independence in combination with the political and economic constraints of Westminster allows these two parts of the party – rigorously balanced budgets and radical activism – to function together. These two parts of the party give the SNP a high degree of political agility.

All three major British political parties – Conservative, Labour, and Liberal Democrat – campaigned for In (although Conservative leaders stayed away from the actual campaigning given how unpopular they are in Scotland). Their campaign was officially named 'Better Together' to sound positive and neutral, and about uniting rather than dividing. Yet their actual campaign was relentlessly negative. The term 'Project Fear' was even coined by the In campaign themselves in an ironic moment of 'office nonsense' that the campaign's director of communications shared with journalists 'after a few pints'.[33]

Project Fear centred on scaremongering about independence, typically on the economic risks around the currency, tax take, and growth. Labour's slogan was literally 'It's not worth the risk'. But the risks were not just economic, as they also seemed to reach every aspect of life. Examples in the media included dying of cancer ('Scottish Independence? We Are Better United – I'm Betting My Life on It'), being bombed by England ('Scottish Independence: England Would "Bomb Scottish Airports To Defend Itself" Lord Fraser Warns'), and Edinburgh Zoo losing its pandas ('Independent Scotland could be banned from using the pound – and lose its pandas').[34] Whether this was ideologically driven or not, the press evidently enjoyed the sensationalism.

The Yes campaign response to Project Fear mirrored the two parts of the SNP: the radical social movement part of the party critiqued and sometimes ridiculed it, while the compromising leaders decided to fight 'objective' analysis with 'objective' analysis of their own. The result was a 670-page document launched by Salmond and Sturgeon in November 2013 that outlined a post-independence approach to everything – from the number of Typhoon jets to the National Lottery.[35] This was not the Scottish Magna Carta that some nationalists had hoped for: as two radical but sympathetic independence activists put it, the document was 'short on messianic declarations, and long in detail'.[36] It did, nevertheless, include promises of better childcare and more generous social security – even if this brought no immediate boost in the polling.[37] The Yes campaign leadership, then, accepted the rules of the game and met Project Fear on its own terms.

The Conservatives and Labour assumed that they would win, and the idea of losing was never built into their calculations.[38] It indeed dominated the polling for the year leading up to the referendum, and it was only after an extraordinary shift in the weeks before polling that Yes had any real chance of winning. Cue panic in Westminster. The three main party leaders – Cameron, Clegg, and Miliband – signed up to a last-minute vow to pursue 'devo max' – i.e. more devolved powers to Scotland, if they won. This has not happened, and probably never will in the terms promised – on the front page of Scottish newspaper the *Daily Record*, presented to look like ancient parchment.[39] The reasons for the result are complex, and so it is difficult to judge how effective these moves were. However, voting behaviour models demonstrate that the key factors were age, political values, Scottish national identity, and – relevant to Project Fear, to a referendum that was actually about in or out, and to a nation with history of unionist-nationalism – perception of whether the union benefits Scotland or not.[40]

Brexit coalitions

Unlike the referendum on Scottish independence, the vote for Brexit was frequently framed alongside Donald Trump's US presidential election victory later that year as a revolt by the left behind, white working classes. For *The Economist*, the Brexit vote 'reveals a sharply polarised country, with a metropolitan elite that likes globalisation on one side and an angry working class that does not on the other'.[41] The 'left behind' is sometimes discussed as a straightforward constituency of voters. However, as pointed towards in the previous chapter, the 'left behind' is better thought of as a legitimising narrative for English nationalists.

But legitimise what, exactly? The English nationalist vision was somewhat fragmented, but Brexiteer elites tended to mobilise around a vision of 'Global Britain': using renewed sovereign powers to pursue free trade and low regulation, with Anglosphere relations at the fore (i.e. the old Commonwealth dominions of Australia, Canada, and New Zealand, and sometimes India).[42] These elites are most prominently clustered around the Eurosceptic wing of the Conservative Party. In this world, Global Britain speaks to a part of English nationhood that aims to project British power across the globe: to be a 'rule-maker' rather than a 'rule-taker', so that those English gifts of liberty, rule of law, and free trade can shape both the world and Britain's interests for the better. In this vision, the Anglosphere are Britain's 'true friends'.[43] They share those same values, and are committed to one another through historical blood ties and whiteness.[44] An English-led project to cement British power might sound paradoxical, especially when England is rhetorically subsumed into Britain, but some of the history surveyed above would suggest otherwise.

This project is sometimes characterised as parochial and as underpinned by a pathetic nostalgia for empire and British power. This is not quite right. There may be elements of this (at least one fantasy is the notion that a CANZUK trading agreement can replace the economic benefits of the EU single market). But Global Britain is evidently not about simply harking back to the past, even if the British Empire is a key part of what denotes Britain's greatness for the English nationalist elites.[45] And as the historian Robert Saunders has pointed out, the arguments and logic of Remain are sensitive to the same criticism: the arguments about Britain being better placed to shape Europe in the union rather than out can also be characterised as imperialist.[46] As for parochial, for these English nationalist elites leaving the EU was not about a turn inward, in the style of post-imperial nationalisation. Rather it is better thought of as a project that aims to re-globalise Britain – to turn back outward – through reclaiming sovereignty, to make the state more British, to make it work better for the British peoples. A nationalisation project, in other words.

'Global Britain' is hardly a vote-winning vision. But the 'left behind' narrative provides English nationalists with a mandate and a people whose behalf they can act upon. And the combination of anti-elite and anti-immigration Euroscepticism provided a way of mobilising in an age of austerity. However, the vote for Brexit cannot be explained by the simple mobilisation of the white working classes, because rural voters in the South also typically voted for Brexit. Social theorist Alan Finlayson presents an elegant typology for analysing the lines of conflict during the Brexit referendum.[47] The typology is founded on a distinction between reactions to 'cultural' globalisation and 'economic' globalisation, although these might be better thought of as cosmopolitanism and global economic integration respectively. These reactions can be pro or anti. By cross-referencing these reactions Finlayson generates four different positions, as plotted on the table below.

		Open global integration (economic globalisation)	
		Pro	Anti
Cosmopolitanism (cultural globalisation)	Pro	(1) Remain Typical profile: Rich, metropolitan, centrist Values progress	(2) Remain Typical profile: Young, graduate, renters Values equality
	Anti	(3) Leave Typical profile: Baby boomer, homeowner, Southern Values status quo	(4) Leave Typical profile: Poor, Northern, "left behind" Values place

The key dividing line between Leave and Remain groups is horizontal rather than vertical, thereby suggesting that that conflicts over Brexit are divided by reactions to cosmopolitanism rather than by reactions to global economic integration. Finlayson argues that the Remain campaign's mistake was to think that the referendum was actually about leaving the EU. Their campaign focused on the economic risks of disrupting or leaving the single market (Project Fear 2.0), and was therefore talking to groups 1 and 3, but did not win much over of 3. The Leave campaign, however, understood that the referendum was not really about the EU, and their focus on immigration ('Take back control') was able to coherently target groups 3 and 4. The distinction between economic and cultural globalisation may be simple. As Chapters 3 and 4 showed, this idea of cosmopolitanism cannot be divorced from the politics of immigration, which in turn cannot be divorced from the global economy.

This coalition between Southern and rural baby boomers, Northern 'white working class', and English nationalist elites is unusual. Most of the Brexit elites are more than sympathetic towards Thatcherism; and Thatcherism is a typical explanation for the economic decline of Northern industrial heartlands. The coalition was first brought together through immigration, and then sustained, as we will see later and in Chapter 6, by the desire to 'get Brexit done' and related culture wars. The Brexit vote was indeed interpreted by some elites – including the then prime minister Theresa May – as a backlash against immigration (and therefore 'cultural globalisation'). In the Conservative leadership election (and de facto process for next prime minister) following Cameron's resignation after the vote, May quickly positioned herself as the custodian for anti-immigration sentiment. 'The Brexit vote', May argued during her campaign, 'gave us a very clear message, that we couldn't allow freedom of movement to continue as it had done hitherto'.[48]

Immigration was one of the key reasons for the referendum in the first place. The Conservative 2015 general election manifesto promised to hold a referendum on Britain's EU membership, as part of a strategy to trap Labour, nullify UKIP, and disempower the Eurosceptic wings of their party.[49] The Conservative strategy for the 2015 election had some similarities with their 2010 campaign: they tried to trap Labour, this time with immigration rather than austerity. In doing so, they also aimed to neutralise the threat from UKIP. UKIP won the most votes in the 2014 European Parliament elections, months after Romanian and Bulgarian citizens were granted open access to the UK labour market in January 2014 as part of their EU accession. They also hoped to appease the noisy Eurosceptics within their own party.

However, the Conservative leadership hoped that they would never hold the referendum, with the potential extension of coalition government with the Lib Dems tying their hands. Cameron and Osborne did not want Britain to leave the EU. The plan was an ambitious renegotiation of Britain's role in an ever closer union, including new immigration controls, to win over the British public. Meanwhile, and more privately, there were long rumblings about maintaining the power of the City of London, especially with the threat of greater integration (especially via Eurobonds or a financial transactions tax) and the prospect of more treaties following the Eurozone crisis.[50] Cameron hoped to capitalise on the Eurozone crisis by using the referendum and threat of leaving to steer the EU away from federalism. Yet when it came to the official negotiations in 2016, he could offer very little to the public, with the main promise to limit some in-work benefits for EU migrants. Alongside the misguided Conservative promise to cap annual migration net in 'the tens of thousands' – misguided for many reasons, including that freedom of movement was an entrenched commitment of the EU – this represented another promise on immigration broken.[51] British geopolitical hubris strikes again (see Chapter 3).

Project Fear: the sequel

The Remain campaign realised early on that they needed to move the debate away from immigration, because they accepted that they could not benefit from the issue no matter how it was presented.[52] With the EU virtually unsellable, they focused on how risky it would be to leave in terms of unemployment, dented GDP growth, and losses in household income. Business was on side.[53] As was most of the City.[54] Trade unions too, even.[55] Plus seemingly the entirety of the world elite: the IMF, the G7, Barack Obama (and even James Bond) all issued warnings, alongside a procession of bleak projections from the Treasury.[56] Chancellor George Osborne claimed that a vote for Leave would necessitate an emergency budget to retrench public spending further, a claim that was ridiculed as 'the punishment budget'.[57] Almost all of the elite lined up behind the Remain campaign and egged on Project Fear. As Adam Tooze puts it, 'the total alignment of interests and expertise that it presented could not but appear uncanny'.[58] With the power of hindsight, Project Fear – with its emphasis on myth busting and scaremongering through statistics and economic logic – seems incredibly misjudged. The 'It's the economy, stupid' campaign style was the epitome of the pre-2008 share-the-proceeds-of-growth politics that was increasingly failing in the post-crash context of austerity and scarcity.

The Leave campaign responded to Project Fear differently from the SNP. The SNP had to straddle between maintaining their reputation for governing competence at Holyrood and mobilising voters in support of national transformation into the unknown. The Leave campaigners, however, needed only to concern themselves with the latter. As with the Scottish independence referendum, all three major British political parties sided with the status quo by officially campaigning for Remain. Project Fear was not just driven by a naive assumption that whoever had the most compelling economic analysis would win. Their gamble was by refusing to say anything on immigration and thereby drawing a line between reasonable and unreasonable

politics, Leave would be trapped.[59] With no economic forecasts to
support their risky propositions, they would be forced into the world
of unreasonable politics of immigration bashing and racism – a
place which many of their leading lights from the official campaign,
such as Boris Johnson and Michael Gove, would be unwilling to
go. This is where the role of Nigel Farage and his unofficial Leave
campaign was crucial. Farage could say the unsayable without
worrying about the political implications. Although the official and
unofficial campaigns did not get on, they nevertheless formed a de
facto partnership: Johnson and the official campaign would dog-
whistle, while Farage and the unofficial campaign would just openly
whistle.[60]

Meanwhile, the official Leave campaign made some infamously
dubious promises about the benefits of leaving the EU. There was
no 670-page plan. This cavalier attitude and lack of planning was
interpreted at the time (and sometimes still today) as a weakness
of the campaign – which it would have been by the old rules of the
game. The Leave campaign recognised that the game was over. This
shift was symbolised during a famous moment during one of the
televised debates on the referendum. In response to a warning that
leaving the European Union would damage the UK's GDP growth,
an audience member responded with 'that's your bloody GDP, not
ours'.[61] Swathes of voters had lost faith in the state telling the truth,
especially over immigration, and had grown suspicious of the kind
of value and reasoning that places economics (forecasts, statistics,
growth) over politics (collective choice and agency).[62]

In many analyses, this represented 'post-truth' politics – indeed,
it was 2016 word of the year.[63] Connecting the Brexit vote to Trump's
victory later that year, many observers have explained these shocking
electoral results as the triumph of emotions over reason.[64] This
entails a shift away from a rational and reasonable process where
political decisions are evidence-based and risk-assessed, and towards
an emotional and unreasonable politics whereby enlightened progress
is debased by emotion and nationalism – with Remain as the former
and Leave as the latter. Less sophisticated accounts, meanwhile,
point to the supposedly sudden acceptance of lying in politics. While
it seems undeniable that there has been a qualitative shift in the
way that society relates to knowledge and facts as highlighted through
the referendum campaigns, post-truth does not really stand up to

scrutiny as an explanation of the Brexit vote. As William Davies points out, dubbing this approach 'Project Fear' was clever, as 'a supposedly dispassionate analysis is cannily reframed as emotional manipulations'. The supposed rational side was using emotion, even if unwittingly. As for lying and bullshit, that 'punishment budget' promised by Remain never did happen.

Even the official Leave campaign slogan of 'Take back control' was condemned as misleading. The slogan was criticised for its ambiguity and its link to dubious claims ('We send the EU £350 million a week. Let's fund our NHS instead'), but in hindsight it is clear that the ambiguity was a strength. The 'Take back control' slogan was very well calibrated for the coalition of English nationalist elites, 'left behind' voters, and affluent Eurosceptics. Control over what? Ostensibly an abstract control of British sovereignty, but also controlling immigration and supporting the NHS. Take control away from who? The Leave campaign's stand with the ordinary people and left behind against the power of the scandalised, technocratic, and out-of-touch British state and EU. And give it *back* to which people? The British people – a people who are racialised as white, as against immigrants, because you cannot be left behind if you're not meant to be carried along in the first place. Project Fear only helped legitimise this coalition. Surveys conducted during the campaigns show that 41 per cent of voters thought that Remain represented the establishment, compared to 19 per cent for Leave.[65]

The coalition brought together by the Brexit referendum was sustained and strengthened by the perpetual desire to 'get Brexit done'. The Brexit vote caught Remain and their interests by complete surprise. The majority of the elite – included many politicians and especially those who had governed for the last two decades, most business and finance, and various organs of the state – seemed to be on the side of Remain. Many of these Remainers and the institutions they were a part of started to scrutinise the prospect of leaving the EU as soon as the vote happened. This included subjecting Brexit to democratic accountability, proper procedure, and, in some cases, subterfuge and bad faith to delay exit in the desperate hope of a second referendum that might reverse the decision. At the extreme end, this Remainer position edged towards conspiracy theories about foreign interference and illegitimate use of data.

This further strengthened the coalition between English nationalist elites and various Brexit voters: a sense of injustice that a national and direct democratic decision was being secretly upturned, with this too edging towards conspiracy theory. The *Daily Mail* famously accused judges of being saboteurs. The then prime minister Theresa May's slogan became 'Brexit means Brexit'. Remainers v. Leavers became the most important political and cultural cleavage in Britain. As we will see in Chapter 6, these positions morphed into a culture war, upon which different visions of the British nation rest.

Conclusion

Capitalist development always produces inequalities across a territory, and so nationalism is always there, to one extent or another. The interesting question is how potent it is at any one moment, and when and why that potency fluctuates with the times.

English and Scottish nationalisms both have a strange long-and-recent history; long in its origins, but recent in its effects. In times of crisis and scarcity, both aim to remake the British nation-state. Brexit aims to restore and consolidate it; Scottish independence to break it. Scottish nationalists could mobilise 45 per cent of the Scottish electorate by promising a better life under self-rule, free of an English-dominated British state. English nationalists could mobilise 52 per cent of the British electorate – mostly in England – by combining an anti-elite populism with anti-immigration Euroscepticism. It is no coincidence that both nationalist movements found increased public support in post-crash times. Austerity politics, wage stagnation, and weak economic growth intensified, twisted, and created conflicts over who should get what, when, and how – including struggle over the boundaries of the nation and protecting those deemed most valuable.

Along with Corbyn's Labour Party, these were the two most viable nationalisation projects in the post-crash era. Both movements have excelled at questioning the constitution of Britain in the midst of capitalist crisis and austerity, in part by mobilising people around a disquiet over the status quo and the elite that reproduces it. However, only one movement won its referendum. And while the margins may seem small as percentages, each centile represents hundreds of thousands – if not millions – of individual voters, with their own motivations and interests, lifestyles, and rhythms. Ultimately, one nationalisation project won the formal authority needed to be realised, the other did not.

Those constitutional dilemmas – in or out, union or not – did not and will not go away. The two will continue to intertwine. There were two feasible routes to Anglo-British reconstitution in the post-crash years. Although Britain only has the authority to follow one of these routes at present, these two questions of reconstitution will continue to intertwine. The independence referendum strengthened English nationalism. The first thing Cameron did after the Scottish referendum was to promise greater powers for England.[66] While the result may seem to solidify England and Scotland's union, or at least put off the issue of another referendum for another generation or so, it was almost immediately weakened by the Brexit result. With Scotland voting overwhelmingly to Remain, Brexit means renewed calls for Scottish independence and increasing justification for another referendum. Yet without EU membership, questions about the economic model for an independent Scotland are opened back up.

The British responses to COVID-19 provide further evidence to Scottish nationalists that ending the union would be in Scotland's best interest (see Chapter 7). For English nationalists, the future seems unclear. Without the EU to punch up to, it is not clear what is next for English nationalists once Brexit is delivered, besides pursuing greater cultural and economic links with the Anglosphere. Yet retreat could be as likely as expansion. Situated in the longue durée, we are perhaps in the middle of a slow and inevitable English nationalisation, as England retreats from empire, Europe, and even Britain itself, and back into the geographical territory of England. Were it not for a few thousand Scottish voters, Britain alone could have been England (and Wales) alone. Perhaps it will be soon enough.

6

Unleashing Britain's potential

For the last three and a half years, this country has felt trapped, like a lion in a cage. We have all shared the same frustration – like some super-green supercar blocked in the traffic. We can see the way ahead. We know where we want to go – and we know why we are stuck.

Boris Johnson, Introduction to 2019 Conservative Party
Manifesto, *Get Brexit Done: Unleash Britain's Potential*

Alongside getting Brexit done, Boris Johnson was elected as prime minister in December 2019 with the promise to 'unleash Britain's potential'. The Conservative manifesto promised a diverse array of policies and interventions to achieve this: creating a 'fair and just society' by ensuring equality of opportunity through improving schooling; 'strengthening the great Union between the United Kingdom's four nations', sometimes referred to as the 'awesome foursome'; drastically increasing public research and development spending, 'giving the NHS its biggest ever cash boost', and the creation of freeports; but also to 'strengthen academic freedom and free speech in universities' and continue to support a 'dynamic free market economy'. All this was in the name of levelling up Britain's underdeveloped and 'left behind' regions. By leaving the EU, 'we can release that lion from its cage and take this amazing country forwards'.

Freeports and free speech. Brexit and increased NHS spending. Levelling up and Global Britain. Redistribution of resources and renewed free trade. This combination of ideas, policies, and promises may appear incoherent and contradictory. 'Economically left wing' and 'culturally right wing' is a common analysis. This incoherent or pick 'n' mix claim is less relevant when the Johnson government is analysed for what it is, in the terms of this book's framework: as a nationalisation project, to 'get Brexit done'. In narrow terms, getting Brexit done means leaving the European Union, and so realigning the political and national boundaries of the United Kingdom. In broader terms, getting Brexit done can mean almost anything. As Chapter 5 showed, the referendum on leaving the EU was as much about Britain's relationship to the world and what kind of nation it ought to be as it was about the EU itself. It is therefore an opportunity for nation-state building in the post-war and post-imperial manner. The Attlee government used opportunities to do just that, the fruits of which Britain lives with today. It was, however, a decidedly inward-facing nationalisation project, which repatriated and controlled capital. The English nationalist vision outlined in Chapter 5 is more outward-facing. So what kind of nationalisation project will the Johnson government build? What kind of nation-state configuration do they envisage?

This is a difficult question to answer. Writing in early 2021, it is less than two years since Johnson won the 2019 election. The early energies of the government were consumed by getting Brexit indeed done, and then were overwhelmed by the response to the coronavirus pandemic (the topic of Chapter 7). This chapter therefore looks at the 2019 campaign and Johnson's first few months in government with his parliamentary majority to get an indication of the direction and character of the accompanying nationalisation project, which will likely still shape their agenda in any post-pandemic, 'new normal' world. Despite some interesting interventions designed at levelling up while pursuing a Global Britain tradition, such as freeports and immigration reform, there is little indication that the Johnson government is properly committed to a post-war style nationalisation project beyond ensuring that the UK exits from the EU and securing its own power. Key here is the so-called 'war on woke', part of the wider culture wars that continue the Brexit-era conflict over the informal boundaries of nationhood. This project, and the strategic dilemmas that direct it, have their origins in the development of Britain's evolution from an empire-state-nation to a nation-state, which were intensified and twisted by the conflicts of the post-crash decade.

Nationalisation as statecraft

Depending on who you asked at the time, this new government represented either a post-neoliberal pivot back to a one-nation Conservatism with its spending pledges, or the final Thatcherite realisation of Singapore-on-Thames with its commitment to Brexit and accompanying patriotic flexing.[1] Later, it became conventional to imply both takes were correct, and that the government can be characterised as economically left wing and culturally right wing.[2] This may come across as contradictory or ideologically incoherent, the latter being a claim that is often put to the Johnson government. How important ideological coherence is to a government is certainly questionable. And, indeed, one of the themes of this book is to challenge the distinction between economic and cultural factors as a way of organising the analysis of politics (as its simplifying assumptions are unable to capture the complexity of lived experience, thereby hindering rather than helping our explanations). The nationalisation framework of this book offers a way around this, and, in doing so, an answer to the apparent contradictory political and ideological character of the Johnson government.

The Johnson government is and must be a nationalising project insofar as its mandate was to 'get Brexit done'. By leaving the European Union, the formal borders of the UK's economic authority will be and was made significantly more national – especially with respect to the labour market, but also in terms of fiscal boundaries, regulation, and other areas. Indeed, on being elected, the Johnson government used its energies in getting the Brexit deal through Parliament, thereby paving the way to make political boundaries more congruent with national boundaries. However, as the Introduction outlined, nationalisation is not just about the formal boundaries of the nation-state. This state-building (or state-consolidating) process can also entail nation-building and/or redistributing resources to those national peoples who were promised a lift up. After a decade of conflict – scarcity, austerity, possible Scottish independence – getting Brexit done presented the Johnson government with the mandate and capacity to remake the nation. On leaving the European Union, the UK has new powers and a thrust to reintegrate into the global economy. As Chapter 5 highlighted, there is and was little reason to think that this would be inward-facing like post-war and post-imperial nationalisation, where the combination of state ownership, welfare state building, and capital controls made an empire-state-nation into something resembling a nation-state. English nationalist elites never saw leaving the EU as a turn inward. Rather, it was a way of re-globalising Britain through reclaiming sovereignty.

However, we should always be wary of reading ideological intentions into Conservative governments. The most famous political science account of the Conservative Party is the theory of 'statecraft': that the party is driven by developing winning electoral strategies rather than by ideology.[3] While ideas such as the free market were important to party projects such as Thatcherism, these work alongside the core purpose of the Conservative Party: 'the art of winning elections'.[4] In practice, statecraft might entail developing policies targeted at those parts of the electorate that are necessary to win a parliamentary majority. Another strategy is to defeat and diminish political opposition (like the trap set for Miliband from Chapter 1). The theory of statecraft helps account for the differences between Cameron, May, and Johnson, as new times call for new strategies. It may also give a clue as to how the Conservatives have ruled for almost the entirety of the 2010s (and likely at least the first half of the 2020s). And so the Johnson government is nationalising but not necessarily driven by a nationalist ideology. That may seem odd by the conventional terms of nationalism, where it is treated as an aggressive, inward-looking, and, above all, dogmatic ideology. The Johnson government is nationalising to the extent that it keeps the party in power.

This nationalisation-as-statecraft evidently coheres as an electoral strategy. However, it produces dilemmas that have shaped the Johnson government's approach and Britain's post-EU nationalisation. The Johnson government faces quite a few dilemmas as a result, however. For instance, all governments wish for strong economic growth, especially come re-election, yet almost all experts agree that leaving the EU will dampen the UK economy. Or, if Brexit was made in England, then how can it be enacted for all four constitutive nations of the union? The dilemma we will focus on here, however, is encapsulated by Andrew Gamble as the tension between Global Britain and levelling up: the national conditions required for global economic and financial integration (Global Britain) typically render progressive-redistributive policies more difficult (levelling up) by producing greater inequalities, impacting tax revenue, and diluting state authority.[5] In the terms of this book, this is the dilemma of outward-facing nationalisation. It is a product of the electoral coalition that underpins the government, which itself is a product of the intensified and twisted political conflict of the post-crash decade.

2019 was the Brexit election that 2017 was supposed to be. The Conservative's promise to 'get Brexit done' meant openly courting Leave voters and those dissatisfied with the lack of progress in leaving the EU. Although the decline in party affiliation based on social class has been a long-term trend, Brexit pushed this dealignment further, with once Labour strongholds turning blue.[6] Johnson's election win was underpinned by a similar electoral coalition to the Brexit vote (see Chapter 5). In the narrative of the election, this challenge became known as winning over the so-called 'red wall', a stretch of constituencies sweeping from west to east across North Wales, through Merseyside and onto Yorkshire and Tyneside, that have almost always voted Labour. This quickly became a cliche for Northern marginal constituencies (or even just the North in general).

There are clear overlaps between the 'left behind' and 'red wall' as categories. In public discourse, the red wall ended up as an extension of the left behind for newer times, albeit without the explicit racialisation provided by 'white working class'. The 'legitimate concerns' of red wall voters ended up being discursively mobilised in a similar way to Brexit voters, often to make an implicit claim: that the nation – and its wealth and services – should belong to and benefit these groups, but that they are currently being ignored by an out-of-touch metropolitan elite. As the previous chapters have shown, these phenomena have their origins in the development of Britain's evolution from an empire-state-nation to a nation-state, but were intensified and twisted by the conflicts of the post-crash decade. And also like the left behind, the red wall's influence was somewhat overstated, as the Conservatives also retained much of their traditional support.

Although this 'get Brexit done' strategy brought them power in the form of a strong parliamentary majority, it is also a weak basis for governing. Johnson's 'blue collar and red trouser' electoral coalition is far from stable.[7] He admitted as much in his victory speech: 'those who voted for us Conservatives for the first time ...

you may only have lent us your vote'.[8] The challenge is deeper than just keeping voters happy. Combining a post-EU nationalisation project that implements both Global Britain and levelling up seems an impossible task: embracing Britain's free trade heritage, while also redistributing resources and industry to the peripheral regions of the country. The two seem to run up against one another, one outward-facing, the other inward, with respect to global economic integration. Aside from the various infrastructure projects and 'pork barrel' local funds,[9] there are two interventions that signify the Johnson government's attempts to resolve this dilemma: Australia's points-based immigration system, and the creation of up to ten 'freeports'. We will look at each policy proposal in turn.

Global Britain v. levelling up

Both freeports and the immigration points systems were policy suggestions from a notorious 2012 book entitled *Britannia Unchained* – which also resembles the 'unleashing' imagery central to the 2019 campaign. *Unchained* was written by a group of newly elected backbench Conservative MPs, who argued that the Cameron government was not neoliberal or patriotic enough. Some of its five authors went on to become prominent figures in the Johnson government: Priti Patel and Dominic Raab found themselves in two of the three big jobs as Home and Foreign Secretary respectively, while two others – Kwasi Kwarteng and Liz Truss – were appointed to key roles in business and trade. The book was not well received. The review in the *Sunday Times* described it as 'neither notable nor well-written'.[10] Most publicity focused on their denigration of 'coffee-sipping' and 'lazing around' British students who prefer degrees in media and business, and so are unlikely to 'ever compete with the Asian work ethic'.[11]

This focus on cultural decline was consistent with their wider analysis: that British values of self-help, innovation, and family have been destroyed by 'statists', while former colonies such as India and Singapore are reaping the benefits of those same untarnished values. As one passage in their preceding book, *After the Coalition*, put it: 'If Britain's historic values are good enough for newly growing Asian economies, they should also be good enough for Britain today.'[12]

Familiar foes crop up: the post-war compact, New Labour, the EU, identity politics, feminists, health and safety – but also the Cameron government, who are seen as neither liberal or conservative enough, and who did not go far enough on austerity and remain committed to high spending on the NHS. The UK is pessimistic and not patriotic enough: 'Britain has lost confidence in itself, and what it stands for. Britain once ruled the Empire on which the sun never set. Now it can barely keep England and Scotland together.'[13] Britain thus needs to be unchained – from the EU, and from 'the statists' – to restore and renew itself, through self-help, a smaller state, and free markets.

This kind of neoliberal nationalism does not neatly correspond with the Johnson agenda.[14] Reading *Unchained*, one might be surprised that the majority of its authors would end up in a government promising greater NHS funding and deficit-financed infrastructure spending. Yet there are many overlaps between *Unchained* and the 2019 Conservative manifesto: Euroscepticism, science, national symbolism – and freeports and immigration.

Although some variant of a points-based immigration system has existed since the late-2000s (and will be familiar to anyone who has been forced to navigate the tiered system of visas), the *Unchained* group have been calling for an 'Australian points-based system' for years. This 'Australian' concept was also used in the 2019 campaign as a way to signal that post-Brexit Britain will have greater control outside of the single market. Rather than pitched in the racialised terms of Enoch Powell, the arguments around a points-based system are more meritocratic: a transparent calculation of deservingness that gives a sense of fairness, of everyone being treated equally on the basis of meritocracy.[15] In both *Unchained* and the 2019 Conservative manifesto it is matched with the sense that immigration is part of what holds Britain back: that by relying on migrant labour, the UK has somehow become lazy and lax in its own training and education. For *Unchained*, this is reflected in the generosity of welfare, the laziness of students, and labour regulations that (supposedly) empower bad workers.

In 2020, Home Secretary and *Unchained* author Priti Patel announced the points-based system for when Britain transitioned out of the European Union in January 2021. The new system gives points on the basis of: job offer, skill level, English language, and salary – with extra points for higher salaries, jobs in shortage occupations, and relevant PhDs (with further extra points for STEM (science, technology, engineering, mathematics) subjects). The Home Office announcement whiffed of Global Britain: that this new system is global-oriented rather than biased towards Europeans; it 'prioritises the skills a person has to offer, not where they come from'; and so 'works in the interests of the whole of the UK'.[16] The aim, the Home Office says, is to reduce overall migration. Patel, meanwhile, splashed 'promise delivered' across her cheery, upbeat social media postings. While this may help some of the strategic dilemmas – solidifying support for the Leaver coalition despite getting Brexit done, for instance – it also creates new tensions. Leaving the EU and the new points-based system means that the UK has the most limited geographical reach of labour it has ever had. In April 2020, British farms helped coordinate special charter flights of Romanian workers 'amid a continuing recruitment crisis in the agriculture sector'.[17] This was despite minister George Eustice's call for the British population to create a 'land army' of agriculture workers and related 'Feed the Nation' campaign.[18] It is making it more difficult for other employers too to appoint workers from overseas, such as in universities, where they are sorely needed.

In Johnson's 'Brexit Address to the Nation' on 31 January 2020, immigration was first on a list of how the state would use 'these new powers, this recaptured sovereignty, to deliver the changes people voted for'.[19] Freeports were second. Freeports are a type of special economic zone, which are regulatory spaces within a state's jurisdiction offering special incentives (such as lower taxes and liberalised customs) to attract investment and generate economic growth. In this case, freeports would be physical spaces within the territory of the UK but legally outside of, or at least different to, UK customs and regulation (i.e. 'offshore'). If that's the 'free' part, then the 'port' part is because they will focus on existing seaports (which special economic zones don't have to be). The 2019 Conservative manifesto pledged to create ten freeports, spread across the country, to help 'level up' the nation. Freeports are used commonly across the global economy, and their particular shape and format is dependent on national strategy. Unsurprisingly then, the proposed UK model of freeports aims to suspend some duties to stimulate manufacturing, processing, and re-export.[20]

Freeports make a short appearance in *Britannia Unchained*,[21] but they are a pet project of Chancellor Rishi Sunak. While a backbench MP in 2016, Sunak wrote a paper on freeports for the Thatcherite think tank *Centre for Policy Studies*, with a title that nicely encapsulates their appeal for the Johnson government: *The Free Ports Opportunity: How Brexit could boost trade, manufacturing and the North*. The influence of this paper can be seen in the government consultation launched in February 2020 – there are segments that are literally copy and pasted. Freeports are presented as industrial strategy, with the aim of rebalancing the economy both in terms of sector (towards manufacturing) and region (towards the North). Sunak argues they could create 86,000 jobs in some of the poorest areas of the UK. Freeports will stimulate a post-Brexit economy. There's also something to the name of them. Freeports are often considered synonymous with 'free zones' or 'special economic zones', but those two terms do not have the Global Britain ring of maritime conquest or the levelling up focus on post-industrial port towns. Freeports, Sunak outlines, will 're-connect Britain with its proud maritime history as a trading nation and act as a beacon of British values, signalling the country's openness to the world'.[22] Freeports, then, have the potential to generate growth and jobs despite Brexit, level up the nation while globalising, and unite the country rather than divide it – all the while, unleashing a suppressed maritime-and-manufacturing British tradition and the potential of deprived communities.

If something seems too good to be true, then it probably is. Indeed, reading the typically pro-liberalisation press – *the FT, the Economist* – it is difficult to find an argument in favour of freeports. Freeports 'are no panacea ... their utility may be tiny';[23] they 'are economically trivial and politically expensive', and 'for a country such as the UK the proposal is basically pointless'.[24] Sunak's sums on job creation are dodgy: he took the 420,000 jobs across the 250 free zones in the US, assumed that all these jobs were created anew by these zones (which they were not), and then simply adjusted the number for the smaller size of the UK labour market.[25] In fact, many economists seem to agree that freeports in the UK will not generate new economic activity, but will instead just move it around the UK.[26] This was indeed the experience of the Thatcher and Osborne-era 'enterprise zones'.[27] With a finite amount of freeports available, and a commitment to spread them across the country, the proposal is likely to put different port towns in competition with one another – for example, Tees Valley versus Tyneside in north-east England.[28] The Scottish government, meanwhile, is sceptical, with their Minister for Trade and Investment Ivan McKee commenting that: 'We remain concerned that the focus of freeports may be positioned to compete on low-cost, low-wage, low-value opportunities with which they are often associated globally.'[29] The criticism from the Labour Party was starker still, with warnings of deeper inequality, tax abuse, and illicit activity.[30] As one op-ed puts it, 'instead of "levelling up" the economy, they would entrench the power of corporations and deepen market competition'.[31]

With so much criticism, it seems legitimate to ask why bother with freeports at all. For all their potential economic flaws and drawbacks, freeports are perhaps best understood less as an economic programme and instead as a political strategy and part of a nationalising narrative. It is surely no coincidence that Blyth – perhaps the quintessential red wall constituency, partly because it was the first of those seats to 'crumble' during the election night coverage – is predicted to be home to one of the first freeports. If so, this will follow the £35m that the town has already been allocated from the government's 'future high streets' and 'stronger towns' fund.[32] Freeports ticks the boxes of the outward-facing nationalisation that is at the heart of Johnson's strategy: imagining Britain as a coherent and governable whole after Brexit, with the boundaries of economic authority enacted back around the Isles, but with an outward-facing orientation. What this looks like in practice is another thing: aiming to restore growth by asking poorer peripheral towns to compete against one another for tax breaks that will divert economic activity to their towns over local alternatives – in the name of 'uniting and levelling up' and 'unleashing Britain's potential' – is far from a guarantee.

Culture wars

On to culture wars. Rather than interventions to reorient Britain's global economic integration to lift up underdeveloped regions, the main way that the strategic dilemmas of the 'blue collar and red trouser' coalition has been kept together is through so-called 'cultural' issues. The 'cultural' issues are many: contesting feminist, trans, and antiracist advances for greater equality; defending the legacy of the British Empire; and promoting Britain's supposed historical glories, especially in education and curricula. These issues perhaps coalesce most clearly around the issue of 'free speech'.

Over the last decade, a loose network of activists, comedians, online personalities, academics and journalists from a range of diverse political positions – socialist, centrist, libertarian, conservative, far right – has emerged who together seek to defend free speech against 'wokeness', the latest incarnation of 'political correctness gone mad'. The underlying definition of free speech within this network seems to focus on the right to offend and call into question issues around race, gender, and sexuality – and Brexit. Interestingly, the network seems largely Anglospheric. From a British perspective, the network includes traditionally conservative outlets such as the *Telegraph* and the *Daily Mail*, but also many outsiders who congregate online on platforms such as YouTube and Twitter. Other key players in this network include: Toby Young, the controversial founder of a 'free speech union'; the remnants of the Revolutionary Communist Party, now in the form of the free speech absolutists *Spiked*; alt-right YouTube personalities such as Paul Joseph Watson, 'Sargon of Akkad', and 'Count Dankula' (all three of whom joined UKIP, the latter two running as candidates); and political scientists, such as Eric Kaufmann. Globally, this taps into the so-called 'intellectual dark web' which includes websites like *Quillette*, personalities such as Jordan Peterson, and the alt-right including *Breitbart* and Steve Bannon. By working in defence of free speech, this network present themselves as shackled.

A thread can be sewn through the course of the book to this point, explicitly from the rise of the 'metropolitan elite' onwards, that constitutes these so-called 'culture wars'. 'So-called' because there is some uneasiness around the 'culture wars' term. A sense perhaps that 'war' is hyperbole or, to the contrary, that it trivialises what is at stake. Alternatively, there is a sense that these conflicts do not really matter, that they are a distraction, that they are 'very internet'. It has its own jargon. For the self-styling shackled, its antagonists are snowflakes and social justice warriors; critical race theory and cultural Marxism its spectre; no platforming and cancel culture its scourge. 'Culture war' is often spoken with an eye-roll or written with scare quotes, as Twitter being Twitter. It is derided and parodied as an 'industry', whereby technology such as social media is weaponised, therefore making its users wary that other users are communicating in bad faith.[33] There is a now familiar news and social media cycle: contrive free speech controversies to get 'cancelled', and then gain attention from news platforms and social media users for apparently being censored. This is best encapsulated by British actor Laurence Fox, who sprung from the political wilderness to national (or at least internet) fame through his appearance on *Question Time*, where he argued that 'to call me a white privileged male is to be racist'. Now seemingly a full-time anti-woke (and later, anti-lockdown) activist of sorts on Twitter, his public existence is dependent on creating constant controversies.

There is, however, much use and value in the 'culture war' concept. To see why, we can return to its US origins, where the term is often attributed to sociologist James Davison Hunter. His 1991 book compared the state of the US to Kulturkampf – a nineteenth-century Protestant–Catholic battle over education in Bismarckian, nation-building Germany. The divide between orthodox and progressive readings of US culture mimicked the religious conflict of that time, Hunter noted. The 'most fundamental ideas about who we are as Americans are now at odds' because of incompatible world views.[34] Hunter showed how these cultural divisions structured many political issues in the US including gender, sexuality, race, the family, and religion. Hunter's analysis was amplified through an infamous speech by paleoconservative politician Patrick Buchanan at the 1992 Republican National Convention. Buchanan stated that 'there is a religious war going on in this country. It is a cultural war, as critical to the kind of nation we shall be as the Cold War itself. For this war is for the soul of America.' In doing so, he denounced the Democratic Party as supporting abortion, radical feminism and the 'homosexual rights movement'.[35] The speech has a mixed legacy within Republican politics. It is sometimes disapprovingly cited as a reason why Clinton won the 1992 election, but many observers pointed to how its terms dominated the 2012 Republican primaries to the extent that it reshaped bipartisanship.[36] The inspiration for Buchanan's 'culture war' slogan was apparently Hunter's book.[37]

Like many concepts developed in the backstages of scholarship, 'culture war' emerged on the frontstages of politics, smudged and stretched. In contemporary usage, the term is often used as a metaphor to 'refer to a displacement or supercession of the classic economic conflicts that animated twentieth-century politics in the advanced democracies by newly emergent moral and religious ones'.[38] In this way, 'culture war' is close to synonymous with the kind of 'cultural backlash' thesis that emerged to explain the Brexit vote, along with the divide between cultural and economic factors and the problems that this generates (see the Introduction).

If we reject a hard distinction between economy and culture, then the culture part of culture war is less of an issue. To speak of culture war does not preclude that economic conflict (whatever that may be) is somehow less important. As the Introduction outlined, politics is about who gets what, when, and how – that is, the distribution of resources. That distribution is dependent on two types of boundary: a line between those who get resources and those who do not, and a set of concentric circles that emanate from a core to a periphery like an archer's target to mark those who are most deserving and those who are less so. In this distribution of resources, control and patronage of the state is the most decisive weapon. The point is that culture wars are not merely cultural, whatever that might mean: they involve state power. The two most famous historical examples show this. Bismarck forcibly repressed the political freedoms of the Roman Catholic Church, including in schools, as he considered it a barrier to a united Germany. The liberal–conservative conflict in US politics has ended up shaping the partisan identities and ties of the Democrat and Republicans, who are the only two parties that can realistically take power.

A second feature of a culture war is a binary distinction between two caricatured groups, through which large swathes of the population can be mobilised. It is often pointed out that most British residents do not participate in this kind of conflict, with those who do mostly grouped towards political extremes. Indeed, a recent study found that most political comment on social media is produced by small, politically driven groups.[39] That such findings can generate newspaper headlines is an indication of how smudged and stretched the 'culture war' concept has become. It should be no surprise that the number of participants is low and concentrated. Twitter controversies do not make a culture war; common statements that 'the country has never been so divided' are not meant to be taken literally. In this context the categories of 'Remainers' and 'Leavers' do not map onto who voted in the referendum. They are imaginary groups: those that supposedly value progress and equality pitted against those that supposedly value the status quo and place, or so the narrative goes (see Chapter 5). For those dedicated to Brexit, Remainers are typically the metropolitan elite, those who pushed to reverse the referendum result. Leavers, meanwhile, are framed as wildcat elites, racists, or both. These divides had their origins before the Brexit vote, but the referendum made it possible to mobilise and speak for the '51 per cent' (or '49 per cent'). For Johnson, that '51 per cent' was represented not just by bots and trolls on Twitter, but by the formal authority of the British state.

Politics always involves contesting moral authority, so under what conditions can we reasonably identify a culture war? That is when political conflict – that is, struggle over who gets what, when, and how – is (i) substantially engaged through a binary struggle over moral authority in and boundaries of the *nation*; that (ii) spills out of formal political arenas and into other spaces, such as education, the arts, or religion, all of which can be reasonably referred to as 'cultural' (and are often significant in nation-building); and which (iii) is ultimately a contest over control and patronage of the formal authority of the *state*. In other words, it is a battle over 'culture', to not only define the nation and who it is for, but to use state authority to enforce a vision of it. This kind of conflict is close to synonymous with nationalisation, insofar as it is a battle over the configuration of nation and state. So while culture 'war' may well be hyperbole or metaphor, for the conservatives involved in this kind of struggle *it is a war*, insofar as it is considered a battle to maintain the status, security, and existence of the nation by maintaining its reproduction through the state.

The war on woke

Contesting 'free speech' is a logical and almost inevitable part of culture wars in liberal democracies.[40] If a battle over moral authority in a nation sounds abstract, then the ability to influence news, entertainment, education, and art is concrete. Whose story is told and whose is not becomes itself a site of conflict. This will be refracted through uneven access to different 'cultural' mediums (in the UK, the left is presumed to be better represented in education, the right in media). It is made all the more fraught through an assumption that 'speech' is not simply the communication of information. 'Speech' is also performative: it has a greater power to confer legitimacy to or even bring into reality a particular politics with distributional outcomes. As Hunter points out, those engaged in culture wars will often 'confuse censuring (the legitimate mobilisation of moral opprobrium) with censoring (the use of the state and other legal or official means to restrict speech)'.[41] This is sometimes deliberate. For the claim of being silenced by a greater authority is a proven tactic. As William Davies puts it, culture wars produce 'the strange sight of both sides claiming defeat, so as to mobilise their own forces around a sense of injustice.'[42]

However, it is the Leave side of the battle where free speech is the key complaint. That a British culture war focuses on free speech feels apt given the nation's mythology. Free speech is considered a cherished principle of Western civilisation, and especially central to the political success of England and/or Britain. Each 'silencing' is somehow imbued with these stakes. Brexit is itself a key issue where supporters are supposedly silenced, as previous chapters have shown. A classic Leaver argument is that ordinary people have legitimate concerns over immigration, but were ignored or patronised by the metropolitan elite; the referendum finally gave them a voice; but ensuring that the people have their say is under threat from the Remainer elite. This Remainer–Leaver cleavage started to structure cultural conflict, especially over race. A common claim is that the *woke* (or sometimes just *wokeness* in general) is silencing debate. A brief history of this term will highlight how the term is wrapped up in antiracist struggles for equality, thereby highlighting the continued racialised terms of the Brexit nationalisation project.

The concept of 'woke' has its origins in Black American politics and culture. Its first use is variously located in a 1923 Marcus Garvey book, a 1938 song by Lead Belly, or a 1962 *New York Times* article.[43] Either way, it was used as a call to be aware of racist oppression, and was reborn through a 2008 Erykah Badu song, with the hook 'I stay woke'. During the August 2014 protests in Ferguson, Missouri, following the police shooting of a young Black man, the hashtag #StayWoke was used on Twitter to remind participants to stay aware of oppression and police brutality.[44] This increasing usage of 'woke' was reflected in popular culture. Jordan Peele's 2017 satirical horror film *Get Out* was an allegory about Black oppression: the plot hinged on its Black protagonist forcing himself to himself to stay awake (literally, to dispel hypnosis) to avoid subsumption into and destruction by the hidden racists of white suburbia.[45] When asked why he gave a prominent role to the song 'Redbone' by US musician Childish Gambino in the film, Peele referenced the song's hook – 'stay woke' – as 'that's what this movie is about'.[46]

In 2016, 'woke' was shortlisted for Oxford Dictionaries word of the year (it lost out to 'post-truth'). An accompanying article for Oxford Dictionaries noted how the word was being 'stripped of its gravitas as well as its call for black folks and allies to remain aware of oppression' and was becoming 'racially sanitized for a mainstream audience'.[47] By this point, 'woke' was being used on social media to denote something quite different: a process of personal and political transformation that renders (typically white male) social media users and celebrities aware of gendered, racial, and sexual oppression (akin to 'waking up'). This personal transformation was typically communicated by a social media user consciously 'checking their privilege'. This might be done through posts that try to recognise intersectional struggles, such as calling out problematic behaviour or uploading photos of themselves reading feminist or post-colonial literature.[48] Corporations, too, recognised the potential of reaching politically conscious young people by adopting activist stances in their advertising and product development (with the Kendall Jenner advert for Pepsi an especially infamous instance).[49]

By 2018, wokeness no longer applied to keeping alert about racial oppression and police brutality, but meant a pretentious and public performance of privilege-checking and self-awareness. Among those antiracist communities that propagated the hashtag as part of Black Lives Matter, the term became problematic. Ironically, being consciously 'woke' started to denote a status that was doing the opposite of what was likely intended: trying to show how aware one is, only to demonstrate a deeper, hidden true unawareness of the politics of that performance – a politics that may indeed reproduce, in some ways, the socially constructed hierarchies that are deemed the problem in the first place.

The evolution of the concept was accelerated by conservative and libertarian appropriation of the term. These voices used 'woke' to satirise and attack the supposedly pretentious ideological zealotry of identity politics, to the point where this has now become the dominant usage. Even Barack Obama made headlines for his comments that 'this idea of purity and you're never compromised and you're politically woke, and all that stuff – you should get over that quickly ... the world is messy'.[50] It is now mostly a term of abuse, generalising from the instances of pretentious performances of faux activism to assume some of sort of bad faith or malicious intent to almost anyone who is arguing or campaigning for antiracist and feminist changes. 'Woke' can therefore capture a number of progressive causes – most prominently over race and trans rights, but also issues such as veganism and fatness, and even just socialism or trade unions – into one overarching category. What this category of 'woke' means depends on the situation. Sometimes it is used to imply that activists are acting in bad faith as a way of demonstrating moral superiority or purity. Other times it is claimed that the focus on, say, antiracism, is a front for anticapitalist politics and 'Marxists'.

Either way, these critics position wokeness as silencing groupthink. Which is where free speech comes to the fore. Critics of wokeness play up the ambiguity between censuring and censoring: that many of those who pursue free speech against wokeness are interested in using the principle of free expression to legitimise controversial and sometimes harmful political positions – such as 'legitimate concerns' over immigration or transphobia. These views tend to elicit a reaction, often fierce criticism. Occasionally responses include 'no platforming', a tried-and-tested anti-fascist measure where venues will refuse to host speakers who use hateful speech.[51] Sometimes those eliciting the controversial views will have employment or other opportunities cancelled, sometimes under pressure from social media (hence 'cancel culture'). Critics of woke argue that this censuring is, in effect, censoring: 'monitoring everyone's behavior, words and art for transgressions against their worldview ... Their tactics were illiberal, damaging to a society that believed in the free exchange of ideas and free speech.'[52] This presents a supposed dilemma for all: are you for free speech (and therefore for English, British, and Western values, for the nation); or are you against it (and what it stands for). This is how Farage can argue that 'the real modern fascism [is] the attempt to close down free speech'.[53]

In the pages of the *Daily Mail* or *Telegraph*, meanwhile, 'wokeness' has largely replaced 'political correctness' (as in, it 'has gone mad').[54] Both concepts are typically used in analyses covered in Chapter 3 and 4: that a disconnected metropolitan elite are imposing values on the people, to the extent that they are not able to air their 'legitimate concerns'. Those 'left behind' were racialised as white, and it is no coincidence that 'wokeness' has been coopted as a way to contest and ridicule feminist, trans, and antiracist advances for greater equality (that is, a greater share in the distribution of resources). Through Brexit, both are now attached to a once-in-a-generation constitutional transformation – which the government is promising to get done.

In the grand scheme of things, Conservative governments' interventions have been subtle. After Laurence Fox's *Question Time* appearance, for instance, the government was reported as privately cheering on, with two senior ministers briefing journalists that 'the public are sick of having this crap stuffed down their throats by the media for years. We don't have to go along with it any more.'[55] These kinds of comment can seem paradoxical: punching up, in this case against 'the media', but from a position of state power. Yet both culture war and nationalism both need a sense of inequality to have any purpose (see Chapter 6). Both culture war and nationalism are about taking or consolidating power, which is more justifiable when taking authority away from forces deemed illegitimate.

Education, however, is the main battle site in the Brexit culture war. Universities are considered the stronghold of Remain wokeness, and the main site of conflict over free speech. Farage's quote earlier about the 'real modern fascism' was in reference to 'no platforming' at universities. Over the post-crash years, the moral panic over students has shifted from concerns about violent protests in response to the 2010 tuition fee rises, to wokeness: students violating free speech through no platforming, decolonising the curriculum as 'rewriting history', and the censoring of conservative ideas.[56] Along with the new language of 'snowflakes' and 'safe spaces' and the context of Brexit, this can give this supposed crisis a sense of genuine novelty.

That is not the case. Quashing Catholic control of schooling was a key objective of Bismarck's Kulturkampf. A key flashpoint in the 1990s US culture war was over expanding the literary canon to include works by women and people of colour.[57] Indeed, state-sanctioned mass education was how loose, local cultures were transformed into the kind of homogenous culture that makes a 'nation' in the modern sense.[58] Many Conservative Party speakers were no platformed in the 1980s, leading to the Education (No. 2) Act 1986 that looked to protect free speech on university campuses.[59]

In 2017, the government launched the Office for Students, with an explicit remit to 'regulate' free speech with the ability to apply 'sanctions'.[60] In 2018, the then Universities Minister Sam Gyimah warned of a 'creeping culture of censorship' on university campuses.[61] However, the Joint Committee on Human Rights that was tasked with investigating free speech at universities found no systematic issue with freedom of expression, but that the advice is complex and 'murky'.[62] Yet this has not stopped the controversy. A think tank report by two academics associated with the pro-free speech movement outlined above remade the argument about censorship and conformity.[63] The 2019 Conservative manifesto also returned to the issue with a promise to strengthen free speech.[64] In October 2020, equalities minster Kemi Badenoch hit the headlines for her comments in Parliament on 'critical race theory'. The term has never once been recorded before in Hansard.[65] Although 'critical race theory' is a specific academic body of work centred in US legal scholarship, it has, like 'woke' and 'cultural Marxism', become a catch-all term to denigrate and deflect social justice activism, especially on race.[66] Badenoch declared that the government was 'unequivocally against' the concept.[67] 'We do not want teachers to teach their white pupils about white privilege and inherited racial guilt', she continued, as teaching critical race theory without offering opposing views is 'breaking the law'.

The state, then, under the stewardship of Johnson's Conservatives, is neither neutral or passive in the culture wars, but an active player with an interest. Those close to Johnson constantly briefed journalists that the government should wage a 'war on woke' given that the Brexit referendum and other recent elections have supposedly shown the power of identity politics.[68] Indeed, *The Economist* has reported the Conservatives as purposively taking 'a more assertive line' on race and other identity politics issues in order to appeal to the value of the red wall voters.[69] And this is ultimately what this nationalisation project is about: statecraft.

Conclusion

Culture wars are a site of conflict over the boundaries of the nation, who is core and who is peripheral or outside, and, ultimately, who ought to share in and shape the distribution of the nation's wealth. Culture wars are also a way of legitimising the political projects of the time, in this case, Brexit, and so too the government that has gone all in on it. Has this got anything to do with freeports, with ending austerity, with greater immigration controls? Is this just an incoherent government, who will say and do anything to consolidate support? This chapter has argued that it seems a lot less incoherent when analysed for what it is: a nationalisation project, albeit one driven as much by expediency and statecraft as by nationalist ideology. By way of conclusion, we can return to *Britannia Unchained* to elaborate this.

Although it was panned by many on publication, it found a fan in Conservative thinker Roger Scruton. In a thoughtful review for *Prospect* magazine in 2013, Scruton endorsed *Unchained*.[70] His disapproving note that the authors 'turn to economics whenever they need a conclusive reason for their policies' generates the question of what, exactly, is conservative in this kind of thinking: 'What, in the end, does a conservative seek to conserve, and why?' Despite his concerns, Scruton finds a compelling answer to this question running through *Unchained*: the moral idea of England.

In *Unchained*, those values are identified as responsibility and self-help through individual autonomy and traditional families, free trading and a spirit of innovation, and an organic social order where everyone has their place. It is England. As Robbie Shilliam shows, this can be traced back to Edmund Burke, who argued that Englishness is an 'exceptional ability to engender in its members (the 'little platoons') an orderly independence at every level in the grand hierarchy, as opposed to the disorderly and anarchical terror of revolution'.[71] For Scruton, the aim of conservatism – and what excites him about *Unchained* – is the defence of English order, and that can only come from recognising that these values are passed on through 'civic inheritance'. England is 'a moral idea, and one to which the Tories have always appealed when asked to define what they are for'. The left has understood this 'and therefore set out to deconstruct the idea of England, to show it to be a class-ridden and socially divisive sham'. The Labour Party, Scruton continues, 'has encouraged a school curriculum from which the "we" concept has been more or less excised, with pride in empire replaced by shame at our former belief in it'.

Rather than the idea of England, the left offers the idea of equality. However, the cost of implementing equality is huge, especially because it goes against conserving the natural order, which is why it goes hand in hand with fiscal excess. People are 'de-skilled and de-schooled in the name of equality'. In this world view, free speech is not really about expression at all. As the authors of *Unchained* explain, 'people are now seen as a product of their background and experience – not as free agents ... Where there is no free will, there can be no responsibility.' Rediscovering England means unleashing the nation from the equality culture of the left and the European Union, and challenging these ideologies across all spheres, including education. As Scruton warns, continued membership of the EU – 'to march with Nick Clegg into a transnational future' – means 'leaving England on the dust-heap of history'. The alternative is let that lion out of its cage.

Even though the pick 'n' mix character of the Johnson government is best explained by strategic responses to electoral dilemmas, there is nonetheless a coherence to the project that can be seen when analysed through the lens of nationalisation rather than left–right and state-market. The biggest barrier to this project was something completely unexpected, the topic of the next chapter: the coronavirus pandemic.

7

Locked down

On Thursday 26 March 2020, at 8 pm exactly, in neighbourhoods up and down the country, the British nation came out onto the street. People leant out of windows and stood on balconies. Some were banging pots and pans, some were clapping, even dancing. Many were whooping and having a good time. This was the first 'clap for carers', three days after the first lockdown. Everyone was ordered to stay indoors to limit physical human interaction and therefore the transfer of coronavirus. The economy was frozen. Some work, however, had to continue outside of the home, including the NHS. The clap was for them.

And it was not just the ordinary people who showed gratitude. Their Royal Highnesses the Prince George, Prince Louis, and Princess Charlotte joined in. As did many inanimate objects. The Kelpies – a public sculpture of horse heads in Falkirk – was lit blue to represent the NHS. As was the Wembley Stadium arch, Tower Bridge, the top of the Shard, and the London Wheel. Blackpool Tower beamed out a blue heart.

For the second clap on 2 April, the majority of broadcast media 'paused' so that viewers could get outside without missing TV.[1] As the clap continued for many weeks, the Queen described it as an 'expression of our national spirit'.[2] In the words of the *Guardian*, it was a ritual that 'united the nation'.[3] Befitting a national moment, the clap seemed to cut across class, race, and gender, as well as political divides (this was one ritual in which both Johnson and Corbyn happily participated). It was a moment of national feeling: ordinary Britons, displaying unity, keeping calm and carrying on, celebrating their brave heroes, in the battle against an existential threat.

The timing was interesting and significant for Britain's post-EU nationalisation. As Chapter 6 argued, the Johnson government was pursuing nationalisation-as-statecraft. Aside from getting Brexit done, this nationalisation project centred on forging a narrative of unleashing Britain's potential – including the so-called 'war on woke' – to hold together its unlikely electoral coalition. Whether their nationalisation project of levelling up would have been further developed or not is difficult to know due to, of course, the coronavirus pandemic that consumed the Johnson government within months of gaining their parliamentary majority in December 2019. During the early days of the pandemic, many commentators predicted a deepening nationalism: lockdown and wartime spirit, virus xenophobia, border closings, vaccine and equipment hoarding, and, indeed, the kind of patriotic spirit produced by the clap for carers. What kind of patriotic moment was this? And what would this mean for the post-crash nationalisation of Britain?

Although public displays of patriotism and national feeling were multiple and amplified in that first lockdown period in the spring of 2020, this chapter argues that the immediate nationalising impact of lockdown is surprisingly limited. The reasons for this are numerous, and include the emergency character of it, the much-documented incompetence, and the priority of a technocratic and economy-first response. Rather than nationalising per se, the chapter will show that the moment is akin to the kind of proto-nationalisation we saw in Chapters 1 and 2 with austerity: the mobilisation of the nation as an imagined community, especially through Britain's core myths of wartime, the NHS, and carrying on. Lockdown Britain therefore represents the kind of fork in the road where, like the financial crisis and its fallout, many futures are now possible. However, those futures will emerge from the conflict of this last decade, and so are likely be contested on a state-nation rather than state-market axis – including the potential break-up of Britain.

'Whatever it takes'

The political dilemma of coronavirus is clear enough. On the one hand, the virus is deadly, especially to the elderly and those with underlying health conditions, so do everything to stop it. The virus spreads through touching, coughing, exhaling even. Stop human interaction and movement through locking people down in their homes, and the virus can be controlled. Otherwise the NHS will be overwhelmed. Yet, on the other hand, to stop human movement puts limits on some productive economic activity, therefore putting at risk jobs, livelihoods, and even Britain's entire system of wealth creation. Lockdown too fast and too much, the argument went, the people will rebel against restrictions and the economy will tank. The consequence would be scarcer resources and the inevitable conflict that such a situation produces. Hence the narrative became 'health v. the economy'.

This is not the place to go over these debates all over again. In-depth accounts have demonstrated just how unprepared the British state was for a pandemic and just how incompetent the Johnson government was in its response.[4] The broad contours, however, are relevant in respect to the Johnson government's nationalisation project analysed in Chapter 6. Many experts now agree that Britain locked down too late. The first case in Britain was recorded on 29 January 2020, and the following day the threat level was raised from low to moderate. The weeks that followed have been characterised as 'lost' until Johnson finally announced a full lockdown starting on 23 March.[5] On 3 March, Johnson's advice was still that 'we should all basically just go about our normal daily lives' but wash our hands while singing happy birthday twice.[6] In the meantime, Italy, France, and Spain all imposed lockdowns, while Germany built a mass test-and-trace system.[7] In those weeks, Britain took a liberal, 'open for business' approach, with some measures such as social distancing introduced. This was soon criticised as the 'herd immunity' approach: protect the most vulnerable, but let most people get infected creating effective immunity in the long term while maintaining as much economic activity as possible.[8] Johnson's plan to 'unleash Britain's potential' by uniting and levelling up was hardly a priority.

A full lockdown finally started on 23 March. A lot happened quickly: almost every resident had their personal freedoms curtailed via state-sanctioned force; productive economic activity was deliberately disrupted and frozen; and there was unprecedented state intervention into the economy, including paying the wages and salaries of workers unable to work. Chancellor Rishi Sunak committed to do 'whatever it takes' to get through the crisis (echoing the then President of the European Central Bank Mario Draghi's famous and famously effective promise during the Eurozone crisis in 2012). Sunak initially committed over £330 billion in measures.[9] The Bank of England cut interest rates to a record 0.1 per cent and expanded its quantitative easing programme, first in March and then again in June and November, outstripping the previous measures between 2009 and 2013.[10] Previous research has shown how QE is in effect a redistributive measure to favour asset-holders.[11] These were supported by later inventions of a similar ilk, including a VAT cut for some sectors, and the exemption on stamp duty (a tax on house purchases) was increased from £125,000 to £500,000.[12] And there were, of course, the various furlough schemes, to which we return later.

It is a cliche that in times of emergency, people turn to both state and nation. The state can provide the resources required for security. It can use its sovereign powers to intervene in a way that no other institution can. This included many moves that could be described as nationalising, insofar as they involved bailouts and state control. The nation, meanwhile, can be united through a shared enemy – in this case, a virus. And so it was unsurprising to see that coronavirus presented an opportunity for the global far right to renew their nativist and xenophobic rhetoric. In Hungary, Victor Orbán claimed that: 'We are fighting a two-front war: one front is called migration, and the other one belongs to the coronavirus. There is a logical connection between the two, as both spread with movement.'[13] In the US, Donald Trump was one of many to refer to coronavirus as 'the Chinese virus' in reference to its origins in Wuhan, which can be seen as part of his wider anti-China strategy. This combination of state intervention and nativism has the potential to be nationalising, especially if it involves restricting resources such as job support or vaccines to ethnic natives, stepping back from international cooperation, or further more-than-temporary control of movement across borders.

Yet this did not really happen in the UK. Not only did Johnson avoid the kind of nativist or xenophobic rhetoric used by superficially similar 'populist' leaders such as Trump and Orbán, but there was little attempt to engage in the kind of nationalising tactics that may otherwise have been available. As set out in Chapter 6, the Johnson nationalisation project is driven by expediency as much as ideology. It was no surprise, then, to see it placed on the back-burner during lockdown, especially given the well-documented issues the Johnson government had in coming to terms with the pandemic. Rather than nationalist in terms of nation-state building, the lockdown period was mostly nationalist in the only way that Britain seems to understand: national symbols and myths in ritualistic displays of patriotism.

One gigantic national effort

The collective, shared experience of being locked down was unparalleled in modern times. In the 'fight' against an existential enemy, with the vulnerable 'shielding' while others worked on the 'frontline', there is little wonder that nationhood helped legitimise freezing the economy and the severe restrictions on movement. In the fear and uncertainty, those symbols of post-colonial British nationhood – the NHS, the Blitz spirit, keeping calm, carrying on – helped create a patriotic moment.

Emergency powers require justification, and promising to protect the people against an existential threat is a strong one. The result is warlike rhetoric. 'The inescapable need for state involvement', as Nicholas Mulder puts it, 'helps explain why the war economy is a favorite metaphor of the technocratic imagination'.[14] In Britain, it may as well be a legal requirement to do so with reference to those myths of post-colonial British nation-state-building: the Second World War, the People's War; and the NHS, the reward for those sacrifices. The Queen's emergency address to the locked-down nation – a similar format to her annual Christmas messages and so one of the many signals during the first lockdown that these were not normal times – was memorable for its comparison to wartime (and the continued relevance of Dame Vera Lynn's wartime classic 'We'll Meet Again').

Boris Johnson announced the first national lockdown through a video announcement. Seated in front of a Union Jack flag, he warned of a 'huge national effort'. After weeks of weak measures and keeping Britain open for business, 'the time has come', Johnson explained, 'for us all to do more' by following the instruction to stay home.

Predictably, Johnson justified these measures through appeal to the nation:

> Each and every one of us is obliged to come together and halt ... I know that as they have done so many times in the past the people of this country will rise to that challenge and we will come through it stronger than ever. We will beat the coronavirus, and we will beat it together. And so therefore I urge you at this moment of national emergency to stay at home, protect our NHS and save lives.

Contained within that last sentence was the slogan for the first lockdown: 'Stay home. Protect the NHS. Save lives.' All three parts of the slogan were presumably equal in importance, linked together in one chain of action. Yet as Johnson had argued earlier in the address, the moment of 'real danger' was overwhelmed health systems. As William Davies points out, the ambition to 'protect the NHS' was so prominent that it started to eclipse the third part of the slogan to 'save lives'.[15] The NHS is one of the founding myths of post-colonial British national identity (see Chapter 3) and so looking to protect it is a ready-made justification for cutting across class and party divides. It also fudges concerns (which are prominent on the Conservative backbenches) that locking down was a vast overreaction.

The military metaphors during lockdown have been aplenty. Early on in the first lockdown the UK was short on ventilators, then a key piece of equipment in keeping alive those suffering from COVID-19. Matt Hancock announced in the *Sunday Telegraph* a 'call to arms' for manufacturers based in Britain to transform their production so that they could build ventilators and other NHS equipment.[16] Although this kind of militarised rhetoric should not be surprising given the existential threat that any pandemic poses, Hancock was not afraid to ramp it up. He went on to explain how 'our generation has never been tested like this':

> Our grandparents were, during the Second World War, when our cities were bombed during the Blitz. Despite the pounding every night, the rationing, the loss of life, they pulled together in one gigantic national effort.[17]

Gearing production towards a warlike effort, for the nation, would be a clear instance of nationalisation, as it is intervening in life to encourage or force a greater alignment of activities with the reproduction of the nation. Hancock's call to arms is a limited example, however.

The military metaphors do not really stretch to characterising the COVID-19 economic interventions in an especially meaningful way. As many observers have pointed out, a 'war economy' typically means mass mobilisation into production; yet the coronavirus response can be characterised as mass *de*mobilisation.[18] Rather than mobilising a war economy, the military metaphors and emergency measures are better thought of an extension of a common feature of modern governing. Susan Sontag wrote in her famous analysis of disease and metaphor that:

> Abuse of the military metaphor may be inevitable in a capitalist society, a society that increasingly restricts the scope and credibility of appeals to ethical principle, in which it is thought foolish not to subject one's actions to the calculus of self-interest and profitability.[19]

This kind of justification has been especially prevalent in post-crash politics, where a variety of emergencies have been enacted to legitimise non-transformative state intervention. In Britain, the key examples are austerity and quantitative easing, but emergency government is perhaps best characterised by the Eurozone crisis.

In other words, the military metaphors are better thought of as a way of legitimising lockdown. By locking down, Johnson proclaimed to the nation we are making sure that the virus won't win; the virus is 'beatable' as 'we have the resolve and the resources to win the fight'. The vulnerable were asked to 'shield' and 'shelter', for example.[20] Key workers, meanwhile, have also been categorised as 'frontline workers', invoking the part of the army that is closest to the enemy in battle, sprinkling a symbolic value and heroism onto their representation. The British population have responded to Johnson and Hancock's call to pull together as one, insofar as much of the patriotic sentiment around lockdown has been bottom-up rather than top-down. Commemorating those who supposedly 'sacrificed' themselves on the frontline for their nation is in keeping with Britain's practice of militarist national rituals (see Chapter 3).

The clap for carers was created by Annemarie Plas, a Dutch woman living in London, who was inspired by similar rituals in Europe. She posted details of the clap on her social media, where it quickly spread (via Victoria Beckham) and was picked up by traditional media outlets.[21] Although politicians participated in the clap, with Plas eventually getting an invite to meet Johnson at Downing Street, the ritual was very much an organic process. Although there has been critique and contestation, the clap for carers was considered a positive experience by many, with anecdotes of NHS workers overwhelmed by emotion, of clappers meeting their neighbours for the first time and building bonds, and of those locked down having something to look forward to.[22]

Whether the Queen and the *Guardian* are right in claiming the clap united the nation or not, it does not preclude the ritual from criticism. It was contested, adapted, and eventually dropped. Thanking NHS staff and other workers for their 'sacrifices' can overlook or justify poor working conditions. One health worker described it as 'a sentimental distraction from the issues facing us' such as provision of personal protective equipment or delayed lockdown.[23] A mental health nurse in Birmingham remarked that 'it was lovely to start with', but that now 'I just want a pay rise, or maybe a tax-free month, or something like that'.[24] Like military commemoration, the clap started light but then 'thickened into something more forceful and censorious, potentially something angrier'.[25] Indeed, each weekly clap seemed less enthusiastic and more fraught than the last: two months after the first clap, 50 per cent of respondents in a YouGov poll said it became less meaningful and more politicised at it went on.[26] The founder, Plas, called it off towards the end of May as lockdown was easing because she felt it was becoming political. 'The narrative around it was changing', explained Plas. 'It was also up to them [politicians] to pick up the bill and start doing more than just applaud, because the applause was actually for us normal people.'[27] Part of a nationalisation project this was not.

Similar patriotic rituals and celebrations were created and adapted, with mixed success. On the one hand, there was 'Captain Tom' – Tom Moore, an ex-army officer who served in Burma in the Second World War – who aimed to walk 100 laps of his garden before reaching his hundredth birthday to raise money for the NHS. His target was £1,000. Within a month, he had raised almost £40 million; within the year, he was knighted, published a book, did over 800 press interviews, and had a Number 1 single. Captain Tom is a heart-warming tale that feels almost beyond the boundaries of politics, even if his story – the NHS and the Second World War, military hero and charity fundraising, white, ordinary, and stoic – would win British nationhood bingo. On the other hand, ex-reality TV participant and now presenter Ben Fogle – a kind of upper-class cultural envoy – tried to jump on the bandwagon by announcing a national birthday singalong to the Queen: 'Let our song bring good cheer not just to Her Majesty but to the whole nation #singforthequeen.'[28] His idea was met with what felt like universal disdain and mockery (one joke being that if the original clap had perhaps not genuinely united the nation, then the reaction to Ben Fogle's idea might still). Fogle's failure shows the limits of the clap, and also highlights how the original clap for carers was not just unthinking acquiescence to patriotic mores but instilled with meaning and choice: supporting 'frontline workers', which has as much a class-based resonance as it does national.

Nationalising salaries?

This patriotic moment, then, was not necessarily a nationalising moment, at least immediately. It may help create the conditions for a nationalisation project in a similar way to how the prudent public household, sense of moral decline, wartime nostalgia, and patterns of distribution and conflict of the austerity era helped set the scene for the competing nationalisation projects of the mid-2010s: Brexit, Scottish independence, and Corbyn's Labour. Indeed, it may, but at the time of writing (mid-2021) it is too early to say (although this a theme returned to in the Conclusion).

Beyond patriotic rituals and symbols, furloughing represented the clearest opportunity for nationalisation. A recap: by ordering everyone to stay indoors, the British state chose to pause swathes of productive, economic activity, in a way that was previously deemed a political impossibility. The 2020 recession was unique because it was deliberate. Productive economic activity was deliberately frozen with the hope of preserving it, so that it could be thawed and reanimated at a later date when human circulation and interaction was no longer permeated by death (or the NHS overloaded). Preserving the economy requires tremendous resources. For businesses that could no longer operate, the state in effect paid their workers anyway – partly to sustain them, partly to preserve their jobs.

This furloughing of workers is something Britain has never before seen. The Coronavirus Job Retention Scheme (later relaunched as the Job Support Scheme) describes itself: keep people in work even when businesses are not operating, by the state paying up to 80 per cent of wages. In hindsight this seems like a normal and even sensible policy. Yet let us not forget how profound this was. Even at late as 20 March 2020, the *Financial Times* sounded sceptical: even though 'past [economic] taboos are rapidly evaporating', they raised concerns about the practicalities of means testing.[29] During the height of the first lockdown in April and May, over 8 million jobs were on furlough.[30] Initially running until July of that year, the scheme was extended along with the second and third lockdowns. Overall, the scheme is estimated to have supported 9.9 million workers in 2020, at an estimated cost of £54 billion.[31] The Self-Employment Income Support Scheme, introduced later, is estimated to have cost £20 billion.[32] Meanwhile, between March and November unemployment-related benefit claimants increased by 1.4 million.[33] The standard rate in Universal Credit was increased by £20 per week at a cost of £8 billion.[34]

In the first few weeks after being announced, it was fairly commonplace to see furloughing described as nationalisation, as in bringing a substantial part of the country's private sector wage bill into state ownership. On 20 March, ITV political editor Robert Peston asked 'Will Rishi Sunak's temporary nationalisation of the economy rescue us?'[35] On the same day, the *Financial Times* described furloughing as a way to 'effectively nationalise' salaries.[36] However, this framing fell away quickly, and for good reason. It is a stretch to characterise furloughing as nationalisation, in either senses of the concept. For furloughing is evidently not 'state ownership': it is temporary support in an emergency, and no control or power over capital or labour is conferred to the state. Neither was it justified in a nationalist or patriotic way. Sunak justified the scheme by saying that 'we said we would stand together with the British people, and we meant it', but this kind of rhetoric was feeble.[37] Rather than being named 'The Great British Job Saver', or whatever, it was technocratic and emergency, and is in no way connected to any purpose of transforming the economy for the nation's benefit.

This helps reinforce how the two definitions of nationalisation outlined in the Introduction – public (rather than state) ownership and making state congruent with nation – are connected, insofar as the first is a subtype of the second, which is a wider category. The purpose of state ownership as 'nationalisation' as exercised in post-war Britain is not about state ownership per se, but about collective, democratic control for and by the national peoples, thereby making the nation and state more congruent. Without this nationalising purpose, state ownership is not 'nationalisation'. This rhetorical oddity is a minor feature of British political discourse, such as when the bailout and then ownership of Royal Bank of Scotland in 2008 is sometimes described as nationalisation, but often with scare quotes to indicate that it is somehow not proper. Likewise, furloughing was a technocratic response to an emergency; it was done for the national peoples. Any attempt to claim otherwise would struggle for justification.

Unlike much of the British coronavirus response, the furloughing scheme was introduced smoothly. In a prestigious annual lecture, Former Cabinet Secretary Sir Gus O'Donnell praised it as a 'success story'.[38] A *Financial Times* editorial was similarly positive.[39] In these analyses, the successes are often couched in terms of policy efficiency, maintaining the economy, and staving off lost jobs and unemployment. We can push further in the terms of this book, however, to how the furlough scheme is in effect an anti-conflict device and, further, likely averted significant privation and hardship for many. This is in contrast to the other proto-nationalisation period studied in this book, where austerity was legitimated through stoking conflicts between the deserving and undeserving.

Furloughing nevertheless had distributional effects. Work that is dependent on social interaction was more likely to struggle in lockdown, and so meant that sectors like hospitality, restaurants, and entertainment were especially hit. Young women in poorly paid jobs were most likely to be furloughed. One in six female employees work in shutdown sectors, compared to one in seven male.[40] This intersects with age: at least 35 per cent of female employees aged under 25 work in those areas, compared to less than 10 per cent of male employees ages 45–54.[41] However, the largest disparity is earnings, with those earning less far more exposed to potential furloughing: 34 per cent of employees in the bottom tenth of the earnings distribution work in shutdown, compared to just 5 per cent of those in the top tenth.[42]

Meanwhile, around 2 million employees had their wages in effect fall below the national living wage as some employers did not provide the 20 per cent top up in addition to the 80 per cent covered by the state.[43] Many poorer households needed to use savings: 50 per cent of those with less than £1,000 in savings used their savings for everyday spending during the first lockdown, compared to 19 per cent of those with £20,000 or more in savings. (This doesn't account for the significant segment of households with no savings.)[44] More than one in eight furloughed workers defaulted on a debt repayment.[45]

Furloughing did indeed have regressive distributional effects, but its main effects were in using state resources to keep people in jobs when the economy was frozen, thereby averting conflict and scarcity. This was completely unthinkable, especially given the age of austerity and its associated imperatives. In hindsight, it is incredible how fast furloughing became normal. There was little attempt to make this nationalising, either rhetorically or substantially: the state has no extra authority or interaction with those being furloughed, and the justifications for it were evidently a technocratic response to an emergency.

Keep cooking and carry on

Furloughing did indeed prevent a scarcity of jobs and the intensified conflict that would accompany that. And despite the patriotic moment of the nation coming together, there was of course conflict.

Food is one resource over which there was considerable scarcity in lockdown, although of a particular type. Chapter 2 showed how food was a key battleground in the politics of austerity, ranging from ensuring that the nation doesn't go hungry through emergency food provisioning such as food banks, to demonstrating one's cultural capital and commitment to thrifty living by consuming in a suitably kitsch and/or frugal manner. Throughout this period there was no scarcity of food, despite the hunger and conflict. There was more than enough to go around. The issue was ensuring that everyone had the resources (i.e. income) to access their required calories through market mechanisms.

One of the lived experiences of early lockdown was the prospect of genuine food scarcity. This gave way to hoarding. Befitting wartime, hoarders were framed as those putting individual interests above the nation; there was severe condemnation for anyone seen to be profiting from the panic. That toilet roll was the key in-demand item added a surreal edge. Fears of genuine food scarcity during the first lockdown proved, for the most, unfounded – flour was in short supply for a while – but the anxieties were real and uneven. With movement restricted, it is little surprise that as the nation retreated into the home, cooking – and baking especially – caught the imagination. Yet the wartime aesthetic seems peculiarly British. TV chef and food campaigner Jamie Oliver created a new show literally called *Keep Cooking and Carry On*. Channel 4 launched *Keeping Crafting and Carry On*, which presented crafting in that well-worn feminised aesthetic of the make-do-and-mend austerity housewife, this time returning to the past to 'restore pride' in British homes.[46] Meanwhile the 'austerity cook' Jack Monroe was given a TV presenting slot on a new (albeit short-lived) show, *Daily Kitchen Live*, which aimed to 'provide inspiration for people struggling at home with limited food resources'.[47]

While lockdown meant endless photos of sourdough on social media, it also meant the most severe food insecurity crisis in post-war history.[48] With economic insecurity a major driver of food insecurity, recessions are likely to increase demand for emergency food provision. Indeed, the lockdown demand for emergency food relief, such as food banks, quadrupled, with estimates that 16 per cent of the population faced food insecurity during the first lockdown.[49] The economic effects of the lockdown were exacerbated by the restrictions on movement. The 1.5 million people categorised as clinically vulnerable were unable to shop for food because of strict instructions to shield themselves, while families with tight finances that relied on free school meals faced the prospect of providing more meals than normal.

For the clinically vulnerable, the state provided food parcels directly.[50] It provided those officially shielding from the virus with a grocery box with food to last one individual a week. The parcels were provided by Brakes and Bidfood, two of the main food wholesalers in the UK. In the words of the government, it was the 'biggest effort to deliver supplies to those in need since World War Two', directly invoking the communal feeding centres set up in the form of 'British restaurants' that fed the nation during wartime (see Chapter 2).[51] Direct food provisioning to households by the British state is unparalleled in post-war history, let alone at this 'scale, speed and complexity'.[52] Unsurprisingly, the scheme faced serious challenges. Many of the boxes provided food that did not meet basic nutritional guidelines, and some were 'not appropriate for meeting the nutritional, cultural or dietary needs of their recipients', such as relying on specific cultural or linguistic norms.[53] Some issues came from the centralised and privatised character of the provision, especially in England. The Welsh government tried to add fresh (and Welsh) produce to the boxes.[54] In Scotland, there was greater co-production with local services, leading to a more holistic and joined-up approach that meant the scheme was incorporated with other forms of support.[55] As with furloughing, any possibility of a nationalising transformation beyond temporary crisis management was resisted.

The government has provided free school meals to children from low-income families in England for some time. With schools closed in lockdown, families with tight finances that relied on free school meals faced the prospect of providing more meals than normal. The government therefore introduced a national voucher scheme to provide those families with the equivalent of £15 per week for each eligible child. The scheme was administered by schools, who had the choice of providing a packed lunch or distributing the vouchers to families.[56] After initially provided for the Easter holidays, the scheme was expanded to cover May half-term break. In response to pressure from a variety of campaigners – including, most prominently and unusually, the footballer Marcus Rashford – the government was forced into an embarrassing U-turn by extending the scheme over the summer holidays at a cost of £120 million. The same happened again in November on whether to extend the vouchers across the Christmas holidays. Once again, Rashford was central. The year ended with Rashford 'a fully fledged national hero'.[57] He was no stranger to good causes.[58] But volunteering is one thing; successfully lobbying for a change in government policy is another.

Like 'clap for carers', Rashford was somehow political and apolitical all at once. He provoked a typical culture wars response, both in the old and new styles. The old style invoked Philip Hollobone from Chapter 2, with one Conservative MP asking 'where is the slick PR campaign encouraging absent parents to take some responsibility for their children? ... I do not believe in nationalising children, instead we need to get back to the idea of taking responsibility.'[59] In the new style, Rashford was criticised for being 'woke' and 'virtue signalling', which he perfectly dispelled by tweeting: 'On a serious note though, what is virtue signalling?'[60] (This term was in the news because the BBC issued new impartiality guidelines that banned news staff from 'virtue signalling' on social media).[61] The problem for culture warriors is that Rashford does not read from the woke script. Supported by the international agency Roc Nation Sports, Rashford has displayed a maturity and political deftness that belies his 22 years.[62] In his letter to MPs in June 2020 that kicked off the controversy, he wrote: 'This is not about politics; this is about humanity. Political affiliations aside, can we not all agree that no child should be going to bed hungry?'[63] After the first of his successful interventions, Rashford tweeted in celebration of the U-turn: 'Just look at what we can do when we come together. THIS is England in 2020.'[64] Whether Rashford meant England because he was sensitive to the devolved character of service provision (a theme returned to below), or because, like many before him, he had simply muddled England and Britain is unclear. It is nevertheless startling for its nationalising tone.

Paying for COVID-19

It may seem strange that when the state is spending £55 billion on furloughing that it also refuses to extend a meal voucher scheme for the school holidays. Conservative MPs were whipped to vote against Labour's motion to extend the school voucher provision into the October half-term. It would cost too much, they argued, and the state cannot afford it.[65] So while the age of austerity seemed over, prudence was still the way in some situations.

Even before the pandemic, the Johnson government had signalled their intent to break away from the Cameron-Osborne playbook. In the midst of lockdown in April 2020, Johnson ruled out public spending cuts: 'It's certainly not going to be part of our approach.'[66] Economists seem to agree. In October 2020, The *Financial Times* ran the headline 'The week that austerity was officially buried', reporting how Carmen Reinhart, a pro-austerity economist and now Chief Economist at the World Bank, recommended that governments should borrow: 'First you worry about fighting the war, then you figure out how to pay for it.'[67] Similar messages came from the IMF and OECD.[68] There is indeed general agreement that there is little to immediately worry about with the debt and deficit, especially as the UK's borrowing costs are extremely low. Bizarrely, both Cameron and Osborne claimed that the UK's response was only possible due to their deficit cutting. Critics, including the *Financial Times* editorial board, naturally pointed to the decade of austerity's impact on the social safety net, while austerity's hit on preparedness was a key theme in *The Times'* inside story of what went wrong in the UK's initial response.[69] But there is a time when the costs of these interventions is likely to become subject to conflict, when debates about 'balancing the books' emerge. What then?

Three camps are emerging.[70] At one end of the spectrum are those who see the lockdown interventions as further evidence of how the 'magic money tree' can be put to progressive or even radical use. Modern Monetary Theory, for instance, is controversial and heterodox: quantitative easing has shown how money creation really works but ends up inflating asset prices and therefore benefitting the already wealthy. It could even suggest that the traditional fiscal imagination of raising revenue and then spending it is completely wrongheaded: the state creates money through expenditure. An alternative could use those same mechanisms for social good.

At the other end of the spectrum are those still versed in austerity orthodoxy. This seems to include Sunak himself. In an October 2020 Twitter video in response to a question from the public – 'Whose money are you spending?' – Sunak cheerily replied 'Your money!', and explained that this is why he is careful with money to avoid burdening future generations.[71] Similarly, BBC political correspondent Laura Kuenssberg was criticised by a range of economists for bringing back the household metaphor in November 2020: 'This is the credit card, the national mortgage, everything absolutely maxed out … for next few years, there is really no money.'[72] It was perhaps unsurprising then that the November 2020 spending review included yet another pay freeze for Britain's 5.5 million public sector workers, two years after an eight-year freeze was ended. This was referred to by critics as a 'cap for carers'.[73]

A third camp can be identified in something like a middle ground between the 'magic money tree' and yet more austerity. There are many options here, with wealth taxes generating considerable energy. The independent Wealth Tax Commission proposed a one-off levy of 1 per cent on the value of assets, limited to £1 million per household.[74] Whatever the specifics, the idea of a wealth tax 'to pay for COVID' has received encouraging noises and endorsements from across the political spectrum.[75] The editorial boards of both the *Guardian* and *Financial Times* have written positively of the prospect. The Treasury have been reported as considering taxes on the wealthy, and the Treasury Committee has explored through its Tax After Coronavirus inquiry.[76] Research into public attitudes highlights such a move would gain considerable support from voters, with 74 per cent of people wanting to see wealth taxed more, including 64 per cent of Conservative voters and 88 per cent of Labour voters.[77] 'To pay for COVID' is the discourse, and this has been criticised as short-sighted.[78] However, many taxes – including British income tax – have been introduced as emergency, temporary measures to fund unforeseen events such as wars, and then hung around for a while afterwards (to put it mildly in the case of income tax). Although any implementation is far off and will inevitably be fraught, that wealth taxes are even being discussed in this way indicates a level of popularity unthinkable ten years ago. Much of that is down to concerns about inequality that characterise the austerity years (see Chapter 4).

A 'national wealth tax' to pay for COVID is certainly conceivable. It is also imaginable as a nationalist move. After the Second World War, the Labour Party made a similar move in rebuilding after crisis (see Chapter 1 and Chapter 4). The contemporary Labour Party could make it part of a pitch to strengthen Britishness à la 'a new Jerusalem', with everyone playing their part to recover and level up the nation. At the time of writing, however, there is no indication that new Labour leader Keir Starmer would pursue this. His approach so far has been either a bland caricature of pre-crash centrism or biding time with a general election likely years away. As things stand, any nationalising shifts in post-lockdown Britain seem more likely to be breaking up rather strengthening the union. It is more likely to be constitutional rather than ideological, and to emerge from Scotland rather than London.

Health ministers were to 2020 what central bankers were to 2008.[79] In the UK context, we can include devolved leaders in that statement. The governance of lockdown has been, at times, approaching a constitutional mess. Westminster has a tendency towards centralising control, but many of the relevant powers – including on lockdown itself – are devolved. This includes the NHS. When Boris Johnson addressed the British nation on lockdown, as he often did, he technically only had authority over England, but he either did not realise or did not care. In his 10 May television address on easing lockdown, for example, Johnson spoke as if the measures applied to the whole of the UK, just hours after Sturgeon had requested public clarity.[80] One former Downing Street official was reported to observe that there was 'an almost colonial mindset'.[81] And so the different UK nations had had different lockdown rules. There was a time when those in England could drive as far as they wanted for leisure, while those in Wales were told to 'stay local'. In one instance, the Welsh police arrested a woman from England who had taken a trip into Wales, a hundred miles from home. She complained was that she was following the rules: 'Boris Johnson said that you can'.[82] At the time of research, in January 2021, travel is not permitted between England and Scotland:[83] a powerful if temporary nationalising measure.

Both Sturgeon and Scottish nationalism have been strengthened by lockdown. Sturgeon has looked to avoid politicising the pandemic, early on declaring that she 'could not be less interested' in normal politics at that moment.[84] But the devolved politics has been delicate. The Scottish government led by Sturgeon has the authority to call lockdowns in Scotland, but lacks the economic power to fund them. In principle, the situation suits no one: with their limited fiscal and monetary powers, the Scottish government cannot fund the interventions necessary to pay for lockdown, while the Treasury bemoan lockdown decisions taken in Scotland that they have little choice but to support and fund.[85]

Although Scotland's coronavirus record is similar to England's, Sturgeon has been judged as a far more capable and competent leader. When the UK messes up, such as with the delayed lockdown, this can easily be framed as the fault of England and of London in particular. It has not just been delayed lockdown however. Promises over NHS Test and Trace have been consistently broken. Johnson's chief advisor Dominic Cummings told a scarcely believable story about breaking lockdown restrictions. A steady stream of controversies over corruption and clientelism have quietly rippled through since lockdown: friends of the Conservative Party have been appointed to prominent roles, and contracts for personal protective equipment have been given to inappropriate firms with strong political ties, all with a lack of transparency justified by the emergency.[86] A December 2020 poll shows support for Scottish independence at an all-time high, with 58 per cent indicating an intention for Yes compared to 42 per cent for No.[87]

The distribution of authority through devolution has played into Sturgeon's hands: go along with the UK on the big decisions, blame any issues on Johnson and London and shine a light on the corruption, while ensuring crystal-clear communication to Scottish voters.[88] Meanwhile, Johnson has given himself the title of Minister for the Union, called devolution a 'disaster', and created a 'union unit' in Number 10 to combat Scottish nationalism and preserve the British nation.[89] In one of their first tasks, they failed to get the Union Jack printed on the Oxford vaccine kits. This may all seem like just a quirk of devolution, and in a way it is. But devolution itself is not a random feature of the UK (see Chapter 5). Rather it is itself part of the evolution – or crisis – of Britain: from initial union, to empire, to nation, into Europe and out, and now to this. The prospect of Scottish overdevelopment through independence is ever plausible. At the SNP conference in November 2020, Sturgeon told delegates that she had 'never been so certain' the country will achieve independence.[90]

Conclusion

This chapter has highlighted how, if anything, the pandemic and lockdown derailed rather than continued the Johnson nationalisation project. The logic of lockdown was to preserve the economy – freezing it in place to thaw and reanimate it when movement is permitted again. This deliberate act of economic sabotage was legitimised through nationhood, including the clap for carers. This has helped give British nationhood an extra lease of life. But preserving the *nation-state* itself, in addition to its symbols and identity, will require that economic reanimation to go more than smoothly, and even provide development for the whole of Britain – including Scotland, former industrial areas (the left behind and red wall), carers, those individuals and businesses hit by Brexit, and many others, including their racial, gender, sexual, and ableist interactions. The costs and conflicts of this economic preservation are and will be various and vast. It may prove to cost Britain its nation-state.

Conclusion

As I sit down to finalise this conclusion, the European Championships in international football have just started. Austria's victory over North Macedonia during the first round of games was marred by controversy. Austrian striker Marko Arnautović celebrated his goal furiously: shouting, finger pointing, restrained by his teammates. Arnautović has roots in Serbia, who have a strained relationship with Albania. It is alleged that Arnautović's fury was aimed at North Macedonia's Gjanni Alioski, who has Albanian roots. The North Macedonian governing body issued a clear rebuttal of this offensive xenophobic outburst: 'We are always against nationalism, discrimination and all other forms of insults and outbursts that are not in the spirit of football and values that we all stand together.' These comments were widely reported by outlets covering the tournament.

Having just finished writing a book about nationalism in which one theme is the confusing character of the concept, the phrase 'We are always against nationalism' caught my attention, especially because it effectively equates nationalism with insult. Perhaps the intention was to indicate that nations are welcome but their politics ('nationalism') are not. Or perhaps it was simply lost in translation. Either way, I thought it interesting that such a statement could be issued by a national football federation during a competition to find out which European nation is the best at football.

Dividing up the world into nations seems so natural that it barely registers as nationalism. But there are many others ways – with some edging towards credibility and others not even close – that one could divide up Europe into teams for the sake of a football tournament, each with their own intriguing prospects: residency (in effect, the best players from each country's domestic leagues); region (think Scandinavia v. Iberia); language (with the possibility for a Celtic-heritage team including Ireland, Scotland, Wales, Cornwall, and Brittany); or age (and therefore footballing legend Cristiano Ronaldo leading a team of fellow 36 year-old Europeans).

But, no, these ideas won't do, because it is the nations that work – or, to be more precise, it is *nation-states* that do. After all, some European stateless nations like Padania and Abkhazia are not eligible to participate in formal international football tournaments. Rather it is that combination of nation and state that is so compelling and meaningful, which in turn confers a degree of legitimacy onto the idea that nations and states belong together.

State-nation histories

That nationalism is a confusing or stretched concept is one reason there is value in the concept of nationalisation, even though the two concepts evidently overlap. Nationalisation – defined as when the boundaries of the state are made more congruent with the boundaries of the nation – is a way to bring together nation and state in our analyses. While nationalism, in contrast, can take many guises, in the final analysis, its ultimate quest is for some kind of power, most likely in the form of control or patronage of a state. If politics is about the distribution of resources – or, in other words, who gets what, when, how – then the state is a justified site to direct one's political energies, as that is where the most power lies.

The state distribution and regulation of resources is bounded in two ways: formally through an in-or-out logic, and informally through a core-periphery logic. That state and nation boundaries seem like such a natural fit is itself a result of nationalism. Yet nation-states are but a recent feature of European politics; city-states, empires, and regional federations do not have closely aligned state and nation boundaries. Nationalisation is the process when those sets of state boundaries are made to more closely align with national boundaries. In other words, it is to make the state more national.

Recent British history looks different through this lens. Rather than just the triumph of the state over market or Keynesianism over liberalism, the post-war British settlement was also a post-imperial settlement that started to forge a new kind of British state-nation configuration. This book's central thesis is that the global financial crisis and its aftermath has generated another nationalising process: with Brexit, the formal boundaries of Britain's economic authority have been made as national as they have ever been. The relations between state and nation have changed in ways that were utterly unforeseen prior to the financial crash. Taking oneself back to the pre-crash world of no boom and bust is challenging, but it felt like a one-way street towards the erosion of state sovereignty characterised by a centrist political consensus.

Brexit is of course the centre of this nationalising thrust. But, as the book has highlighted, two other viable nationalising projects – Corbyn's Labour Party and Scottish independence – also gained momentum during this decade. And there have been other nationalising processes in addition to or alongside leaving the European Union, including the restriction of NHS services, the emergence of new political constituencies such as the left behind and red wall, and the increased prevalence of pro-military campaigns amid wartime nostalgia. As the book has shown, these wider nationalising processes have their origins in Britain's evolution from an empire-state-nation to a nation-state, but were intensified and twisted by the conflicts of the post-crash decade.

The decade following the global financial crisis saw the Coalition austerity project, sluggish economic recovery, and increased wealth and income inequality amid a succession of revelations that scandalised the elite. If politics is about who gets what, when, and how, then conflict over resource distribution is inherent to all social situations. Hard times, however, produce a social impulse towards consolidation: to draw in those nation-state boundaries, to protect those who are conferred greater value by virtue of being core to the nation. This is especially the case when the then government – an emergency-like coalition brought together by a promise to save Britain from indebtedness – insists that there are not enough resources to go around and that the nation should return to past glories to rediscover the ways of thrift and prudence. The existing battle lines of Britain – over those formal and informal boundaries of the nation-state – were intensified and twisted by the austerity, scarcity, and inequalities of the crash and its aftermath.

This has been a book, then, about how the political response to the global financial crisis has generated questions and conflict over

– and, ultimately, the transformation of – Britain's state-nation configuration. There is at the time of writing – mid-2021 – only one nationalisation project in the ascendency: Johnson's government, and his post-Brexit plan to level up Britain by unleashing its potential, although this vision was somewhat derailed by the pandemic. As this suggests, the UK's formal exit from the EU in January 2020 does not mark the end of that nationalising phase nor some sort of final victory over the other two nationalising projects of the decade. Conflict over resource distribution will continue to evolve and twist, but they will evolve and twist from these existing patterns. What will happen to Johnson's project?

State-nation now

One implication of this book is that the future of the UK will be defined by shifting configuration of state and nation rather than just by state and market.

The financial crash and the decade since has seen many changes in state-market relations. Austerity, quantitative easing, and then the lockdown interventions have transformed the relationship between state and market in profound and unforeseen ways. Yet there has been no 'great transformation' in the underlying ideas of economic policy in a way that mirrors the rise and fall of Keynesianism in the post-war era. Nor has there been a pendulum swing from the supposed market-led order of the pre-crash years to a new state-led order. While there have been significant state interventions over the past decade, much of this has been technocratic fixes to avert emergency. We may well therefore conclude that we live in an 'interregnum', in which the transformative potential of the global financial crisis is yet to be realised.[1]

This kind of analysis is guided by a previous historical event, in which capitalist crises coincided with a 'paradigm shift' in the key ideas of economic policy-makers to generate a specific kind of political and economic change. But, history, of course, has no preordained pattern. There is no reason why that specific kind of change has to happen again. While we search for how the 2008 crash has or has not transformed state-market relations or generated new ideas on how to do this, we risk missing the obvious conflict and transformation that is right in front of us: that is, conflict and transformation in state-nation relations, including territorial, constitutional, and, yes, nationalist. This will not suddenly end.

The Johnson government is of this decade. While it is still common to hear that it is right wing on culture and left wing on economics – a seeming contradiction, a supposed ideological paradox – focusing on state-nation configuration rather than state-market offers a different analysis: it is a nationalising government. Nationalism does not map onto left–right or state-market: it can be liberal, conservative, or socialist. While post-imperial nationalisation was an inward turn even with the Commonwealth, post-EU nationalisation is different, as Global Britain and its associated policies such as freeports suggest. Like lungs inhaling and exhaling, it is simultaneously inward and outward: inward because Brexit draws the formal boundaries inward to be congruent with a respective nation; but outward too because there is no intention to become protectionist.

Yet the current Conservative government is nationalising only so far as it keeps the party in power. While traces of an English ideology are visible when the Johnson government and its key players are analysed forensically, their commitment to levelling up the so-called left behind will weaken if it is no longer politically expedient. As I write this, two recent by-election results suggest that the post-Brexit electoral realignment is continuing to change along a Leave–Remain axis. In May 2021, the Conservatives won Leave-majority Hartlepool from Labour for the first time, but in June they lost the Remain-majority Chesham and Amersham to the Lib Dems. While the Hartlepool result was foreshadowed thanks to the 'red wall' narrative, Chesham and Amersham came as a shock: the Tories not only lost the seat but a huge majority. And so begins the 'blue wall' narrative, with analysts identifying the other Conservative Remain-majority seats that could conceivably flip to the Lib Dems. Other analysts have speculated that this shock defeat is a result of the Conservatives' preoccupation with keeping the red wall on side, thereby neglecting their traditional base.[2] That traditional base do not need levelling up, and will probably be content with traditional Tory offers of low taxes, which will run up against the 'splurges' needed to level up.

Despite this nationalising thrust, the Johnson government could end up overseeing the end of Britain. Johnson is evidently committed to the union between England and Scotland in principle and in rhetoric. He enjoys speaking of 'the awesome foursome' and put himself in charge of the Number 10 'union unit'. Yet symbolic gestures cannot distract from the Englishness of Brexit or dent the continued promise of overdevelopment that Scottish independence offers. Brexit has aligned the formal boundaries of the British nation and state; but it was a project of English ideology, mandated by English voters, delivered by an English government. The formal boundaries of the UK have been redrawn on English terms. The implications of this mismatch might make post-EU nationalisation as nation-breaking as it is nation-building.

Leaving one union is presumably enough for Johnson. Yet, if the framework of this book is to be taken seriously, the prospect of Britain's break-up will not be averted by printing Union Jacks on COVID-19 vaccines or by talking up the 'awesome foursome'. Nationalism feeds off inequality – or, more precisely, nationalism thrives when a relative low status produced by capitalist growth provides a basis to mobilise an ethnically homogenous group to take power away from (supposed) oppressors. To save the union, then, distribute resources more evenly across the territory.

That may sounds like an obvious platitude, especially given Cameron and Osborne's broken promise to 'rebalance' the British economy away from the south and finance.[3] Yet it is interesting how discourse around 'rebalancing' and the break-up of Britain are so disconnected. While rebalancing is seen as economic, Scottish independence is perceived in mainstream political discourse as a cultural phenomenon, as in 'identity politics'. So long as nationalism is conflated with nationhood, patriotism, and so on, this point will be continually missed. How else to explain the presumption that Scottish independence rose from the 1970s onwards because Scottish people suddenly started feeling more Scottish, rather than due to the inequalities of the union, the decline of post-imperial Britain, and the prospect of windfalls from North Sea oil. To put it starkly, the union needs growth, not flags. Otherwise, England will find itself alone, eventually.

Culture wars are another key pillar of the Johnson nationalisation project. Like talk of the 'awesome foursome', here too there is a sense of distraction through symbolism – these conflicts are ephemeral and very online, and so disconnected from the real world.

Being named as culture wars can sometimes be taken to imply that they are about identity politics and other issues that are separate from or even irrelevant compared to the hard reality of economic distribution and class. The term 'culture wars' is unfortunate, but it is able to capture the concerted and intensified pushback against antiracist and feminist advances, both prospective and achieved. This is nationalising to the extent that they conflict over where the informal boundaries of the nation-state should be drawn, and so who ought to be valued and protected via access to and share in the nation's wealth.

Culture wars are thus a fundamentally distributive issue. People of colour, women, trans people, and others, continue to face inequalities and systematic barriers to the good life, while those with relative status and privilege will continue to feel threatened by those advances. For this reason, these conflicts are not going to suddenly disappear, although they will evolve over time. Recall that this kind of conflict over 'culture' has not sprung from nowhere. 'Woke' is to Johnson's nationalisation project, what 'scrounger' was to austerity, and those conflicts over deservingness a decade ago were racialised and gendered too.

The key question is not whether these conflicts will continue or not, but to what extent they will form the basis for formal party political competition. As immigration declines from its status as the salient issue of British politics, it is unclear whether this kind of conflict offers any party the opportunity to mobilise a parliamentary majority. The Johnson government has shown, in relative terms, and compared to, say, Orbán in Hungary, a cautious endorsement of anti-wokeness. However, that the Tories lost that recent by-election in the affluent Home Counties to the Lib Dems is hardly a ringing endorsement of the power of culture wars to unite their shaky electoral coalition. Starmer, meanwhile, has shown little appetite for endorsing antiracist, feminist, and pro-trans causes. There was the possibility that culture wars and the battle over free speech might take on a new coronavirus flavour, as an imaginary Venn diagram of Brexiteers, 'free speech' advocates, and lockdown sceptics would show considerable overlap between the three. But as the lockdowns of 2020 and early 2021 recede into history, this seems less significant. But this does bring up a significant question: what are the implications of the pandemic and lockdown for nationalisation thrust in British politics?

State-nation futures

In the pre-crash world it felt as if there was only one future available. The pandemic represents yet another fork in the road where, like the financial crisis and its fallout, many futures are now possible. Yet the relationship between lockdown and nationalisation is complex. On the one hand, lockdown was a patriotic moment that coincided with state intervention at a scale and intensity that justify comparisons with wartime. On the other hand, those interventions were a technocratic response to emergency which derailed the government from their own post-EU nationalisation project of restoring Global Britain while levelling up. There are a couple of directions this could take.

In one scenario, the pandemic could lead to redrawn political battle lines. From a British perspective, it will be noted that the pandemic coincided with when Britain formally left the EU in January 2020. The successful vaccine roll-out will convince enough Scottish voters that their future lies with the union rather than alone. The post-Brexit electoral geography will cement itself as the new normal of British politics, with the Conservatives as the only party capable of a parliamentary majority as the de facto party of England after coming good on their promises to 'level up'. And so the conflicts over state-nation boundaries that characterised the post-crash decade will give way to a new and unforeseen pattern of conflict that will characterise a new era. Future historians will mark the outbreak at the beginning of 2020 the turning point from one era to another. Nationalisation will be neither here nor there.

In an alternative scenario, the nationalising thrust in British politics intensifies rather than withers. The Labour Party decide to mirror the Conservative strategy of targeting Leave constituencies by appealing to Remain constituencies through socially liberal policies matched with an equivalent promise of levelling up after the hard times of the pandemic. United by commitments to redistribution, party political competition between Labour and Conservative is reduced to their respective positions in the culture war, and the next general election rehashes the battles over Brexit, including over the informal boundaries of Britishness. And so while Britain's status outside of the EU is not a realistic option, conflict over Britain's state-nation configuration nevertheless intensifies.

However, speculating on whether there will be more or less nationalism is not really in keeping with the framework of the book. It is, after all, difficult to assess Brexit or the Johnson government on these terms, with the latter combining an outward-facing Global Britain and an inward-facing levelling up agenda. We can also presume that the basic feature of nationalism – that states should have nations and that nations should have states – will stay in tact. So rather than speculating on more or less, we can instead look for patterns that suggest whether the pandemic and lockdown hinder or help opportunities for nationalist mobilisation, and therefore continued conflict over (and further transformation of) Britain's state-nation configuration.

The clap for carers was a demonstration of who and what is valued in Britain, albeit symbolic. Without care, the economy and nation are nothing, and lockdown reinforced this anew with its patriotic rituals. Care was 'the buzzword of the moment': during lockdown, people cannot help but notice how life itself depends not just on NHS staff, but all care provision, as well the other labour that helps sustain this infrastructure, such as supermarket workers and bus drivers.[4] Some have speculated about whether this has fostered a sense of dependency and vulnerability among the nation, to the point where voters might be open to a more redistributive politics.[5] How this 'current affective mood of heart-felt appreciation' is 'translated into demands for material change' is an important question.[6] The 'cap for carers' – the pay freeze for Britain's 5.5 million public sector workers, including NHS staff, announced in November 2020 – shows how immediately limited this kind of mooted shift in meaning can be in the face of state authority. It's the longer game that matters, however, especially with state support, including furloughing to end, thereby raising the prospect of mass unemployment, especially among low-paid workers.[7]

These new inequalities will develop their own lines of conflict, but, either way, will present new opportunities for nationalist or class political mobilisation. Based on the conflict of the last decade, mobilisation against inequality is more likely to take the form of fiscal populism through wealth taxes – in which the nation reclaims its rightful wealth from a small, immoral elite that have cheated their way to riches – rather than through rejigging capital–labour relations to redistribute resources through the social relations of employment. Wealth taxes may sound like the classic state v. market battle, but the lines of conflict are to be fought on a state-nation axis: about one's responsibilities to the nation and wider citizenship in a tax haven world rather than about the crowding out effects of tax on investment or the deservingness of the mega-wealthy. The state *has* intervened through furloughing and other measures, and the old justifications for meritocracy are worn out. The Patriotic Millionaire movement – where rich individuals club together to encourage greater taxation of the wealthy – highlights the direction of travel in this regard.[8] This kind of revenue could help fund a Green New Deal in the style of President Biden's American Rescue Plan and American Jobs Plan. The potential for nationalisation here is evident.

It is not clear who would have an interest in developing this potential. Unless the Lib Dems stage a remarkable comeback, the future of Britain has three possible paths, each with their own ideology and party political representative: continued English nationalism with the Conservatives; Scottish independence through the SNP; and socialism (broadly conceived, given Starmer) and the Labour Party. Given that a second Scottish independence referendum has been ruled out by the current Conservative government, and the Conservatives are the incumbents, then Labour are in the most interesting position. This is especially so as they are the odd one out in this schema, with no nationalist ideology.

To some extent, of course, the Labour Party must be a nationalist party, insofar as trying to form a government to hold authority they recognise the legitimacy of the nation-state, even if they are begrudging and pragmatic in that implicit endorsement. Yet taken-for-granted principles aside, the party has a complicated relationship with nationalism, as does any political project or ideology with origins in class-based representation. Class and nation have historically been considered by British leftist intellectuals as zero-sum and incompatible.[9] This awkwardness is reflected in both factions of the party. The New Labour project dealt with this through a mix of multicultural civic nationalism and defending the Empire with a commitment to global finance, humanitarian intervention, and the EU. Corbyn, meanwhile, took some opposing stances: a mix of anti-imperialism and antiracism with a national economic strategy and Euroscepticism. Starmer initially seemed like he was going to forge his own Third Way between these two factions with his promise to maintain Corbynite economic policies, but as of mid-2021 he seems to have jettisoned that plan.

These two factions do at least share one commitment in common: looking back to the post-war Attlee government with pride. For many Corbyn supporting socialists, the spirit of '45 remains the crowning achievement of the party and a blueprint for state-over-market. While in Starmer's February 2021 speech outlining his economic vision, he played up the comparisons to 1945, arguing that 'I believe people are now looking for more from their government – like they were after the Second World War.'[10] In both cases, the nostalgia only works through incomplete analysis, because the Attlee government was as nationalist as it was socialist. It depended on colonial extraction, a Commonwealth labour market, and excluding Black and Asian British subjects from new national institutions such as the NHS. The second major moment of British nationalisation – Brexit – was similarly racialised. While Scottish nationalism can mobilise without recourse to race because of its aim of self-determination outside of the British union, there has never been an instance of successful English or British nationalist mobilisation that hasn't worked through race and racism. As Paul Gilroy memorably put it: 'Brit[ish] nationalism cannot be purged of its racialised contents any more easily than a body can be purged of the skeleton that supports it. Doubtless, the full implications of that realisation will one day transform the conduct of British political life.'[11]

Nationalism, then, is damaged goods, and beyond the pale in its English and British forms for socialists and the Labour Party. However, nationalisation, as a concept with some overlap, is evidently not. As Green New Deals, infrastructure plans, and industrial strategies become the practical options of how to 'build back better', those looking to mobilise will also need to realise that the legitimacy of the state – especially when intervening at great cost – is tied to the nation, just as the legitimacy of the nation is tied to the state.

Acknowledgements

Although the two have barely a passage in common, this book has its origins in the PhD I started in 2010 and completed in 2014. It's been a long journey, and so my debts are considerable!

I'd therefore like to start by thanking a number of teachers, friends, and colleagues who have mentored and supported me over this last decade: David Bailey, Stephen Bates, Rebecca Bramall, André Broome, Andy Hindmoor, Genevieve LeBaron, Johnna Montgomerie, Amin Samman, Len Seabrooke, Sven Steinmo, and Mat Watson.

Other debts are from the process of writing this book, which I began in November 2016 with the proverbial Book.docx. Since then, a number of friends and colleagues were generous enough to read and comment on draft material and/or meet with me to discuss the book or give advice, for which I am grateful. Thank you to Josh Baker, Victoria Basham, Jacquie Best, Matt Bishop, Mark Blyth, Ben Clift, Erica Consterdine, Laurence Cooley, Rhys Crilley, Will Davies, Kate Dommett, Andrew Gamble, Maya Goodfellow, Ellie Gore, Colin Hay, Andy Hindmoor, Tom Hunt, Hannah Lambie-Mumford, Michael Jacobs, Jamie Johnson, Scott Lavery, Genevieve LeBaron, Jonna Nyman, Owen Parker, Ed Pemberton, Charlotte Rommerskirchen, Simon Rushton, Anastasia Shesterinina, Rhiannon Spear, Burak Tansel, Jo Tidy, Merisa Thompson, and Joe Turner.

A few extended thankyous: Ed Pemberton provided research assistance at the very beginning of this project and has otherwise sharpened my thinking. A number of book-writing workshops with Jo Tidy and Joe Turner shaped the project, especially on race – as did Ellie Gore. Josh Baker, Rhys Crilley, and Jamie Johnson have together provided countless hours of support and relief. Erica Consterdine coached me through the politics of immigration.

Genevieve LeBaron and Tom Hunt suggested the title. Kate Dommett brought me baked goods to keep me going. Many of the key ideas in this book were developed in discussion with Scott Lavery, who was also a much-valued source of support and advice during the final year of writing. Many friends – including Tom and Lovell, and Jamie and Jenny – were kind enough to ask how the book was going without judgement, and to always lend support and an ear. Thank you all.

I presented the ideas from the book at a number of seminars and conferences, including the European International Studies Association (EISA) 2017 in Barcelona, my own Department of Politics in 2017, a workshop in Amsterdam in 2018, European Workshops in International Studies (EWIS) 2018 in Groningen, the Political Studies Association (PSA) 2018 in Nottingham, a Review of International Political Economy (RIPE)/New Political Economy (NPE) workshop in 2019, and an in-house work-in-progress session at the Sheffield Political Economy Research Institute (SPERI) in 2020. Thank you to all the participants at those events for your helpful comments and suggestions.

Much of the work for this book was undertaken in the SPERI offices, and I'd like to thank all my colleagues there past and present for providing such a stimulating and supportive environment. I am also fortunate enough to be based in a department and at a university which backed me in taking nearly a decade to transform my PhD research into a book, and where I have many stimulating and smart colleagues.

Thank you to Tom Dark at Manchester University Press for all his support – and especially for convincing me to make the book more ambitious (even if I did have to rewrite nearly the whole thing!). Two anonymous reviewers provided useful feedback on the proposal which shaped the book. Much later on, an anonymous reader offered a series of generous and very incisive comments on the draft manuscript for which I am extremely grateful, as implementing them has significantly improved the book.

A big thank you to Jamie Johnson and Andy Hindmoor. Without Jamie this book would look very different, and without Andy I doubt there would be a book at all.

And finally a special thank you to Jonna and my family for all of the support on every step of the way.

Notes

Introduction

1 www.youtube.com/watch?v=sm5ghIn4nwQ [accessed 24 October 2020].
2 'Network Rail', *Gov.uk*, http://orr.gov.uk/about-orr/who-we-work-with/industry-organisations/network-rail [accessed 11 March 2019].
3 David Litterick, 'Statisticians Wrangle over Network Rail Accounting Treatment', *Telegraph*, 1 November 2002, www.telegraph.co.uk/finance/2832095/Statisticians-wrangle-over-Network-Rail-accounting-treatment.html [accessed 11 March 2019].
4 Heather Stewart, 'Network Rail to be "Government Body", Adding £30 billion to UK National Debt', *Guardian*, 17 December 2013, www.theguardian.com/business/2013/dec/17/network-rail-public-body-uk-national-debt [accessed 11 March 2019].
5 Susan Strange, *The Retreat of the State: The Diffusion of Power in the World Economy* (Cambridge: Cambridge University Press, 1996); Matthew Watson and Colin Hay, 'The Discourse of Globalisation and the Logic of No Alternative: Rendering the Contingent Necessary in the Political Economy of New Labour', *Policy & Politics*, 30/4 (2003).
6 'FactCheck: No More Boom and Bust?', Channel 4 News, 17 October 2008, www.channel4.com/news/articles/politics/domestic_politics/factcheck%2Bno%2Bmore%2Bboom%2Band%2Bbust/2564157.html [accessed 22 October 2020].
7 John Christensen, Nick Shaxson, and Duncan Wigan, 'The Finance Curse: Britain and the World Economy', *British Journal of Politics & International Relations*, 18/1 (2016).
8 David Edgerton, *The Rise and Fall of the British Nation: A Twentieth-Century History* (London: Penguin, 2018), p. 467; Office for National Statistics, 'Ownership of UK Quoted Shares: 2018' (14 January 2020), www.ons.gov.uk/economy/investmentspensionsandtrusts/bulletins/ownershipofukquotedshares/2018 [accessed 22 October 2020].

9   World Health Organization, 'How WHO is Funded', www.who.int/
    about/planning-finance-and-accountability/how-who-is-funded [accessed
    25 June 2021].

10 Robbie Shilliam, *Race and the Undeserving Poor: From Abolition to
    Brexit* (Newcastle-upon-Tyne: Agenda Publishing, 2018); Gurminder
    K. Bhambra, 'Brexit, Trump, and "Methodological Whiteness": On
    the Misrecognition of Race and Class', *British Journal of Sociology*,
    68/S1 (2017).

11 Sir William Blackstone, *Commentaries on the Laws of England, Book
    the First* (1765), available at: www.gutenberg.org/ebooks/30802, p.
    235, emphasis in original [accessed 11 March 2019].

12 Shilliam, *Race and the Undeserving Poor*; Bhambra, 'Brexit, Trump,
    and "Methodological Whiteness"'.

13 Edgerton, *The Rise and Fall of the British Nation*, p. 265.

14 Pippa Norris and Ronald Inglehart, *Cultural Backlash: Trump, Brexit,
    and Authoritarian Populism* (Cambridge: Cambridge University Press,
    2019); Roger Eatwell and Matthew Goodwin, *National Populism: The
    Revolt against Liberal Democracy* (London: Penguin, 2018).

15 Norris and Inglehart, *Cultural Backlash*, pp. 44–5.

16 Eatwell and Goodwin, *National Populism*, pp. x, xvi.

17 Ibid., pp. 5–7.

18 Norris and Inglehart, *Cultural Backlash*, pp. 487–91.

19 Karl Polanyi, *The Great Transformation: The Political and Economic
    Origins of Our Time* (Boston, MA: Beacon Press, 1944/1957). See also
    M. Blyth, *Great Transformations: Economic Ideas and Institutional
    Change in the Twentieth Century* (Cambridge: Cambridge University
    Press, 2002); Colin Hay, 'Crisis and the Structural Transformation
    of the State: Interrogating the Process of Change', *British Journal of
    Politics & International Relations*, 1/3 (1999).

20 Martijn Konings, *The Emotional Logic of Capitalism: What Progressives
    Have Missed* (Redwood City, CA: Stanford University Press, 2015),
    p. 114.

21 Martijn Konings, 'Imagined Double Movements: Progressive Thought
    and the Specter of Neoliberal Populism', *Globalizations*, 9/4 (2012); Tom
    Hunt and Liam Stanley, 'From "There Is No Alternative" to "Maybe
    There Are Alternatives": Five Challenges to Economic Orthodoxy
    after the Crash', *Political Quarterly*, 90/3 (2019); L. Seabrooke, 'Why
    Political Economy Needs Historical Sociology', *International Politics*,
    44/4 (2007).

22 Colin Hay, 'Brexistential Angst and the Paradoxes of Populism: On the
    Contingency, Predictability and Intelligibility of Seismic Shifts', *Political
    Studies*, 68/1 (2020).

23 Charles Tilly, *Coercion, Capital, and European States, AD 990–1990* (Oxford: Blackwell, 1990), p. 1.

24 Benedict Anderson, *Imagined Communities: Reflections on the Origin and Spread of Nationalism* (London: Verso Books, 1983/2006), p. 6.

25 Nira Yuval-Davis, 'Gender and Nation', *Ethnic and Racial Studies*, 16/4 (1993); Tom Nairn, *The Break-Up of Britain: Crisis and Neo-Nationalism* (London: Verso, 1981); Ernest Gellner, *Nations and Nationalism* (Ithaca, NY: Cornell University Press, 1983/2008).

26 Sivamohan Valluvan, *The Clamour of Nationalism: Race and Nation in Twenty-First-Century Britain* (Manchester: Manchester University Press, 2019).

27 Gellner, *Nations and Nationalism*, p. 6.

28 Charles Tilly, *Durable Inequality* (Berkeley, CA: University of California Press, 1998), pp. 171–2.

29 D. Beetham, *The Legitimation of Power* (Basingstoke: Palgrave, 1991), p. 127.

30 Partha Chatterjee, *The Nation and Its Fragments* (Princeton, NJ: Princeton University Press, 1993); Frantz Fanon, *The Wretched of the Earth* (London: Penguin, 1961/2001).

31 Nairn, *The Break-Up of Britain*, p. 61.

32 Yuval-Davis, 'Gender and Nation'.

33 Ibid., p. 629.

34 Patricia Hill Collins, 'It's All in the Family: Intersections of Gender, Race, and Nation', *Hypatia*, 13/3 (1998).

35 Gurminder K. Bhambra, 'Colonial Global Economy: Towards a Theoretical Reorientation of Political Economy', *Review of International Political Economy*, 28/2 (2020), p. 11.

36 Tilly, *Durable Inequality*, p. 25.

37 Norman Davies, *The Isles: A History* (London: Macmillan, 1999).

38 Linda Colley, *Britons: Forging the Nation, 1707–1837* (New Haven, CT: Yale University Press, 1992/2005).

39 Andrew Gamble, *Between Europe and America: The Future of British Politics* (Basingstoke: Palgrave Macmillan, 2003), p. 20; Nairn, *The Break-Up of Britain*, p. 12.

40 Nairn, *The Break-Up of Britain*, p. 129.

41 Eric J. Hobsbawm and Chris Wrigley, *Industry and Empire: From 1750 to the Present Day* (London: Penguin, 1999), p. 26; David Richardson, 'The British Empire and the Atlantic Slave Trade, 1660–1807', in P.J. Marshall (ed.), *The Oxford History of the British Empire, Volume II: The Eighteenth Century* (Oxford: Oxford University Press, 1998).

42 Martin Lynn, 'British Policy, Trade, and Informal Empire in the Mid-Nineteenth Century', in Andrew Porter (ed.), *The Oxford History of the*

British Empire, Volume III: The Nineteenth Century (Oxford: Oxford University Press, 1999); John Gallagher and Ronald Robinson, 'The Imperialism of Free Trade', *The Economic History Review*, 6/1 (1953).

43   Bhambra, 'Colonial Global Economy', p. 11.
44   Michael Kenny and Nick Pearce, *Shadows of Empire: The Anglosphere in British Politics* (Cambridge: Polity, 2018); Ben Wellings, *English Nationalism, Brexit and the Anglosphere: Wider Still and Wider* (Manchester: Manchester University Press, 2020); Duncan Bell, *The Idea of Greater Britain: Empire and the Future of World Order, 1860–1900* (Princeton, NJ: Princeton University Press, 2009).
45   Edgerton, *The Rise and Fall of the British Nation*, pp. 1–42.
46   Andrew Gamble, *Britain in Decline: Economic Policy, Political Strategy and the British State* (Basingstoke: Macmillan, 1981/1994).
47   Gamble, *Between Europe and America*, p. 2; Edgerton, *The Rise and Fall of the British Nation*.
48   Edgerton, *The Rise and Fall of the British Nation*, p. 27.
49   Ibid., pp. xxi, 25; Shilliam, *Race and the Undeserving Poor*, p. 55.
50   Edgerton, *The Rise and Fall of the British Nation*, p. 141.
51   This formulation is informed by William Davies, *The Limits of Neoliberalism: Authority, Sovereignty and the Logic of Competition* (London: Sage, 2016); Melinda Cooper, *Family Values: Between Neoliberalism and the New Social Conservatism* (New York: Zone Books, 2017); Angus Cameron and Ronen Palan, *The Imagined Economies of Globalization* (London: Sage, 2004).
52   Nairn, *The Break-Up of Britain*. For two recent contrasting scholarly texts, see Michael Kenny, *The Politics of English Nationhood* (Oxford: Oxford University Press, 2014); Wellings, *English Nationalism, Brexit and the Anglosphere*.
53   Gamble, *Between Europe and America*, p. 231.
54   Ailsa Henderson et al., 'How Brexit Was Made in England', *British Journal of Politics & International Relations*, 19/4 (2017).
55   Wellings, *English Nationalism, Brexit and the Anglosphere*.
56   Harold Dwight Lasswell, *Politics: Who Gets What, When, How* (Cleveland, OH: World Publishers, 1950); B.J. Kerkvliet, 'Everyday Politics in Peasant Societies (and Ours)', *Journal of Peasant Studies*, 36/1 (2009).
57   Cabinet Office, 'The Coalition: Our Programme for Government', policy paper (20 May 2010), p. 15, available at: www.gov.uk/government/publications/the-coalition-our-programme-for-government [accessed 30 August 2021].
58   Paul Krugman, 'The Austerity Delusion', *Guardian*, 29 April 2015, www.theguardian.com/business/ng-interactive/2015/apr/29/the-austerity-delusion [accessed 25 October 2020].

59 Imogen Tyler, *Revolting Subjects: Social Abjection and Resistance in Neoliberal Britain* (London: Zed, 2013).

60 Shilliam, *Race and the Undeserving Poor.*

61 Kerkvliet, 'Everyday Politics in Peasant Societies (and Ours)'; J.M. Hobson and L. Seabrooke, *Everyday Politics of the World Economy* (Cambridge: Cambridge University Press, 2007).

62 Jamie M. Johnson, 'Beyond a Politics of Recrimination: Scandal, Ethics and the Rehabilitation of Violence', *European Journal of International Relations*, 23/3 (2017).

Chapter 1

1 www.youtube.com/watch?v=IldMnsymDo0 [accessed 6 February 2018].

2 Krugman, 'The Austerity Delusion'.

3 Scott Lavery, *British Capitalism after the Crisis* (Basingstoke: Palgrave Macmillan, 2019), pp. 79–108.

4 Ibid., pp. 80–93. See also Peter Burnham, 'New Labour and the Politics of Depoliticisation', *British Journal of Politics & International Relations*, 3/2 (2001); Ben Clift and Jim Tomlinson, 'Credible Keynesianism? New Labour Macroeconomic Policy and the Political Economy of Coarse Tuning', *British Journal of Political Science*, 37/1 (2006); Matthew Watson, 'The Split Personality of Prudence in the Unfolding Political Economy of New Labour', *Political Quarterly*, 79/4 (2008).

5 Lavery, *British Capitalism after the Crisis*, pp. 93–7. See also Andrew Hindmoor, *What's Left Now?: The History and Future of Social Democracy* (Oxford: Oxford University Press, 2018); Jim Tomlinson, 'From "Distribution of Industry" to "Local Keynesianism": The Growth of Public Sector Employment in Britain', *British Politics*, 7/3 (2012).

6 Lavery, *British Capitalism after the Crisis*, p. 103, emphasis added.

7 Colin Hay, 'Good Inflation, Bad Inflation: The Housing Boom, Economic Growth and the Disaggregation of Inflationary Preferences in the UK and Ireland', *British Journal of Politics & International Relations*, 11/3 (2009).

8 Matthew Watson, 'New Labour's "Paradox of Responsibility" and the Unravelling of Its Macroeconomic Policy', *British Journal of Politics & International Relations*, 15/1 (2013), p. 8; Helen Thompson, 'UK Debt in Comparative Perspective: The Pernicious Legacy of Financial Sector Debt', *British Journal of Politics & International Relations*, 15/3 (2013), pp. 474–5.

9 Graeme Weardon, 'IMF Warns Countries are "Playing with Fire" over Debt Disputes', *Guardian*, 17 June 2011, www.theguardian.com/

business/2011/jun/17/imf-debt-crisis-recovery-warning [accessed 27 September 2020]. See also Ben Clift, *The IMF and the Politics of Austerity: In the Wake of the Global Financial Crisis* (Oxford: Oxford University Press, 2018), pp. 150–75.

10 Andrew Gamble, 'Austerity as Statecraft', *Parliamentary Affairs*, 68/1 (2015).

11 Liam Stanley, 'Governing Austerity in the UK: Anticipatory Fiscal Consolidation as a Variety of Austerity Governance', *Economy and Society*, 45/3–4 (2016).

12 Gamble, 'Austerity as Statecraft'.

13 David Cameron, 'Together in the National Interest', speech to Conservative Party conference, 6 October 2010.

14 David Cameron, 'The Age of Austerity', speech to Conservative Party spring conference, Cheltenham, 26 April 2009.

15 George Osborne, 'We're Building a Better Future for Britain', speech to Conservative Party spring conference, 5 March 2011.

16 David Cameron, 'The PM Has Had His Boom and His Reputation Is Now Bust', speech to Conservative Party conference, Birmingham, 28 September 2008.

17 David Cameron, 'We Need Economic Change', speech (unknown venue), 7 November 2008.

18 David Cameron, 'Transforming the British Economy', speech in Shipley, West Yorkshire, 28 May 2010.

19 Mike Berry, 'The UK Press and the Deficit Debate', *Sociology*, 50/3 (2016).

20 Lucy Barnes and Timothy Hicks, 'Making Austerity Popular: The Media and Mass Attitudes toward Fiscal Policy', *American Journal of Political Science*, 62/2 (2018).

21 Liam Stanley, 'What Six Public Opinion Graphs tell us about Austerity', *SPERI Blog* (8 July 2015), http://speri.dept.shef.ac.uk/2015/07/08/public-opinion-graphs-austerity/ [accessed 21 June 2021].

22 Malcolm Sawyer, 'The Tragedy of UK Fiscal Policy in the Aftermath of the Financial Crisis', *Cambridge Journal of Economics*, 36/1 (2012), p. 206.

23 'Leaked Memo shows Miliband was Warned over Deficit, Immigration and Welfare in 2010', *LabourList.org*, 5 August 2015, https://labourlist.org/2015/08/leaked-memo-shows-miliband-was-warned-over-deficit-immigration-and-welfare-in-2010/ [accessed 6 February 2018].

24 Philip Cowley and Dennis Kavanagh, *The British General Election of 2015* (Basingstoke: Routledge, 2016), p. 74.

25 Mark Blyth, *Austerity: The History of a Dangerous Idea* (Oxford: Oxford University Press, 2013).

26 David Graeber, *Debt: The First 5,000 Years* (New York: Melville House, 2011).

27 Paul Rock, *Making People Pay* (London: Routledge & Kegan Paul, 1973); Joe Deville, *Lived Economies of Default: Consumer Credit, Debt Collection and the Capture of Affect* (Abingdon: Routledge, 2014).

28 Gustav Peebles, 'The Anthropology of Credit and Debt', *Annual Review of Anthropology*, 39 (2010).

29 Graeber, *Debt*, pp. 121–2.

30 Chris A. Gregory, 'On Money Debt and Morality: Some Reflections on the Contribution of Economic Anthropology', *Social Anthropology*, 20/4 (2012); Graeber, *Debt*.

31 George Lakoff, 'Metaphor, Morality, and Politics, or, Why Conservatives Have Left Liberals in the Dust', *Social Research*, 62/2 (1995).

32 Friedrich Nietzsche, *On the Genealogy of Morals* (Cambridge: Cambridge University Press, 2007 [1887]), p. II:4.

33 Sara Ahmed, *Cultural Politics of Emotion* (Edinburgh: Edinburgh University Press, 2014).

34 Ben Anderson, 'Affective Atmospheres', *Emotion, Space and Society*, 2/77–81 (2009); Angharad Closs Stephens, 'The Affective Atmospheres of Nationalism', *Cultural Geographies*, 23/2 (2016).

35 *Michael McIntyre's Comedy Roadshow*, 4 July 2009, BBC One, https://learningonscreen.ac.uk/ondemand/index.php/prog/010611A1 [accessed 10 Jan 2019].

36 Matthew Watson, 'Headlong into the Polanyian Dilemma: The Impact of Middle-Class Moral Panic on the British Government's Response to the Sub-Prime Crisis', *British Journal of Politics & International Relations*, 11/3 (2009); Matthew Watson, 'Constituting Monetary Conservatives Via the "Savings Habit": New Labour and the British Housing Market Bubble', *Comparative European Politics*, 6/3 (2008).

37 Alan Finlayson, 'Financialisation, Financial Literacy and Asset-Based Welfare', *British Journal of Politics & International Relations*, 11/3 (2009); Watson, 'Constituting Monetary Conservatives'; Matthew Watson, 'Planning for a Future of Asset-Based Welfare? New Labour, Financialized Economic Agency and the Housing Market', *Planning Practice & Research*, 24/1 (2009).

38 Johnna Montgomerie and Mirjam Büdenbender, 'Round the Houses: Homeownership and Failures of Asset-Based Welfare in the United Kingdom', *New Political Economy*, 20/3 (2015); Watson, 'Planning for a Future of Asset-Based Welfare?'

39 Alan Finlayson, 'Planning People: The Ideology and Rationality of New Labour', *Planning Practice and Research*, 24/1 (2009); Watson, 'Headlong into the Polanyian Dilemma'.

40 Watson, 'The Split Personality of Prudence', p. 583.
41 Herman M. Schwartz and Leonard Seabrooke, 'Varieties of Residential Capitalism in the International Political Economy: Old Welfare States and the New Politics of Housing', *Comparative European Politics*, 6/3 (2008), p. 249; Herman M. Schwartz, 'Housing, the Welfare State, and the Global Financial Crisis: What Is the Connection?', *Politics & Society*, 40/1 (2012).
42 Colin Hay, 'Pathology without Crisis? The Strange Demise of the Anglo-Liberal Growth Model', *Government and Opposition*, 46/1 (2011), p. 14.
43 Watson, 'Constituting Monetary Conservatives'; Paul Langley, *The Everyday Life of Global Finance: Saving and Borrowing in Anglo-America* (Oxford: Oxford University Press, 2008).
44 *Newswipe with Charlie Brooker*, 29 March 2009, BBC Four, https://learningonscreen.ac.uk/ondemand/index.php/prog/00E76DD1?bcast=31968331 [accessed 11 January 2019]. See also James Brassett, 'British Comedy, Global Resistance: Russell Brand, Charlie Brooker and Stewart Lee', *European Journal of International Relations*, 22/1 (2016).
45 Watson, 'Headlong into the Polanyian Dilemma'.
46 Ibid., p. 438.
47 James Brassett and Chris Clarke, 'Performing the Sub-Prime Crisis: Trauma and the Financial Event', *International Political Sociology*, 6/1 (2012), p. 5.
48 Liam Stanley, 'The Everyday Politics of the Age of Austerity: Crisis and the Legitimation of Fiscal Consolidation in the UK' (Unpublished PhD thesis: University of Birmingham, 2014).
49 Liam Stanley, '"We're Reaping What We Sowed": Everyday Crisis Narratives and Acquiescence to the Age of Austerity', *New Political Economy*, 19/6 (2014).
50 Ibid.
51 Ahmed, *Cultural Politics of Emotion*, p. 103.
52 Ibid., pp. 103–6.
53 Gesa Helms, Marina Vishmidt, and Lauren Berlant, 'Affect & the Politics of Austerity: An Interview Exchange with Lauren Berlant', *Variant*, 39/40 (2010).
54 Stanley, '"We're Reaping What We Sowed"'.
55 Martijn Konings, 'The Spirit of Austerity', *Journal of Cultural Economy*, 9/1 (2016), p. 92.
56 Tracey Jensen, 'Tough Love in Tough Times', *Studies in the Maternal*, 4/2 (2012).
57 Ahmed, *Cultural Politics of Emotion*, p. 109.
58 Ibid.

59 This formulation is informed by Davies, *The Limits of Neoliberalism*; Cooper, *Family Values*; Cameron and Palan, *The Imagined Economies of Globalization*.

60 Rebecca Bramall, *The Cultural Politics of Austerity: Past and Present in Austere Times* (Basingstoke: Palgrave Macmillan, 2013); Owen Hatherley, *The Ministry of Nostalgia* (London: Verso, 2016).

61 Bramall, *The Cultural Politics of Austerity*; Hatherley, *The Ministry of Nostalgia*.

62 Konings, 'The Spirit of Austerity', p. 98.

63 Liam Byrne, '"I'm Afraid there is No Money." The Letter I will Regret for Ever', *Guardian*, 9 May 2015, www.theguardian.com/commentisfree/2015/may/09/liam-byrne-apology-letter-there-is-no-money-labour-general-election [accessed 12 January 2019].

Chapter 2

1 Greg Hurst, 'The MPs who Can't Stop Talking', *The Times*, 26 February 2006, https://web.archive.org/web/20070216112003/http://www.timesonline.co.uk/tol/news/politics/article735429.ece [accessed 17 March 2017].

2 James North, 'Tory MP Suggests Poor Families "Could Learn from War Generation about Cooking Good Food on a Tight Budget"', *Mirror*, 19 January 2017, www.mirror.co.uk/news/uk-news/tory-mp-suggests-poor-families-9651428 [accessed 17 March 2017].

3 Lauren Berlant, *Cruel Optimism* (Durham, NC: Duke University Press, 2011), pp. 103–5.

4 Simon Glaze and Ben Richardson, 'Poor Choice? Smith, Hayek and the Moral Economy of Food Consumption', *Economy and Society*, 46/1 (2017); Bethan Evans, 'Anticipating Fatness: Childhood, Affect and the Pre-Emptive "War on Obesity"', *Transactions of the Institute of British Geographers*, 35/1 (2010).

5 Royal College of Surgeons, *Smokers and Overweight Patients: Soft Targets for NHS Savings?* (London: Royal College of Surgeons, 2016), www.rcseng.ac.uk/-/media/files/rcs/library-and-publications/non-journal-publications/smokers-and-overweight-patients–soft-targets-for-nhs-savings.pdf [accessed 31 July 2018].

6 Rowena Mason, 'David Cameron Calls on Obese to Accept Help or Risk Losing Benefits', *Guardian*, 14 February 2015, www.theguardian.com/politics/2015/feb/14/david-cameron-obese-addicts-accept-help-risk-losing-benefits [accessed 31 July 2018].

7   Caroline Wheeler and Alex Stevenson, '"Too Fat to Work" to be put on Celeb Diet by Tories', *Express*, 14 September 2014, www.express. co.uk/news/uk/510666/Tory-diet-plan-for-those-too-fat-to-work; www.cambridgeweightplan.com/whats-the-plan [accessed 31 July 2018].

8   Hannah Lambie-Mumford, 'The Growth of Food Banks in Britain and What They Mean for Social Policy', *Critical Social Policy*, 39/1 (2018).

9   www.trusselltrust.org/news-and-blog/latest-stats/end-year-stats/ [accessed 31 July 2018].

10 Ibid.

11 Hannah Lambie-Mumford, '"Every Town Should Have One": Emergency Food Banking in the UK', *Journal of Social Policy*, 42/1 (2013).

12 Ibid., p. 76.

13 Ibid., p. 77.

14 Hansard, 2013, column 812, https://publications.parliament.uk/pa/ cm201314/cmhansrd/cm131218/debtext/131218-0003.htm [accessed 30 September 2021].

15 'Tory Peer Apologises for Saying "Poor Can't Cook"', BBC News, 8 December 2014, www.bbc.co.uk/news/uk-politics-30379431 [accessed 31 July 2018].

16 Lambie-Mumford, '"Every Town Should Have One"', p. 85.

17 Pat Caplan, 'Big Society or Broken Society?: Food Banks in the UK', *Anthropology Today*, 32/1 (2016), p. 11; Kingsley Purdam, Elisabeth A. Garratt and Aneez Esmail, 'Hungry? Food Insecurity, Social Stigma and Embarrassment in the UK', *Sociology*, 50/6 (2016), p. 1080; Paul Cloke, Jon May and Andrew Williams, 'The Geographies of Food Banks in the Meantime', *Progress in Human Geography*, 41/6 (2017), p. 11.

18 Hannah Lambie-Mumford and Elizabeth Dowler, 'Rising Use of "Food Aid" in the United Kingdom', *British Food Journal*, 116/9 (2014).

19 Rachel Loopstra et al., 'Austerity, Sanctions, and the Rise of Food Banks in the UK', *BMJ*, 350 (2015); Rachel Loopstra et al., 'Impact of Welfare Benefit Sanctioning on Food Insecurity: A Dynamic Cross-Area Study of Food Bank Usage in the UK', *Journal of Social Policy*, 47/3 (2018); Aaron Reeves, Rachel Loopstra and David Stuckler, 'The Growing Disconnect between Food Prices and Wages in Europe: Cross-National Analysis of Food Deprivation and Welfare Regimes in Twenty-One EU Countries, 2004–2012', *Public Health Nutrition*, 20/8 (2017).

20 Laura Pitel, 'Chancellor Tackles Surplus with an Austerity Diet', *The Times*, 21 February 2014, www.thetimes.co.uk/article/chancellor-tackles-surplus-with-an-austerity-diet-cjwhnlgw628 [accessed 31 July 2018]. Cited in Glaze and Richardson, 'Poor Choice?', p. 134.

21 Ina Zweiniger-Bargielowska, *Austerity in Britain: Rationing, Controls, and Consumption, 1939–1955* (Oxford: Oxford University Press, 2000);

Louise Amoore, *The Politics of Possibility: Risk and Security Beyond Probability* (Durham, NC: Duke University Press, 2013), pp. 34–48.

22 Zweiniger-Bargielowska, *Austerity in Britain*, p. 14.

23 Ibid., pp. 102–3.

24 Source: Mass Observation, Topic Collection: FOOD 1937–1953, 62-2-C Cafes 1940. Emphasis in original.

25 Zweiniger-Bargielowska, *Austerity in Britain*, pp. 161–2.

26 Ibid., p. 163.

27 Peter Atkins, 'Communal Feeding in War Time: British Restaurants, 1940–1947', in Ina Zweiniger-Bargielowska (ed.), *Food and War in Twentieth Century Europe* (Farnham: Ashgate, 2011).

28 Zweiniger-Bargielowska, *Austerity in Britain*, p. 74; Atkins, 'Communal Feeding in War Time', p. 140.

29 Atkins, 'Communal Feeding in War Time'. See also www.theoldfoodie. com/2016/01/the-rural-meat-pie-scheme-britain-ww-ii.html [accessed 1 August 2018].

30 Mass Observation, Topic Collection: FOOD 1937–1953, 67-3-D British Restaurants.

31 Victoria Basham, *War, Identity and the Liberal State: Everyday Experiences of the Geopolitical in the Armed Forces* (Abingdon: Routledge, 2013), pp. 40–2.

32 Ministry of Defence, *The Armed Forces Covenant* (London: Ministry of Defence), https://assets.publishing.service.gov.uk/government/ uploads/system/uploads/attachment_data/file/49469/the_armed_forces_ covenant.pdf [accessed 12 May 2021], cited in Basham, *War, Identity and the Liberal State*, p. 41.

33 Ibid., pp. 40–2.

34 Joanna Tidy, 'Forces Sauces and Eggs for Soldiers: Food, Nostalgia, and the Rehabilitation of the British Military', *Critical Military Studies*, 1/3 (2015).

35 Michael Moran, *The End of British Politics?* (Basingstoke: Palgrave Macmillan, 2017), p. 17.

36 Jensen, 'Tough Love in Tough Times'; Bramall, *The Cultural Politics of Austerity*; Hatherley, *The Ministry of Nostalgia*; Lucy Potter and Claire Westall, 'Neoliberal Britain's Austerity Foodscape: Home Economics, Veg Patch Capitalism and Culinary Temporality', *New Formations*, 80/81 (2014); Nadya Ali, 'Cup-Cakes and Cutbacks: Being Nostalgic About Austerity', *Reading Politics* blog (2012), available at: https:// web.archive.org/web/20151225210209/http://blogs.reading.ac.uk/ readingpolitics/2012/09/24/cup-cakes-and-cutbacks-being-nostalgic- about-austerity/ [accessed 10 September 2021].

37 Bramall, *The Cultural Politics of Austerity*, p. 23.

38 Ibid., pp. 58–83.
39 'The English Allotment Lottery', *Guardian DataBlog*, 10 November 2011, www.theguardian.com/news/datablog/2011/nov/10/allotments-rents-waiting-list [accessed 25 October 2020].
40 Potter and Westall, 'Neoliberal Britain's Austerity Foodscape', pp. 165–6.
41 Ibid.; Ali, 'Cup-Cakes and Cutbacks'.
42 Jensen, 'Tough Love in Tough Times'; Bramall, *The Cultural Politics of Austerity*; Hatherley, *The Ministry of Nostalgia*; Potter and Westall, 'Neoliberal Britain's Austerity Foodscape'; Ali, 'Cup-Cakes and Cutbacks'.
43 Jensen, 'Tough Love in Tough Times', p. 12; Bramall, *The Cultural Politics of Austerity*.
44 Sam Binkley and Jo Littler, 'Introduction: Cultural Studies and Anti-Consumerism: A Critical Encounter', *Cultural Studies*, 22/5 (2008); Aneta Podkalicka and Jason Potts, 'Towards a General Theory of Thrift', *International Journal of Cultural Studies*, 17/3 (2013).
45 David Evans, 'Thrifty, Green or Frugal: Reflections on Sustainable Consumption in a Changing Economic Climate', *Geoforum*, 42/5 (2011).
46 All of these examples are taken from a Facebook group called 'Plague' that shares photos of pastiched versions of the Keep Calm meme.
47 Hatherley, *The Ministry of Nostalgia*, p. 22.
48 Ibid.
49 Jensen, 'Tough Love in Tough Times'; Angus Cameron, Nicola Smith, and Daniela Tepe-Belfrage, 'Household Wastes: Disciplining the Family in the Name of Austerity', *British Politics*, 11/4 (2016).
50 Cameron, Smith, and Tepe-Belfrage, 'Household Wastes', p. 397.
51 BBC Radio 4, *Analysis*, http://news.bbc.co.uk/nol/shared/spl/hi/programmes/analysis/transcripts/05_03_09.txt [accessed 18 September 2018].
52 Kim Allen et al., 'Welfare Queens, Thrifty Housewives, and Do-It-All Mums: Celebrity Motherhood and the Cultural Politics of Austerity', *Feminist Media Studies*, 15/6 (2015), pp. 911–13.
53 Bramall, *The Cultural Politics of Austerity*, p. 139.
54 George Osborne, 'On Fairness', speech to Demos, 21 August 2008.
55 David Cameron, 'The Values that Underpin our Long-Term Economic Plan', speech, 4 March 2014.
56 L.A. Paul, 'What You Can't Expect When You're Expecting', *Res Philosophica*, 92/2 (2015).
57 Val Gillies, 'From Function to Competence: Engaging with the New Politics of Family', *Sociological Research Online*, 16/4 (2011), p. 5.1.
58 Ruth Levitas, 'There May Be "Trouble" Ahead: What We Know About Those 120,000 "Troubled" Families', Poverty and Social Exclusion in the UK Policy Response Series No. 3, 21 April 2012; Tracey Jensen and Imogen Tyler, 'Austerity Parenting: New Economies of Parent-Citizenship',

Studies in the Maternal, 4/2 (2012); Sara De Benedictis, 'Feral Parents: Austerity Parenting under Neoliberalism', *Studies in the Maternal*, 4/2 (2012); Jensen, 'Tough Love in Tough Times'; Nicola Smith, 'Toward a Queer Political Economy of Crisis', in Aida A. Hozic and Jacqui True (eds), *Scandalous Economics: Gender and the Politics of Financial Crises* (Oxford: Oxford University Press, 2016).

59 David Cameron, 'PM's Speech on the Fightback after the Riots', 15 August 2011, cited in De Benedictis, 'Feral Parents'.

60 Raekha Prasad and Fiona Bawden, 'Don't Blame our Parents, say Rioters', *Guardian*, 6 December 2011, www.guardian.co.uk/uk/2011/dec/06/dont-blame-parents-say-rioters (accessed 19 September 2018).

61 Kim Allen and Yvette Taylor, 'Placed Parenting, Locating Unrest: Failed Femininities, Troubled Mothers and Rioting Subjects', *Studies in the Maternal*, 4/2 (2012); Fidelma Ashe, '"All About Eve": Mothers, Masculinities and the 2011 UK Riots', *Political Studies*, 62/3 (2014); Jennie Bristow, 'Reporting the Riots: Parenting Culture and the Problem of Authority in Media Analysis of August 2011', *Sociological Research Online*, 18/4 (2013); Tracey Jensen, 'Riots, Restraint and the New Cultural Politics of Wanting', *Sociological Research Online*, 18/4 (2013).

62 Aisha Phoenix and Ann Phoenix, 'Racialisation, Relationality and Riots: Intersections and Interpellations', *Feminist Review*, 100/1 (2012).

63 www.bbc.co.uk/news/av/uk-14513517/england-riots-the-whites-have-become-black-says-david-starkey (accessed 9 March 2019).

64 Ashe, '"All About Eve"', p. 654.

65 David Matthews, 'Out of the Ashes by David Lammy – Review', *Guardian*, 9 December 2011, www.theguardian.com/books/2011/dec/09/out-ashes-riots-david-lammy-review-matthews (accessed 20 September 2018).

66 www.gov.uk/government/news/encouraging-strong-relationships (accessed 20 September 2018). Harriet Churchill, 'Family Support and the Coalition: Retrenchment, Refocusing and Restructuring', in Majella Kilkey Gaby Ramia, and Kevin Farnsworth (eds), *Social Policy Review, 24: Analysis and Debate in Social Policy* (Bristol: Policy Press, 2012).

67 Cited in Smith, 'Toward a Queer Political Economy of Crisis', p. 242.

68 Fiona Colgan, Chrissy Hunter, and Aidan McKearney, '"Staying Alive": The Impact of "Austerity Cuts" on the LGBT Voluntary and Community Sector (VCS) in England and Wales', TUC Funded Research Report (2014).

69 Martin Mitchell et al., 'Implications of Austerity for LGBT People and Services', NatCen/Unison, 2013, pp. 11, 29.

70 https://cookingonabootstrap.com/2018/09/11/carrot-kidney-bean-burger-recipe/ [accessed 20 September 2018].

71 www.dailymail.co.uk/debate/article-2482111/RICHARD-LITTLEJOHN-Ah-Pesto-Meet-poverty-poster-girls.html [accessed 20 September 2018].

72 www.dailymail.co.uk/debate/article-2848092/So-cruel-hypocrite-SARAH-VINE-describes-food-writer-Jack-Monroe-sent-heartless-tweet.html [accessed 12 May 2021].

73 Melissa Kite, 'Meet Westminster's Cheapest MP: Philip Hollobone', *Telegraph*, 5 April 2009, www.telegraph.co.uk/news/politics/5104564/Meet-Westminsters-cheapest-MP-Philip-Hollobone.html [accessed 17 March 2017].

Chapter 3

1 In the original reporting, Marshall was called Albert Thompson while his case was still ongoing. Amelia Gentleman, 'Londoner Denied NHS Cancer Care: "It's like I'm being Left to Die"', *Guardian*, 10 March 2018, www.theguardian.com/uk-news/2018/mar/10/denied-free-nhs-cancer-care-left-die-home-office-commonwealth [accessed 1 July 2020].

2 Amelia Gentleman, 'Uncovering Windrush: 'Only after Months of Reporting did the Government Apologise', *Guardian*, 10 November 2018, www.theguardian.com/membership/2018/nov/10/windrush-scandal-government-apology-reporting [accessed 1 July 2020].

3 Amelia Gentleman, 'Windrush Row: Javid's Apology Overshadowed by New Removal Figures', *Guardian*, 21 August 2018, www.theguardian.com/uk-news/2018/aug/21/sajid-javid-says-sorry-for-18-windrush-removals-or-detentions [accessed 1 July 2020]; Kevin Rawlinson, 'Windrush: 11 People Wrongly Deported from UK have Died – Javid', *Guardian*, 12 November 2018, www.theguardian.com/uk-news/2018/nov/12/windrush-11-people-wrongly-deported-from-uk-have-died-sajid-javid [accessed 1 July 2020].

4 Amelia Gentleman, 'Windrush Backlog Reaches 3,720 Cases, Home Office Reveals', *Guardian*, 30 April 2020, www.theguardian.com/uk-news/2020/apr/30/windrush-case-backlog-remains-at-3700-home-office-reveals [accessed 1 July 2020].

5 Lisa Murphy, Joanna Dobbin, and Sarah Boutros, 'Understanding Changes to NHS Charging Regulations for Patients from Overseas', *British Journal of Hospital Medicine*, 79/6 (2018).

6 Department of Health, *Visitor & Migrant NHS Cost Recovery Programme: Implementation Plan 2014–16* (London: DOH, 2014), p. 11, https://assets.publishing.service.gov.uk/government/uploads/system/uploads/attachment_data/file/329789/NHS_Implentatation_Plan_Phase_3.PDF [accessed 29 June 2020].

7 Department of Health, 'Updating the Immigration Health Surcharge 2020' (12 March 2020), www.legislation.gov.uk/ukia/2020/30/pdfs/ukia_20200030_en.pdf [accessed 29 June 2020].

8 Ipsos MORI Social Research Institute, *Overseas Visitor and Migrant NHS Cost Recovery Programme: Formative Evaluation – Final Report* (London: Ipsos MORI, 2017), p.vi, https://assets.publishing.service.gov.uk/government/uploads/system/uploads/attachment_data/file/589815/Ipsos_MORI_Cost_Recovery.pdf [accessed 29 June 2020].

9 Maternity Action, *What Price Safe Motherhood?: Charging for NHS Maternity Care in England and its Impact on Migrant Women* (London: Maternity Action, 2018), p. 6, www.maternityaction.org.uk/wp-content/uploads/WhatPriceSafeMotherhoodFINAL.October.pdf [accessed 29 June 2020].

10 Murphy, Dobbin, and Boutros, 'Understanding Changes to Nhs Charging Regulations'.

11 Department of Health, *Implementing the Overseas Visitors Hospital Charging Regulations: Guidance for NHS Trust Hospitals in England* (London: Department of Health, 2004), https://webarchive.nationalarchives.gov.uk/20130105040917/http://www.dh.gov.uk/prod_consum_dh/groups/dh_digitalassets/@dh/@en/documents/digitalasset/dh_081516.pdf [accessed 29 June 2020].

12 Department of Health, *Internal Review of the Overseas Visitor Charging System: Part 2: Analysis of the Overseas Visitor Charging System* (London: Department of Health, n.d.), p. 59, https://fullfact.org/sites/fullfact.org/files/782677R%20Chap%202%20of%20Review%20pages%201-52.pdf [accessed 29 June 2020].

13 Ibid., pp. 48, 59, 85.

14 Ibid., p. 3.

15 Ibid., pp. 37–8.

16 Department of Health, 'Impact Assessment: Visitor and Migrant NHS Cost Recovery – Amending and Extending the Charging Regulations' (19 July 2017), p. 8, www.legislation.gov.uk/ukia/2017/121/pdfs/ukia_20170121_en.pdf [accessed 29 June 2020].

17 Ipsos MORI, *Overseas Visitor and Migrant NHS Cost Recovery Programme*, p. vi.

18 Wendy Webster, 'The Empire Comes Home: Commonwealth Migration to Britain', in Andrew Thompson (ed.), *Britain's Experience of Empire in the Twentieth Century* (Oxford: Oxford University Press, 2012), pp. 122–3; Laura Tabili, 'A Homogeneous Society? Britain's Internal "Others", 1800–Present', in Catherine Hall and Sonya N. Rose (eds), *At Home with the Empire: Metropolitan Culture and the Imperial World* (Cambridge: Cambridge University Press, 2006), pp. 57–9.

19 Randall Hansen, *Citizenship and Immigration in Postwar Britain* (Oxford: Oxford University Press, 2000).

20 Bridget Anderson, *Us and Them?: The Dangerous Politics of Immigration Control* (Oxford: Oxford University Press, 2013), pp. 29–30.

21 Hansen, *Citizenship and Immigration in Postwar Britain*.

22 Erica Consterdine, *Labour's Immigration Policy: The Making of the Migration State* (London: Palgrave Macmillan, 2018), p. 55.

23 Anderson, *Us and Them?*, pp. 38–9.

24 Webster, 'The Empire Comes Home'.

25 Consterdine, *Labour's Immigration Policy*, p. 55.

26 Ibid., pp. 54–7; Anderson, *Us and Them?*, pp. 39–40; Shilliam, *Race and the Undeserving Poor*, pp. 95–6; Ambalavaner Sivanandan, 'Race, Class and the State: The Black Experience in Britain', *Race & Class*, 17/4 (1976), pp. 353–4.

27 Consterdine, *Labour's Immigration Policy*, p. 58; Hansen, *Citizenship and Immigration in Postwar Britain*, p. 195.

28 Gary P. Freeman, 'Can Liberal States Control Unwanted Migration?', *Annals of the American Academy of Political and Social Science*, 534/1 (1994). For a discussion see Consterdine, *Labour's Immigration Policy*, pp. 53–86.

29 Shilliam, *Race and the Undeserving Poor*, p. 92; Chris Waters, '"Dark Strangers" in Our Midst: Discourses of Race and Nation in Britain, 1947–1963', *Journal of British Studies*, 36/2 (1997), p. 290.

30 Anderson, *Us and Them?*, pp. 12–37; Waters, '"Dark Strangers" in Our Midst'.

31 Webster, 'The Empire Comes Home', p. 123.

32 Linda McDowell, 'Old and New European Economic Migrants: Whiteness and Managed Migration Policies', *Journal of Ethnic and Migration Studies*, 35/1 (2009); Kathleen Paul, *Whitewashing Britain: Race and Citizenship in the Postwar Era* (Ithaca, NY: Cornell University Press, 1997), pp. 85–9, 121–7; Shilliam, *Race and the Undeserving Poor*, p. 86.

33 Cited in Johannes-Dieter Steinert, 'British Post-War Migration Policy and Displaced Persons in Europe', in Jessica Reinisch and Elizabeth White (eds), *The Disentanglement of Populations* (London: Springer, 2011), p. 232.

34 Paul, *Whitewashing Britain*.

35 Shilliam, *Race and the Undeserving Poor*, p. 86.

36 Ibid.

37 Webster, 'The Empire Comes Home', p. 123.

38 Alastair Bonnett, 'How the British Working Class Became White: The Symbolic (Re)formation of Racialized Capitalism', *Journal of Historical Sociology*, 11/3 (1998), p. 330.

39 Webster, 'The Empire Comes Home', p. 145.
40 Shilliam, *Race and the Undeserving Poor*, pp. 33–55, Bonnett, 'How the British Working Class Became White', p. 330.
41 Waters, '"Dark Strangers" in Our Midst', p. 213; Nikolas Rose, *Governing the Soul: The Shaping of the Private Self* (Sidmouth: Free Association Books, 1999 [1989]), pp. 15–52.
42 James Hampshire, *Citizenship and Belonging: Immigration and the Politics of Demographic Governance in Postwar Britain* (Houndmills, Basingstoke: Palgrave Macmillan, 2005); Paul, *Whitewashing Britain*.
43 Gurminder K. Bhambra and John Holmwood, 'Colonialism, Post-colonialism and the Liberal Welfare State', *New Political Economy*, 23/5 (2018).
44 Bonnett, 'How the British Working Class Became White', p. 329.
45 Roberta E. Bivins, *Contagious Communities: Medicine, Migration, and the NHS in Post-War Britain* (Oxford: Oxford University Press, 2015), p. 369; Des Fitzgerald et al., 'Brexit as Heredity Redux: Imperialism, Biomedicine and the NHS in Britain', *Sociological Review*, 68/6 (2020).
46 David Feldman, 'Migrants, Immigrants and Welfare from the Old Poor Law to the Welfare State', *Transactions of the Royal Historical Society*, 13 (2003), p. 97.
47 Christopher Kyriakides and Satnam Virdee, 'Migrant Labour, Racism and the British National Health Service', *Ethnicity & Health*, 8/4 (2003); Fitzgerald et al., 'Brexit as Heredity Redux'; Bhambra and Holmwood, 'Colonialism, Postcolonialism and the Liberal Welfare State'.
48 For discussion, see Shamit Saggar (ed.), *Race and British Electoral Politics* (London: UCL Press, 1998).
49 Tom Nairn, 'Enoch Powell: The New Right', *New Left Review*, 61 (1970).
50 Shilliam, *Race and the Undeserving Poor*, p. 96.
51 Consterdine, *Labour's Immigration Policy*, p. 2.
52 Cited in ibid., p. 57.
53 Hannah Jones et al., *Go Home?: The Politics of Immigration Controversies* (Manchester: Manchester University Press, 2017), pp. 73–4.
54 Consterdine, *Labour's Immigration Policy*, p. 179.
55 Tony Blair, speech at press conference following Copenhagen EU Council, 16 December 2002, www.cvce.eu/en/obj/press_conference_held_by_tony_blair_following_the_copenhagen_european_council_16_decembe r_2002-en-2dc11ba8-3b6d-49d1-8bd8-f3b74ab557d3.html [accessed 10 September 2021]; Consterdine, *Labour's Immigration Policy*, p. 178.

56 Ibid.; Maya Goodfellow, *Hostile Environment: How Immigrants Became Scapegoats* (London: Verso Books, 2019), p. 96.

57 Alana Lentin and Gavan Titley, *The Crises of Multiculturalism: Racism in a Neoliberal Age* (London: Zed Books, 2011), p. 2.

58 Ben Pitcher, *The Politics of Multiculturalism: Race and Racism in Contemporary Britain* (Houndmills, Basingstoke: Palgrave Macmillan, 2009), p. 2.

59 Paul Gilroy, *There Ain't No Black in the Union Jack: The Cultural Politics of Race and Nation* (London: Routledge, 2002 [1987]), p. 38.

60 Etienne Balibar and Immanuel Wallerstein, *Race, Nation, Class: Ambiguous Identities* (London: Verso, 1991); Lentin and Titley, *The Crises of Multiculturalism*.

61 Lentin and Titley, *The Crises of Multiculturalism*, p. 3.

62 Ibid., p. 49. For a classic of the 'racism doesn't exist' genre, see A. C. Grayling, 'The Last Word on … Racism', *Guardian*, 4 March 2000, www.theguardian.com/books/2000/mar/04/books.guardianreview8 [accessed 24 June 2020].

63 Lentin and Titley, *The Crises of Multiculturalism*, p. 74.

64 Ibid.

65 Pitcher, *The Politics of Multiculturalism*, pp. 165–6.

66 Ibid., p. 64; Goodfellow, *Hostile Environment*, pp. 118–21; Anderson, *Us and Them?*, p. 101.

67 William Walters, 'Secure Borders, Safe Haven, Domopolitics', *Citizenship Studies*, 8/3 (2004).

68 Anderson, *Us and Them?*, pp. 99–101.

69 Pitcher, *The Politics of Multiculturalism*, pp. 58–72. Quotes taken from the archived British Citizenship website, available at: https://web.archive.org/web/20041123082539/http://www.ind.homeoffice.gov.uk/british_citizenship/english/homepage/what_happens_at_a.html and https://web.archive.org/web/20041123095657/http://www.ind.homeoffice.gov.uk/british_citizenship/english/homepage/what_happens_at_a/ceremony_video.html [accessed 24 June 2020].

70 Katie Bales and Lucy Mayblin, 'Unfree Labour in Immigration Detention: Exploitation and Coercion of a Captive Immigrant Workforce', *Economy and Society*, 47/2 (2018).

71 Lentin and Titley, *The Crises of Multiculturalism*, pp. 31–2; Humayun Ansari, *"The Infidel Within": Muslims in Britain since 1800* (Oxford: Oxford University Press, 2018), pp. 244–54; Webster, 'The Empire Comes Home', p. 157.

72 Ansari, *"The Infidel Within"*, p. 9.

73 Ibid., pp. xvii, 6–14.

74 Nadya Ali and Ben Whitham, 'The Unbearable Anxiety of Being: Ideological Fantasies of British Muslims Beyond the Politics of Security', *Security Dialogue*, 49/5 (2018); Joe Turner, *Bordering Intimacy: Postcolonial Governance and the Policing of Family* (Manchester: Manchester University Press, 2020).

75 McDowell, 'Old and New European Economic Migrants'.

76 Jon E. Fox, Laura Moroşanu, and Eszter Szilassy, 'The Racialization of the New European Migration to the UK', *Sociology*, 46/4 (2012).

77 Duncan Light and Craig Young, 'European Union Enlargement, Post-Accession Migration and Imaginative Geographies of the "New Europe": Media Discourses in Romania and the United Kingdom', *Journal of Cultural Geography*, 26/3 (2009); Fox, Moroşanu, and Szilassy, 'The Racialization of the New European Migration to the UK'.

78 Consterdine, *Labour's Immigration Policy*, p. 225.

79 Helen Thompson, 'Inevitability and Contingency: The Political Economy of Brexit', *British Journal of Politics & International Relations*, 19/3 (2017).

80 Goodfellow, *Hostile Environment*, pp. 92–128.

81 Scott Blinder and Lindsay Richards, *UK Public Opinion toward Immigration: Overall Attitudes and Level of Concern*, Migration Observatory Briefing (Oxford: COMPAS, University of Oxford, 2020).

82 Owen Parker, 'Critical Political Economy, Free Movement and Brexit: Beyond the Progressive's Dilemma', *British Journal of Politics & International Relations*, 19/3 (2017).

83 Consterdine, *Labour's Immigration Policy*, p. 149.

84 Ibid.

85 Scott Blinder, 'Imagined Immigration: The Impact of Different Meanings of "Immigrants" in Public Opinion and Policy Debates in Britain', *Political Studies*, 63/1 (2015).

86 Jones et al., *Go Home?*.

87 Ibid., pp. 11–14, 81.

88 Ibid., p. 81.

89 Institute of Race Relations, *PR and the Selling of Border Controls* (21 May 2009), www.irr.org.uk/news/pr-and-the-selling-of-border-controls/; Christopher Hope, 'Sky returns £400000 to Home Office after Criticism of Sponsored TV', *Telegraph*, 13 September 2008, www.telegraph.co.uk/news/politics/2910565/Sky-returns-400000-to-Home-Office-after-criticism-of-sponsored-TV.html [accessed 24 June 2020].

90 Consterdine, *Labour's Immigration Policy*, p. 78.

91 Matthew J. Goodwin, *New British Fascism: Rise of the British National Party* (Abingdon: Routledge, 2011), p. 11.

92 An argument made in more detail in Goodfellow, *Hostile Environment* and Erica Consterdine, 'Parties Matter but Institutions Live On: Labour's Legacy on Conservative Immigration Policy and the Neoliberal Consensus', *British Journal of Politics & International Relations*, 22/2 (2020).

93 Katharine Dommett, 'The Theory and Practice of Party Modernisation: The Conservative Party under David Cameron, 2005–2015', *British Politics*, 10/2 (2015); Rebecca Partos and Tim Bale, 'Immigration and Asylum Policy under Cameron's Conservatives', *British Politics*, 10/2 (2015).

94 Harold D. Clarke et al., *Austerity and Political Choice in Britain* (London: Palgrave Macmillan, 2015), p. 50.

95 Pitcher, *The Politics of Multiculturalism*, pp. 52–7; Goodfellow, *Hostile Environment*, pp. 118–20.

96 See Dennis Kavanagh and Philip Cowley, *The British General Election of 2010* (Basingstoke: Palgrave Macmillan, 2010), pp. 173–7. For the clip, see www.youtube.com/watch?v=yEReCN9gO14 [accessed 24 June 2020].

97 Ibid., p. 175.

98 Carole Cadwalladr, 'Gillian Duffy: Why She Made the Headlines in 2010', *Guardian*, 19 December 2010, www.theguardian.com/theobserver/2010/dec/19/faces-2010-gillian-duffy [accessed 24 June 2020].

99 Harry Mount, 'Emily is so at Home in Islington Luvvie-Land, a Metropolitan Liberal Allergic to the Ideals of Patriotism and the Self-Reliant Family', *Mail Online*, 22 November 2014, www.dailymail.co.uk/debate/article-2844839/Emily-home-Islington-luvvie-land-metropolitan-liberal-allergic-ideals-patriotism-self-reliant-family.html [accessed 24 June 2020].

100 'Hague rounds on liberal elite', BBC News, 14 December 2000, http://news.bbc.co.uk/1/hi/uk_politics/1070549.stm [accessed 24 June 2020].

101 Jones et al., *Go Home?*, p. 152.

102 Roger Scruton, *England: An Elegy* (London: Continuum, 2006). Cited in Gilroy, *There Ain't No Black in the Union Jack*, p. xxvi.

103 Jones et al., *Go Home?*

104 James Brokenshire, 'Speech to Demos', 6 March 2014, www.demos.co.uk/files/JamesBrokenshireSpeechtoDemos.pdf [accessed 24 June 2020].

105 Lucinda Hiam, Sarah Steele, and Martin McKee, 'Creating a "Hostile Environment for Migrants": The British Government's Use of Health

Service Data to Restrict Immigration is a Very Bad Idea', *Health Economics, Policy and Law*, 13/2 (2018); Luke De Noronha, 'Deportation, Racism and Multi-Status Britain: Immigration Control and the Production of Race in the Present', *Ethnic and Racial Studies*, 42/14 (2019); Nadine El-Enany, *(B)ordering Britain: Law, Race and Empire* (Manchester: Manchester University Press, 2020).

106 E.g. his 2011 and 2013 immigration speeches, available via www.bbc. co.uk/news/uk-politics-13083781 and www.gov.uk/government/speeches/ david-camerons-immigration-speech [accessed 17 July 2020].

107 Feldman, 'Migrants, Immigrants and Welfare', p. 97; Anderson, *Us and Them?*, pp. 12–28.

Chapter 4

1   'White: A Series of Programmes on BBC2', BBC, https://web.archive.org/ web/20080307002258/http://www.bbc.co.uk/white/ [accessed 16 July 2020].

2   'Soaring Crime, Mass Immigration … Why the White Working Class is Fearful for the Future', *Evening Standard*, 6 March 2008, www. standard.co.uk/news/soaring-crime-mass-immigrationwhy-the-white- working-class-is-fearful-for-the-future-6613508.html [accessed 16 July 2020].

3   John Lloyd, 'White Men Unburdened', *Financial Times*, 1 March 2008, www.ft.com/content/8943a7d0-e650-11dc-8398-0000779fd2ac [accessed 16 July 2020].

4   Ibid.

5   'BBC Two Winter/Spring 2008', BBC, 20 November 2007, www.bbc. co.uk/pressoffice/pressreleases/stories/2007/11_november/20/bbctwo_ white.shtml [accessed 16 July 2020].

6   Goodfellow, *Hostile Environment*, p. 172.

7   Shilliam, *Race and the Undeserving Poor*; Gurminder K. Bhambra, 'Brexit, Trump, and "Methodological Whiteness"'.

8   Herbert Blumer, 'Race Prejudice as a Sense of Group Position', *Pacific Sociological Review*, 1/1 (1958); Robert K. Merton, *Social Theory and Social Structure* (London: Free Press, 1968), pp. 279–334.

9   Gellner, *Nations and Nationalism*.

10 Gertrude Himmelfarb, 'The Idea of Poverty', *History Today*, 34/4 (1984), pp. 23–4; Wim Van Oorschot, 'Who Should Get What and Why? On Deservingness Criteria and the Conditionality of Solidarity among the Public', *Policy and Politics*, 28/1 (2000), p. 35; Shilliam, *Race and the*

Undeserving Poor, pp. 25–31; Mitchell Dean, *The Constitution of Poverty (Routledge Revivals): Towards a Genealogy of Liberal Governance* (London: Routledge, 2013).

11 S. Hall, *The Hard Road to Renewal: Thatcherism and the Crisis of the Left* (London: Verso, 1988), p. 47.

12 Michael Bang Petersen et al., 'Deservingness Versus Values in Public Opinion on Welfare: The Automaticity of the Deservingness Heuristic', *European Journal of Political Research*, 50/1 (2011).

13 Watson, 'New Labour's "Paradox of Responsibility"', p. 11.

14 R. Levitas, *The Inclusive Society?: Social Exclusion and New Labour* (Basingstoke: Palgrave, 1998); Tyler, *Revolting Subjects.*

15 Cameron and Palan, *The Imagined Economies of Globalization*; Edgerton, *The Rise and Fall of the British Nation*; Michel Foucault, *The Birth of Biopolitics: Lectures at the Collège De France, 1978–79* (Basingstoke: Palgrave Macmillan, 2008).

16 Cameron and Palan, *The Imagined Economies of Globalization*, pp. 34–6.

17 Levitas, *The Inclusive Society?*, p. 7.

18 Cameron and Palan, *The Imagined Economies of Globalization*, p. 131.

19 Ruth Lister, 'Investing in the Citizen-Workers of the Future: Transformations in Citizenship and the State under New Labour', *Social Policy & Administration*, 37/5 (2003).

20 Davies, *The Limits of Neoliberalism*, p. 44.

21 Watson, 'New Labour's "Paradox of Responsibility"', p. 11.

22 Imogen Tyler, '"Chav Mum Chav Scum": Class Disgust in Contemporary Britain', *Feminist Media Studies*, 8/1 (2008), p. 21.

23 Ibid.

24 Ibid.

25 Philip Mirowski, *Never Let a Serious Crisis Go to Waste: How Neoliberalism Survived the Financial Meltdown* (London: Verso Books, 2013), p. 118.

26 Tracy Shildrick and Robert Macdonald, 'Poverty Talk: How People Experiencing Poverty Deny their Poverty and Why they Blame "The Poor"', *Sociological Review*, 61/2 (2013).

27 Ibid., p. 296.

28 Liam Stanley, 'Legitimacy Gaps, Taxpayer Conflict, and the Politics of Austerity in the UK', *British Journal of Politics & International Relations*, 18/2 (2016); Gill Valentine and Catherine Harris, 'Strivers vs Skivers: Class Prejudice and the Demonisation of Dependency in Everyday Life', *Geoforum*, 53/May (2014).

29 Peter Taylor-Gooby, 'Why Do People Stigmatise the Poor at a Time of Rapidly Increasing Inequality, and What can be Done About it?', *Political Quarterly*, 84/1 (2013).

30 Alan Finlayson, 'The Broken Society Versus the Social Recession', *Soundings*, 44/1 (2010); Tom Slater, 'The Myth of "Broken Britain": Welfare Reform and the Production of Ignorance', *Antipode*, 46/4 (2013).

31 Margaret McCartney, 'Well Enough to Work?', *BMJ*, 342 (2011).

32 May Bulman and Alina Polianskaya, 'Attempted Suicides by Disability Benefit Claimants more than Double after Introduction of Fit-To-Work Assessment', *Independent*, 28 December 2017, www.independent.co.uk/news/uk/home-news/disability-benefit-claimants-attempted-suicides-fit-to-work-assessment-i-daniel-blake-job-centre-dwp-a8119286.html [accessed 13 July 2020].

33 Howard Reed, 'The Distributional Impact of Tax and Social Security Reforms in the UK from 2010 to 2017', *Social Policy and Society*, 19/3 (2020).

34 Ruth Cain, 'Responsibilising Recovery: Lone and Low-Paid Parents, Universal Credit and the Gendered Contradictions of UK Welfare Reform', *British Politics*, 11/4 (2016); Reed, 'The Distributional Impact of Tax and Social Security Reforms'; Frances Ryan, *Crippled: Austerity and the Demonization of Disabled People* (London: Verso, 2019).

35 Adam Tinson, *The Rise of Sanctioning in Great Britain* (London: New Policy Institute, 2015).

36 Adam Whitworth and Elle Carter, 'Welfare-to-Work Reform, Power and Inequality: From Governance to Governmentalities', *Journal of Contemporary European Studies*, 22/2 (2014), p. 110.

37 Tinson, *The Rise of Sanctioning in Great Britain*.

38 Craig Berry, *Austerity Politics and UK Economic Policy* (Basingstoke: Palgrave Macmillan, 2016), pp. 51–68.

39 Loopstra et al., 'Austerity, Sanctions, and the Rise of Food Banks in the UK'; Kayleigh Garthwaite, 'Fear of the Brown Envelope: Exploring Welfare Reform with Long-Term Sickness Benefits Recipients', *Social Policy & Administration*, 48/7 (2014).

40 Hatty Collier, 'Channel 4's *Benefits Street* claims 4.3 million viewers', *Guardian*, 7 January 2014, www.theguardian.com/media/2014/jan/07/tvratings-channel4 [accessed 13 July 2020].

41 Sara De Benedictis, Kim Allen, and Tracey Jensen, 'Portraying Poverty: The Economics and Ethics of Factual Welfare Television', *Cultural Sociology*, 11/3 (2017), p. 348.

42 Ibid.

43 Ibid., p. 339.

44 Cornelia Woll, *The Power of Inaction: Bank Bailouts in Comparison* (Ithaca, NY: Cornell University Press, 2014).

45 Pepper D. Culpepper and Raphael Reinke, 'Structural Power and Bank Bailouts in the United Kingdom and the United States', *Politics & Society*, 42/4 (2014); Woll, *The Power of Inaction*.

46 Matthew Watson, '"Habitation vs. Improvement"and a Polanyian Perspective on Bank Bail-Outs', *Politics*, 29/3 (2009).

47 www.youtube.com/watch?v=WSIUf2hD6Io [accessed 13 July 2020].

48 Andrew Hindmoor, *Twelve Days That Made Modern Britain* (Oxford: Oxford University Press, 2019), p. 249.

49 Ibid., pp. 249–50.

50 M. V. Flinders, 'The Demonisation of Politicians: Moral Panics, Folk Devils and MPs' Expenses', *Contemporary Politics*, 18/1 (2012); Hindmoor, *Twelve Days That Made Modern Britain*, p. 256.

51 Hindmoor, *Twelve Days That Made Modern Britain*, p. 251.

52 Alexi Mostrous and Fay Schlesinger, 'The Comedian and his Sheltered Millions', *The Times*, 19 June 2012, www.thetimes.co.uk/article/the-comedian-and-his-sheltered-millions-r2bmb893qhs [accessed 13 July 2020]. See also Rebecca Bramall, 'A "Powerful Weapon"? Tax, Avoidance, and the Politics of Celebrity Shaming', *Celebrity Studies*, 9/1 (2018).

53 'Carr "Morally Wrong" for Avoiding Tax, says Cameron', *Channel 4*,20 June 2012, www.channel4.com/news/take-that-members-in-tax-avoidance-row [accessed 13 July 2020].

54 Bramall, 'A "Powerful Weapon"?'.

55 Stanley, 'Legitimacy Gaps'; Hunt and Stanley, 'From "There Is No Alternative" to "Maybe There Are Alternatives"'.

56 IPPR Commission on Economic Justice, *Unfair and In Need of Reform: Public Attitudes to the UK Economy* (London: IPPR, 2019).

57 Thomas Piketty, *Capital in the Twenty-First Century* (Cambridge, MA: Harvard University Press, 2014); Richard Wilkinson and Kate Pickett, *The Spirit Level: Why Equality is Better for Everyone* (London: Penguin, 2009).

58 Brett Christophers, Andrew Leyshon, and Geoff Mann, 'Money and Finance after the Crisis: Taking Critical Stock', in Brett Christophers, Andrew Leyshon, and Geoff Mann (eds), *Money and Finance After the Crisis: Critical Thinking for Uncertain Times* (Oxford: Wiley, 2017), p. 10.

59 Johnathan Watkins et al., 'Effects of Health and Social Care Spending Constraints on Mortality in England: A Time Trend Analysis', *BMJ Open*, 7/11 (2017).

60 Philip Cowley and Dennis Kavanagh, *The British General Election of 2017* (Basingstoke: Palgrave Macmillan, 2018), pp. 67–73.

61 Ibid., p. 69.

62 Matt Bolton and F. H. Pitts, 'Corbynism and Blue Labour: Post-Liberalism and National Populism in the British Labour Party', *British Politics*, 15/1 (2020).

63 Ibid., p. 93.

64 Robert Ford and Matthew Goodwin, 'Understanding UKIP: Identity, Social Change and the Left Behind', *Political Quarterly*, 85/3 (2014).

65 Ibid., p. 279.

66 David Goodhart, 'Too diverse?', *Prospect*, 20 February 2004, www.prospectmagazine.co.uk/magazine/too-diverse-david-goodhart-multiculturalism-britain-immigration-globalisation [accessed 16 July 2020].

67 Dominic Casciani, 'Is this Man the Left's Enoch Powell?', BBC News, 26 April 2004, http://news.bbc.co.uk/1/hi/magazine/3652679.stm [accessed 16 July 2020].

68 David Goodhart, 'Why I Left My Liberal London Tribe', *Financial Times*, 17 March 2017, www.ft.com/content/39a0867a-0974-11e7-ac5a-903b21361b43 [accessed 16 July 2020].

69 Shilliam, *Race and the Undeserving Poor*, p. 168.

Chapter 5

1 Nairn, *The Break-Up of Britain*.

2 Tom M. Devine, *Scotland and the Union 1707–2007* (Edinburgh: Edinburgh University Press, 2008), p. 27.

3 Nairn, *The Break-Up of Britain*, p. 179.

4 Ibid., p. 129.

5 David McCrone, 'Scotland out the Union? The Rise and Rise of the Nationalist Agenda', *Political Quarterly*, 83/1 (2012), pp. 72–73. The term originates from Graeme Morton, *Unionist Nationalism: Governing Urban Scotland, 1830–1860* (East Linton: Tuckwell Press, 1999).

6 Scott Lavery, 'Dilemmas of Over-Development: Scottish Nationalism and the Future of the Union', *Verso Blog*, 14 February 2019, www.versobooks.com/blogs/4241-dilemmas-of-over-development-scottish-nationalism-and-the-future-of-the-union [accessed 3 October 2020].

7 '"Day of Reckoning" Post-Yes Vote, says Jim Sillars', *Scotsman*, 12 September 2014, www.scotsman.com/news/politics/day-reckoning-post-yes-vote-says-jim-sillars-1526501 [accessed 3 October 2020].

8 Nairn, *The Break-Up of Britain*.

9 McCrone, 'Scotland out the Union?', p. 74.

10 Ibid., p. 69.

11 James Maxwell, 'British Inequality and the Nordic Alternative', Donaldson Lecture, 2007 SNP conference, *Bella Caledonia*, 24 April 2013, https://bellacaledonia.org.uk/2013/04/24/british-inequality-and-the-nordic-alternative/ [accessed 3 October 2020].

12 Examples from Neil Davidson, 'A Scottish Watershed', *New Left Review*, 89 (2014), p. 19.

13 Examples from Pete Ramand and James Foley, *Yes: The Radical Case for Scottish Independence* (London: Pluto Press, 2014), p. 39.

14 Henderson et al., 'How Brexit Was Made in England'.

15 Ibid.

16 Alex Niven, *New Model Island: How to Build a Radical Culture Beyond the Idea of England* (London: Repeater, 2019).

17 Davies, *The Isles*; Gamble, *Between Europe and America*.

18 Davies, *The Isles*, p. 655.

19 Nairn, *The Break-Up of Britain*.

20 Ben Wellings and Michael Kenny, 'Nairn's England and the Progressive Dilemma: Reappraising Tom Nairn on English Nationalism', *Nations and Nationalism*, 25/3 (2019).

21 Kenny, *The Politics of English Nationhood*, p. 101.

22 Wellings, *English Nationalism, Brexit and the Anglosphere*, p. 60.

23 Niven, *New Model Island*.

24 Kenny, *The Politics of English Nationhood*.

25 Wellings, *English Nationalism, Brexit and the Anglosphere*, p. 60; Ben Wellings, 'Losing the Peace: Euroscepticism and the Foundations of Contemporary English Nationalism', *Nations and Nationalism*, 16/3 (2010).

26 Henderson et al., 'How Brexit Was Made in England'.

27 Wellings, 'Losing the Peace', p. 489.

28 Peter Lynch, 'From Social Democracy Back to No Ideology? – The Scottish National Party and Ideological Change in a Multi-Level Electoral Setting', *Regional and Federal Studies*, 19/4–5 (2009).

29 'Salmond defends Thatcher comments, BBC, 22 August 2008, http://news.bbc.co.uk/1/hi/scotland/7576801.stm [accessed 3 October 2020].

30 The Newsroom, 'Salmond sees Scots in "arc of prosperity"', *Scotsman*, 12 August 2006, www.scotsman.com/news/salmond-sees-scots-arc-prosperity-2470157 [accessed 24 June 2021].

31 McCrone, 'Scotland out the Union?', p. 75.

32 Ramand and Foley, *Yes: The Radical Case for Scottish Independence*, p. 11.

33 Jamie Ross, 'The Man Who Created The Phrase "Project Fear" Says He Has No Regrets', *Buzzfeed News*, 24 May 2016, www.buzzfeed.com/jamieross/fear-we-go-again [accessed 3 October 2020].

34 Examples from https://wingsoverscotland.com/reasons-to-be-fearful/ [accessed 3 October 2020].

35 Scottish Government, *Scotland's Future: Your Guide to an Independent Scotland* (Edinburgh: Scottish Government, 2013).

36 Ramand and Foley, *Yes: The Radical Case for Scottish Independence*, p. 118.

37 Kiran Stacey, George Parker, Mure Dickie, and Beth Rigby, 'Scottish Referendum: How Complacency Nearly Lost a United Kingdom', *Financial Times*, 19 September 2014, www.ft.com/content/5d888e34-3ff0-11e4-a381-00144feabdc0 [accessed 3 October 2020].

38 Ibid.

39 Kathleen Jamie, contribution to 'After the referendum', *London Review of Books*, 36/9 (2014).

40 Charles Pattie and Ron Johnston, 'Sticking to the Union? Nationalism, Inequality and Political Disaffection and the Geography of Scotland's 2014 Independence Referendum', *Regional & Federal Studies*, 27/1 (2017).

41 'After the Vote, Chaos', *Economist*, 25 June 2016, www.economist.com/britain/2016/06/25/after-the-vote-chaos [accessed 3 October 2020].

42 Gamble, *Between Europe and America*, pp. 83–107; Wellings, *English Nationalism, Brexit and the Anglosphere*; Kenny and Pearce, *Shadows of Empire*; Srdjan Vucetic, *The Anglosphere: A Genealogy of a Racialized Identity in International Relations* (Stanford, CA: Stanford University Press, 2011).

43 Wellings, *English Nationalism, Brexit and the Anglosphere*.

44 Vucetic, *The Anglosphere*.

45 Wellings, *English Nationalism, Brexit and the Anglosphere*, p. 38.

46 Robert Saunders, 'Brexit and Empire: "Global Britain" and the Myth of Imperial Nostalgia', *Journal of Imperial and Commonwealth History*, 48/6 (2020).

47 Alan Finlayson, 'Who Won the Referendum?', *Open Democracy*, 26 June 2016, www.opendemocracy.net/en/opendemocracyuk/who-won-referendum/ [accessed 3 October 2020].

48 '"I Know I'm not Showy": Britain's Theresa May in Her Own Words', *Reuters*, 11 July 2016, www.reuters.com/article/us-britain-eu-conservative-may-factbox-idUSKCN0ZR0WQ [accessed 4 June 2021].

49 Cowley and Kavanagh, *The British General Election of 2015*, pp. 12–14; Adam Tooze, *Crashed: How a Decade of Financial Crises Changed the World* (London: Penguin, 2018), p. 544.

50 Tooze, *Crashed*, pp. 545–7; Helen Thompson, 'How the City of London Lost at Brexit: A Historical Perspective', *Economy and Society*, 46/2 (2017).

51 Jamie Grierson, 'UK Government Misses Net Migration Target for 37th Time in a Row', *Guardian*, 24 May 2019, www.theguardian.com/uk-news/2019/may/24/uk-government-misses-net-migration-target-for-37th-time-in-a-row [accessed 3 October 2020].

52 Harold D. Clarke, Matthew J. Goodwin, and Paul Whiteley, *Brexit: Why Britain Voted to Leave the European Union* (Cambridge: Cambridge University Press, 2017), p. 32.

53 Scott Lavery, '"Defend and Extend": British Business Strategy, EU Employment Policy and the Emerging Politics of Brexit', *British Journal of Politics & International Relations*, 19/4 (2017).

54 Thompson, 'How the City of London Lost at Brexit'.

55 Tooze, *Crashed*, p. 550.

56 Hindmoor, *Twelve Days That Made Modern Britain*, p. 103.

57 Lavery, *British Capitalism after the Crisis*, p. 186.

58 Tooze, *Crashed*, p. 551.

59 Ibid.

60 Ibid., p. 552.

61 Douglas Fraser, 'Whose Economy is it Anyway?', BBC, 7 March 2018, www.bbc.co.uk/news/uk-scotland-scotland-business-43317433 [accessed 3 October 2020].

62 William Davies, *Nervous States: How Feeling Took over the World* (London: Jonathan Cape, 2018).

63 Alison Flood, '"Post-Truth" Named Word of the Year by Oxford Dictionaries', *Guardian*, 15 November 2016, www.theguardian.com/books/2016/nov/15/post-truth-named-word-of-the-year-by-oxford-dictionaries [accessed 3 October 2020].

64 John Gray, 'Post Truth by Matthew D'Ancona and Post-Truth by Evan Davis Review – Is This Really a New Era of Politics?', *Guardian*, 19 May 2017, www.theguardian.com/books/2017/may/19/post-truth-matthew-dancona-evan-davis-reiews [accessed 3 October 2020].

65 Clarke, Goodwin, and Whiteley, *Brexit: Why Britain Voted to Leave the European Union*, p. 43.

66 'In Full: David Cameron Statement on the UK's Future', BBC, 19 September 2014, www.bbc.co.uk/news/uk-politics-29271765 [accessed 3 October 2020].

Chapter 6

1 For examples, see 'Boris Johnson is Reinventing One-Nation Conservatism', *Economist*, 2 January 2020, www.economist.com/britain/2020/01/02/boris-johnson-is-reinventing-one-nation-conservatism;

Heather Stewart, 'Johnson's Brexit would be Thatcherism on Steroids, says Corbyn', *Guardian*, 4 November 2019, www.theguardian.com/politics/2019/nov/04/johnsons-brexit-would-be-thatcherism-on-steroids-says-corbyn [accessed 17 November 2020].

2 For examples, see Rachel Sylvester, 'How Right Wing is Boris Johnson?', *Prospect*, 7 January 2020, www.prospectmagazine.co.uk/politics/how-right-wing-is-boris-johnson-election-parliament-brexit; Kate Andrews, 'Boris Johnson is Wasting his Majority with a Left-Wing Agenda', *Telegraph*, 19 May 2021, www.telegraph.co.uk/business/2021/05/19/boris-johnson-wasting-majority-left-wing-agenda/; Andy Beckett, 'The Idea that Johnson is "Moving Left" may be Thatcher's Final Victory', *Guardian*, 7 March 2020, www.theguardian.com/commentisfree/2020/mar/07/boris-johnson-thatcher-conservative-economic-policy-thatcherism [accessed 15 June 2021].

3 Jim Bulpitt, 'The Discipline of the New Democracy: Mrs Thatcher's Domestic Statecraft', *Political Studies*, 34/1 (1986); Gamble, 'Austerity as Statecraft'.

4 Bulpitt, 'The Discipline of the New Democracy'.

5 Andrew Gamble, '"Global Britain" or "Britain First"?', *SPERI Blog* (7 February 2020), http://speri.dept.shef.ac.uk/2020/02/07/brexit-the-conservative-majority-and-the-uk-political-economy-part-2-global-britain-or-britain-first/ [accessed 17 November 2020].

6 David Cutts et al., 'Brexit, the 2019 General Election and the Realignment of British Politics', *Political Quarterly*, 91/1 (2020).

7 'Victory for Boris Johnson's All-New Tories', *Economist*, 13 December 2019, www.economist.com/leaders/2019/12/13/victory-for-boris-johnsons-all-new-tories [accessed 17 November 2020].

8 'Election Results 2019: Boris Johnson's Victory Speech in Full', BBC, 13 December 2019, www.bbc.co.uk/news/election-2019-50777071 [accessed 17 November 2020].

9 Chris Hanretty, 'The Pork Barrel Politics of the Towns Fund', *Political Quarterly*, 92/1 (2021).

10 Dominic Lawson, 'Britannia Unchained Review', *The Times*, 23 September 2012, www.thetimes.co.uk/article/britannia-unchained-by-kwasi-kwarteng-priti-patel-dominic-raab-chris-skidmore-and-elizabeth-truss-p9r39ln5wtt [accessed 17 November 2020].

11 Kwasi Kwarteng et al., *Britannia Unchained: Global Lessons for Growth and Prosperity* (Basingstoke: Palgrave Macmillan, 2012), pp. 13, 42, 56.

12 Kwasi Kwarteng et al., *After the Coalition: A Conservative Agenda for Britain* (London: Biteback Publishing, 2011), Kindle location 259.

13 Kwarteng et al., *Britannia Unchained*, p. 10.

14 On neoliberal nationalism, see Valluvan, *The Clamour of Nationalism*; Adam Harmes, 'The Rise of Neoliberal Nationalism', *Review of International Political Economy*, 19/1 (2012).

15 Jones et al., *Go Home?*, p. 75.

16 Home Office, *The UK's Points-Based Immigration System: Policy Statement* (19 February 2020), www.gov.uk/government/publications/the-uks-points-based-immigration-system-policy-statement/the-uks-points-based-immigration-system-policy-statement [accessed 17 November 2020].

17 Lisa O'Carroll, 'Romanian Fruit Pickers Flown to UK Amid Crisis in Farming Sector', *Guardian*, 15 April 2020, www.theguardian.com/world/2020/apr/15/romanian-fruit-pickers-flown-uk-crisis-farming-sector-coronavirus [accessed 17 November 2020].

18 Steven Morris and Lisa O'Carroll, 'UK Farmers Fear Huge Labour Shortfall Despite Interest in "Land Army"', *Guardian*, 25 March 2020, www.theguardian.com/environment/2020/mar/25/uk-farmers-fear-huge-labour-shortfall-despite-interest-in-land-army [accessed 17 November 2020].

19 www.youtube.com/watch?v=hdYNcv-chgY [accessed 17 November 2020].

20 HM Government, *Freeports Consultation: Boosting Trade, Jobs and Investment across the UK* (London: HMSO, 2020), https://assets.publishing.service.gov.uk/government/uploads/system/uploads/attachment_data/file/878352/Freeports_Consultation_Extension.pdf; Anton Moiseienko, Alexandria Reid and Isabella Chase, 'Free Ports, Not Safe Havens: Preventing Crime in the UK's Future Freeports', RUSI Briefing Paper (London: Royal United Services Institute, 2020) https://rusi.org/explore-our-research/publications/briefing-papers/free-ports-not-safe-havens-preventing-crime-uks-future-freeports [accessed 10 September 2021].

21 Kwarteng et al., *Britannia Unchained*, p. 88.

22 Rishi Sunak, *The Free Ports Opportunity: How Brexit could Boost Trade, Manufacturing and the North* (London: Centre for Policy Studies, 2016), p. 28, www.cps.org.uk/files/reports/original/161109144209-TheFreePortsOpportunity.pdf [accessed 17 November 2020].

23 'What Free Ports Can and Can't Achieve', *Economist*, 8 August 2019, www.economist.com/britain/2019/08/08/what-free-ports-can-and-cant-achieve [accessed 17 November 2020].

24 Alan Beattie, 'Freeports are Economically Trivial and Politically Expensive', *Financial Times*, 19 November 2019, www.ft.com/content/c87c366c-5cc0-4072-9389-e78f4bf5f84b [accessed 17 November 2020].

25 Ilona Serwicka and Peter Holmes, 'What is the Extra Mileage in the Reintroduction of "Free Zones" in the UK?', Briefing paper 28 (Sussex: UK Trade Policy Observatory, February 2019), p. 6, https://blogs.sussex.ac.uk/uktpo/publications/what-is-the-extra-mileage-in-the-reintroduction-of-free-zones-in-the-uk/ [accessed 17 November 2020].

26 Delphine Strauss, 'Freeports Plan for 'Left-Behind' Regions Divides Opinion', *Financial Times*, 10 February 2020, www.ft.com/content/297df8ce-4c31-11ea-95a0-43d18ec715f5 [accessed 17 November 2020].

27 Serwicka and Holmes, 'What is the Extra Mileage in the Reintroduction of "Free Zones" in the UK?'

28 Jim Pickard, Peter Foster, and Chris Tighe, 'Business and Politicians Wary of UK Plan for Low-Tax Trade Zones', *Financial Times*, 12 July 2020, www.ft.com/content/122cdc16-7435-4c7b-85e1-09cd10c1ab7a [accessed 17 November 2020].

29 Ibid.

30 Labour Party, 'Boris Johnson's "Free Ports" are for the Super-Rich to Dodge Taxes and Launder Money – Peter Dowd' (26 July 2019), https://labour.org.uk/press/boris-johnsons-free-ports-super-rich-dodge-taxes-launder-money-peter-dowd/ [accessed 17 November 2020].

31 Quinn Slobodian, 'Rishi Sunak's Free Ports Plan Reinvents Thatcherism for the Johnson Era, *Guardian*, 1 March 2020, www.theguardian.com/commentisfree/2020/mar/01/rishi-sunak-free-ports-thatcherism [accessed 17 November 2020].

32 Richard Partington, 'Levelling up Britain: Blyth's Hopes Rest on Tory Promises of a New Dawn', *Guardian*, 6 March 2020, www.theguardian.com/business/2020/mar/06/levelling-up-britain-blyths-hopes-rest-on-tory-promises-of-a-new-dawn [accessed 17 November 2020].

33 Davies, *Nervous States*, p. 19.

34 James Davison Hunter, *Culture Wars: The Struggle to Control the Family, Art, Education, Law, and Politics in America* (New York: Basic Books, 1991), p. 42.

35 Adam Nagourney, '"Cultural War" of 1992 Moves In From the Fringe', *New York Times*, 30 August 2012, www.nytimes.com/2012/08/30/us/politics/from-the-fringe-in-1992-patrick-j-buchanans-words-now-seem-mainstream.html [accessed 14 December 2020].

36 William G. Jacoby, 'Is There a Culture War? Conflicting Value Structures in American Public Opinion', *American Political Science Review*, 108/4 (2014).

37 Morris P. Fiorina, Samuel J. Abrams, and Jeremy C. Pope, *Culture War: The Myth of a Polarized America* (London: Pearson Longman, 2005), p. 2.

38 Ibid.

39 Michael Savage, '"Culture Wars" are Fought by Tiny Minority – UK Study', *Observer*, 24 October 2020, www.theguardian.com/society/2020/oct/24/culture-wars-are-fought-by-tiny-minority-uk-study [accessed 14 December 2020].

40 Hunter, *Culture Wars*, pp. 225–46.

41 Ibid., p. 246.

42 William Davies, 'The Free Speech Panic: How the Right Concocted a Crisis', *Guardian*, 26 July 2018, www.theguardian.com/news/2018/jul/26/the-free-speech-panic-censorship-how-the-right-concocted-a-crisis [accessed 14 December 2020].

43 Abas Mirzaei, 'Where "Woke" Came From and Why Marketers Should Think Twice before Jumping on the Social Activism Bandwagon', *The Conversation*, 8 September 2019, https://theconversation.com/where-woke-came-from-and-why-marketers-should-think-twice-before-jumping-on-the-social-activism-bandwagon-122713; Aja Romano, 'A History of "Wokeness"', *Vox*, 9 October 2020, www.vox.com/culture/21437879/stay-woke-wokeness-history-origin-evolution-controversy [accessed 14 December 2020].

44 Romano, 'A History of "Wokeness"'.

45 Ibid.

46 www.youtube.com/watch?v=N1YAdd6ERBs [accessed 14 December 2020].

47 'How "Woke" Fell Asleep', *Oxford Dictionaries* (16 November 2016), https://web.archive.org/web/20170105220153/http://blog.oxforddictionaries.com/2016/11/woke/ [accessed 14 December 2020].

48 Amanda Hess, 'Earning the "Woke" Badge', *The New York Times*, 24 April 2016, www.nytimes.com/2016/04/24/magazine/earning-the-woke-badge.html [accessed 14 December 2020].

49 Mirzaei, 'Where "Woke" Came From'.

50 'Barack Obama Challenges "Woke" Culture', BBC, 30 October 2019, www.bbc.co.uk/news/world-us-canada-50239261 [accessed 14 December 2020].

51 Evan Smith, *No Platform: A History of Anti-Fascism, Universities and the Limits of Free Speech* (London: Routledge, 2020).

52 Clint Margrave, 'Is Anti-Woke Becoming the New Woke?', *Areo*, 21 January 2020, https://areomagazine.com/2020/01/21/is-anti-woke-becoming-the-new-woke/ [accessed 14 December 2020]/.

53 'ONCE & FOR ALL Nigel Farage Debunks the Left's Big Lie about Nationalism', *Nigel Farage* (19 May 2020), www.nigelfaragemep.co.uk/once-for-all-nigel-farage-debunks-the-lefts-big-lie-about-nationalism/ [accessed 14 December 2020]. Cited in Smith, *No Platform*, p. 2.

54 Daniel Trilling, 'Why is the UK Government Suddenly Targeting "Critical Race Theory"?', *Guardian*, 23 October 2020, www.theguardian.com/commentisfree/2020/oct/23/uk-critical-race-theory-trump-conservatives-structural-inequality [accessed 14 December 2020].

55 Alex Wickham, 'Divide And Disrupt: Inside Number 10's War Against The Media On Multiple Fronts', *BuzzFeed News*, 8 February 2020, www.buzzfeed.com/alexwickham/boris-johnson-government-war-on-media [accessed 14 December 2020].

56 Smith, *No Platform*.

57 Eric Foner, 'More Pasts Than One', *London Review of Books*, 17/6 (1995), www.lrb.co.uk/the-paper/v17/n06/eric-foner/more-pasts-than-one [accessed 14 December 2020].

58 Gellner, *Nations and Nationalism*, p. 55.

59 Smith, *No Platform*, pp. 156–60.

60 www.officeforstudents.org.uk/advice-and-guidance/student-wellbeing-and-protection/freedom-of-speech/what-can-we-do/ [accessed 25 June 2021].

61 Sean Coughlan, '"Intolerance" Threat to University Free Speech', BBC, 27 March 2018, www.bbc.co.uk/news/education-43544546 [accessed 14 December 2020].

62 'Sam Gyimah hosts free speech summit', *Gov.uk* (3 May 2018), www.gov.uk/government/news/sam-gyimah-hosts-free-speech-summit [accessed 14 December 2020].

63 Thomas Simpson and Eric Kaufmann, *Academic Freedom in the UK* (London: Policy Exchange, 2019), https://policyexchange.org.uk/publication/academic-freedom-in-the-uk/ [accessed 14 December 2020].

64 *Get Brexit Done: Unleash Britain's Potential*, Conservative and Unionist Party Manifesto 2019, p. 37, https://assets-global.website-files.com/5da42e2cae7ebd3f8bde353c/5dda924905da587992a064ba_Conservative%202019%20Manifesto.pdf [accessed 14 December 2020].

65 Trilling, 'Why is the UK Government Suddenly Targeting "Critical Race Theory"?'

66 Kojo Koram, 'What Is "Critical Race Theory" and Why Are Tories Talking About It?', *Vice*, 27 October 2020, www.vice.com/en/article/3anz43/what-is-critical-race-theory-conservative-party [accessed 14 December 2020].

67 'The Conservative Party's Changing Stance on Race', *Economist*, 31 October 2020, www.economist.com/britain/2020/10/31/the-conservative-partys-changing-stance-on-race [accessed 14 December 2020].

68 Robert Shrimsley, 'Boris Johnson Cannot Substitute Culture Wars for Competence', *Financial Times*, 22 June 2020, www.ft.com/content/e09c6f83-d591-4c65-a02c-d3863034fdb3 [accessed 14 December 2020].

69 'The Conservative Party's Changing Stance on Race', *Economist*.
70 Roger Scruton, 'Postmodern Tories', *Prospect*, 21 February 2013, www. prospectmagazine.co.uk/magazine/conservatism-tories-roger-scruton [accessed 14 December 2020].
71 Shilliam, *Race and the Undeserving Poor*, p. 17.

Chapter 7

1 https://clapforourcarers.co.uk/acknowledgements [accessed 18 January 2021].
2 'The Queen's Broadcast to the UK and Commonwealth' (5 April 2020), www.royal.uk/queens-broadcast-uk-and-commonwealth [accessed 18 January 2021].
3 Esther Addley, 'Clap for our Carers: The Very UnBritish Ritual that United the Nation', *Guardian*, 28 May 2020, www.theguardian.com/society/2020/may/28/clap-for-our-carers-the-very-unbritish-ritual-that-united-the-nation [accessed 18 January 2021].
4 Jonathan Calvert and George Arbuthnott, *Failures of State: The Inside Story of Britain's Battle with Coronavirus* (London: Mudlark, 2021).
5 Jonathan Calvert, George Arbuthnott, and Jonathan Leake, 'Coronavirus: 38 Days when Britain Sleepwalked into Disaster', *The Times*, 19 April 2020, www.thetimes.co.uk/article/coronavirus-38-days-when-britain-sleepwalked-into-disaster-hq3b9tlgh [accessed 18 January 2021].
6 David Conn, Felicity Lawrence, Paul Lewis, Severin Carrell, David Pegg, Harry Davies and Rob Evans, 'Revealed: The Inside Story of the UK's Covid-19 Crisis', *Guardian*, 29 April 2020, www.theguardian.com/world/2020/apr/29/revealed-the-inside-story-of-uk-covid-19-coronavirus-crisis [accessed 18 January 2021].
7 Ibid.
8 Calvert and Arbuthnott, *Failures of State*, pp. 167–93.
9 'Chancellor of the Exchequer, Rishi Sunak on COVID19 Response', *Gov.uk* (17 March 2020), www.gov.uk/government/speeches/chancellor-of-the-exchequer-rishi-sunak-on-covid19-response [accessed 18 January 2021].
10 Chris Giles, 'Bank of England Boosts Bond-Buying by £100bn but Slows the Pace' *Financial Times*, 18 June 2020, www.ft.com/content/9c2744f a-5162-489d-b117-18b2df88b6bd [accessed 18 January 2021].
11 J. Green and S. Lavery, 'The Regressive Recovery: Distribution, Inequality and State Power in Britain's Post-Crisis Political Economy', *New Political Economy*, 20/6 (2015).

12 Daniel Harari and Matthew Keep, *Coronavirus: Economic Impact*, House of Commons Library Briefing Paper Number 8866 (London: House of Commons Library, 2020), https://commonslibrary.parliament.uk/research-briefings/cbp-8866/ [accessed 18 January 2021].

13 'Hungary's Orban Blames Foreigners, Migration for Coronavirus Spread', *France24*, 13 March 2020, www.france24.com/en/20200313-hungary-s-pm-orban-blames-foreign-students-migration-for-coronavirus-spread [accessed 18 January 2021].

14 Nicholas Mulder, 'The Coronavirus War Economy Will Change the World', *Foreign Policy*, 26 March 2020, https://foreignpolicy.com/2020/03/26/the-coronavirus-war-economy-will-change-the-world/ [accessed 18 January 2021].

15 William Davies, 'The Great British Battle: How the Fight against Coronavirus Spread a New Nationalism', *Guardian*, 16 May 2020, www.theguardian.com/books/2020/may/16/the-great-british-battle-how-the-fight-against-coronavirus-spread-a-new-nationalism [accessed 18 January 2021].

16 Matt Hancock, 'We must All do Everything in our Power to Protect Lives', *Telegraph*, 14 March 2020, www.telegraph.co.uk/politics/2020/03/14/must-do-everything-power-protect-lives/. Cited in Rachel Malik, 'Hancock's Call to Arms', *LRB Blog* (16 March 2020), www.lrb.co.uk/blog/2020/march/hancock-s-call-to-arms [accessed 18 January 2021].

17 Ibid.

18 James Meadway, 'The Anti-Wartime Economy', *Tribune*, 19 March 2020, https://tribunemag.co.uk/2020/03/the-anti-wartime-economy [accessed 18 January 2021].

19 Susan Sontag, *Illness as Metaphor and Aids and Its Metaphors* (New York: Picador, 1979/1988), p. 99.

20 David Craig, 'Pandemic and its Metaphors: Sontag Revisited in the COVID-19 Era', *European Journal of Cultural Studies*, 23/6 (2020).

21 Emine Saner, '"It was Surreal Watching it": How Life Changed for the Woman behind Clap for Our Carers', *Guardian*, 21 December 2020, www.theguardian.com/lifeandstyle/2020/dec/21/it-was-surreal-watching-it-spread-how-life-changed-for-the-woman-behind-clap-for-our-carers [accessed 18 January 2021].

22 Ibid.; Aamna Mohdin, 'Pots, Pans, Passion: Britons Clap their Support for NHS Workers Again', *Guardian*, 2 April 2020, www.theguardian.com/world/2020/apr/02/pots-pans-passion-britons-clap-their-support-for-nhs-workers-again [accessed 18 January 2021].

23 Addley, 'Clap for our Carers'.

24 Lauren O'Neill, 'NHS Workers Need You to Support them Beyond Clapping', *Vice*, 22 May 2020, www.vice.com/en/article/z3evd8/nhs-clap-for-carers-support [accessed 18 January 2021].

25 Davies, 'The Great British Battle'.

26 YouGov Survey Results, https://docs.cdn.yougov.com/cvz3k50tmj/ Internal_ClapforCarers_200529.pdf [accessed 18 January 2021].

27 Saner, '"It was Surreal Watching it"'.

28 'Ben Fogle Hits Back at 'Mean' Responses to Royal Birthday Song Suggestion', BBC, 16 April 2020, www.bbc.co.uk/news/entertainment-arts-52312392 [accessed 18 January 2021].

29 Martin Sandbu, 'Coronavirus: The Moment for Helicopter Money', *Financial Times*, 20 March 2020, www.ft.com/content/abd6bbd0-6a9 f-11ea-800d-da70cff6e4d3 [accessed 18 January 2021].

30 'Coronavirus Job Retention Scheme Statistics: December 2020', *Gov.uk* (24 December 2020), www.gov.uk/government/publications/coronavirus-job-retention-scheme-statistics-december-2020/coronavirus-job-retention-scheme-statistics-december-2020 [accessed 18 January 2021].

31 Ibid.; Office for Budget Responsibility, *Economic and Fiscal Outlook: November 2020* (London: Office for Budget Responsibility, 2020), https:// obr.uk/efo/economic-and-fiscal-outlook-november-2020/ [accessed 18 January 2021].

32 Ibid.

33 Harari and Keep, *Coronavirus: Economic Impact*.

34 HM Treasury, *Spending Review 2020* (London: HMSO, 2020) p. 12, https://assets.publishing.service.gov.uk/government/uploads/system/ uploads/attachment_data/file/938052/SR20_Web_Accessible.pdf [accessed 18 January 2021].

35 Robert Peston, 'Will Rishi Sunak's Temporary Nationalisation of the Economy Rescue Us?', ITV, 20 March 2020, www.itv.com/news/ 2020-03-20/will-rishi-sunak-s-temporary-nationalisation-of-the-economy-rescue-us-writes-robert-peston [accessed 18 January 2021].

36 George Parker, Chris Giles and Sebastian Payne, 'Sunak Turns on Financial Firepower to Help Workers', *Financial Times*, 20 March 2020, www.ft.com/content/826d465a-6ac3-11ea-a3c9-1fe6fedcca75 [accessed 18 January 2021].

37 Ibid.

38 Gus O'Donnell, 'The Covid Tragedy: Following the Science or the Sciences?', *Institute for Fiscal Studies* (24 September 2020), www.ifs.org.uk/ publications/15045 [accessed 18 January 2021].

39 The Financial Times Editorial Board, 'Weaning Britain's Economy off Furlough' *Financial Times*, 15 September 2020, www.ft.com/content/ e1278947-299a-49f0-8be8-68f3bab79e15 [accessed 18 January 2021].

40 *Sector Shutdowns during the Coronavirus Crisis: Which Workers are Most Exposed?*, Institute for Fiscal Studies (6 April 2020), www.ifs.org.uk/ publications/14791 [accessed 18 January 2021].

41 Ibid.

42 Ibid.

43 *First Wave Furloughing Pushed Two Million Employees Below the Minimum Wage*, Resolution Foundation (3 November 2020), www.resolutionfoundation.org/press-releases/first-wave-furloughing-pushed-two-million-employees-below-the-minimum-wage/ [accessed 18 January 2021].

44 *Lockdown Lessons: What 2020 has to Teach us about the Difficult Weeks Ahead*, Resolution Foundation (5 January 2021), www.resolutionfoundation.org/publications/lockdown-lessons/ [accessed 18 January 2021].

45 Christine Berry, 'The UK's Private Debt Crisis will make this Recession so much Worse', *Guardian*, 5 August 2020, www.theguardian.com/commentisfree/2020/aug/05/uk-private-debt-crisis-recession-coronavirus [accessed 18 January 2021].

46 Jessica Martin, 'Keep Crafting and Carry On: Nostalgia and Domestic Cultures in the Crisis', *European Journal of Cultural Studies*, 24/1 (2020).

47 'BBC One Daytime Announces Daily Kitchen Live, to help Viewers through Lockdown', BBC (2 April 2020), www.bbc.co.uk/mediacentre/latestnews/2020/daily-kitchen-live [accessed 18 January 2021].

48 Hannah Lambie-Mumford, Rachel Loopstra, and Katy Gordon, *Mapping Responses to Risk of Rising Food Insecurity during the COVID-19 Crisis across the UK: Phase one report* (Sheffield: Food Vulnerability during Covid-19, 2020), http://speri.dept.shef.ac.uk/wp-content/uploads/2020/08/Food-Vulnerability-During-COVID-19-first-project-report.pdf [accessed 18 January 2021].

49 Margo Barker and Jean Russell, 'Feeding the Food Insecure in Britain: Learning from the 2020 Covid-19 Crisis', *Food Security*, 12/4 (2020).

50 Hannah Lambie-Mumford, Katy Gordon, and Rachel Loopstra, *Monitoring Responses to Risk of Rising Household Food Insecurity during the Covid-19 Crisis across the UK: Phase two* (Sheffield: Food Vulnerability during Covid-19, 2020), pp. 59–69, http://speri.dept.shef.ac.uk/wp-content/uploads/2020/12/Monitoring-responses-to-risk-of-rising-food-insecurity-during-the-COVID-19-crisis-across-the-UK-FINAL-1.pdf [accessed 18 January 2021].

51 'First Food Parcels Delivered to Clinically Vulnerable People', *Gov.uk* (29 March 2020), www.gov.uk/government/news/first-food-parcels-delivered-to-clinically-vulnerable-people [accessed 18 January 2021].

52 Lambie-Mumford, Gordon, and Loopstra, *Monitoring Responses to Risk of Rising Household Food Insecurity*, p. 59.

53 Ibid., p. 59.

54 Ibid., p. 68.

55 Ibid.

56 Lambie-Mumford, Loopstra, and Gordon, *Mapping Responses to Risk of Rising Food Insecurity*, p. 20.

57 David Olusoga and Peter Olusoga, 'What Marcus Rashford's Campaign for Hungry Children Tells us about the Footballer – and Britain', *Guardian*, 22 December 2020, www.theguardian.com/lifeandstyle/2020/dec/22/what-marcus-rashfords-campaign-for-hungry-children-tells-us-about-the-footballer-and-britain [accessed 18 January 2021].

58 'Marcus Rashford puts Manchester Children First in Coronavirus Crisis', *Guardian*, 20 March 2020, www.theguardian.com/football/2020/mar/30/marcus-rashford-manchester-children-coronavirus-crisis-united-injury [accessed 18 January 2021].

59 'Conservative MP Quits Government Job over Free School Meals', BBC (22 October 2020), www.bbc.co.uk/news/uk-politics-54642788 [accessed 18 January 2021].

60 https://twitter.com/MarcusRashford/status/1321584910654705665 [accessed 18 January 2021].

61 Jim Waterson, 'Virtue Signalling: The Culture War Phrase now in BBC Guidelines', *Guardian*, 30 October 2020, www.theguardian.com/media/2020/oct/30/virtue-signalling-the-culture-war-phrase-now-in-bbc-guidelines [accessed 18 January 2021].

62 Caroline Davies, 'It is Never about Him': How Marcus Rashford became such a Devastating Activist', *Guardian*, 21 November 2020, www.theguardian.com/football/2020/nov/21/how-marcus-rashford-became-such-a-devastating-activist [accessed 18 January 2021].

63 Jacob Steinberg, 'Marcus Rashford: Goalscorer who Forced U-Turn over School Lunches', *Guardian*, 16 June 2020, www.theguardian.com/football/2020/jun/16/marcus-rashford-goalscorer-who-forced-u-turn-over-school-lunches [accessed 18 January 2021].

64 https://twitter.com/marcusrashford/status/1272863210207694848?lang=en [accessed 18 January 2021].

65 Sally Weale and Richard Adams, 'Marcus Rashford in "Despair" as MPs Reject Free School Meal Plan', *Guardian*, 21 October 2020, www.theguardian.com/education/2020/oct/21/marcus-rashford-in-despair-as-mps-reject-free-school-meal-plan [accessed 18 January 2021].

66 Chris Giles, George Parker and Tommy Stubbington, 'Invidious Choices await Sunak in Tackling Cost of Virus Crisis', *Financial Times*, 13 May 2020, www.ft.com/content/e4af50a3-3a8d-4bf3-846f-c2b0ae201ad6 [accessed 18 January 2021].

67 Chris Giles, 'Global Economy: The Week that Austerity was Officially Buried', *Financial Times*, 16 October 2020, www.ft.com/content/0940e381-647a-4531-8787-e8c7dafbd885 [accessed 18 January 2021].

68 Ibid.; Richard Partington, 'OECD: UK Economic Recovery will Lag Behind All Rivals bar Argentina', *Guardian*, 1 December 2020, www.theguardian.com/business/2020/dec/01/government-covid-oecd-uk-growth-forecast [accessed 18 January 2021].

69 The Financial Times Editorial Board, 'Pandemic has Exposed UK's Threadbare Safety Net', *Financial Times*, 12 January 2021, www.ft.com/content/e531b77c-0322-43fa-9d9f-33747f8659ad [accessed 18 January 2021]; *The Times*, 'Coronavirus: 38 Days when Britain Sleepwalked into Disaster'.

70 Gary Stevenson, 'Who should Pay for the COVID Crisis?', *Open Democracy* (11 November 2020) www.opendemocracy.net/en/oureconomy/who-should-pay-covid-crisis/ [accessed 18 January 2021].

71 https://twitter.com/RishiSunak/status/1321802739320500224 [accessed 18 January 2021].

72 David Wastell, 'Economists Urge BBC to Rethink 'Inappropriate' Reporting of UK Economy', IPPR (30 November 2020), www.ippr.org/blog/economists-urge-bbc-rethink-inappropriate-reporting-uk-economy [accessed 18 January 2021].

73 'Chancellor Confirms "Cap for Carers" in Spending Review', Tax Justice UK (25 November 2020), www.taxjustice.uk/blog/chancellor-confirms-cap-for-carers-in-spending-review [accessed 18 January 2021].

74 www.ukwealth.tax/ [accessed 18 January 2021].

75 For example, Richard Partington, 'Sir Gus O'Donnell Calls for Wealth Tax as Part of UK's Covid-19 Response', *Guardian*, 2 July 2020, www.theguardian.com/business/2020/jul/02/sir-gus-odonnell-calls-for-wealth-tax-as-part-of-uk-covid-19-response-boris-johnson [accessed 18 January 2021].

76 Emma Agyemang, 'Q&A: How Would a Wealth Tax Work?', *Financial Times*, 19 May 2020, www.ft.com/content/2b62c3fb-7e52-45c1-a5c0-8970fa3f6a5b; https://committees.parliament.uk/work/465/tax-after-coronavirus/ [accessed 18 January 2021].

77 Tax Justice UK, *Talking Tax: How to Win Support for Taxing Wealth* (Bristol: Tax Justice UK, 2020) www.taxjustice.uk/uploads/1/0/0/3/100363766/talking_tax_-_how_to_win_support_for_taxing_wealth.pdf [accessed 18 January 2021].

78 Michael Jacobs, 'Taxes will have to Rise at Some Point, but Right Now We Need the Government to Spend, Spend, Spend', *Independent*, 19 July 2020, www.independent.co.uk/voices/uk-economy-coronavirus-government-spend-austerity-taxes-deficit-debt-a9627006.html [accessed 18 January 2021].

79 Chris Giles, 'Central Bankers have been Relegated to Second Division of Policymakers', *Financial Times*, 1 October 2020, www.ft.com/content/42ca35d8-37ab-4e50-8a4d-7d3d93864cc5 [accessed 18 January 2021].

80 Robert Shrimsley, Peter Foster, Jim Pickard, Mure Dickie, Andy Bounds and Chris Tighe, 'Will Coronavirus Break the UK?', *Financial Times*, 21 October 2020, www.ft.com/content/05bcdeed-ce2d-4009-a3b c-cf9bb71c43d5 [accessed 18 January 2021].

81 Ibid.

82 Ibid.

83 'Coronavirus (COVID-19): Travel and Transport', *Gov.scot*, 18 January 2021, www.gov.scot/publications/coronavirus-covid-19-guidance-on-travel-and-transport/ [accessed 18 January 2021].

84 Shrimsley et al., 'Will Coronavirus Break the UK?'

85 Ibid.

86 Peter Geoghegan, 'Cronyism and Clientelism', *London Review of Books*, 42/21 (2020), www.lrb.co.uk/the-paper/v42/n21/peter-geoghegan/ cronyism-and-clientelism [accessed 18 January 2021].

87 Conor Matchett, 'Poll Shows Scottish Independence Support Surging to Joint Record Levels as SNP Set for Majority', *Scotsman*, 17 December 2020, www.scotsman.com/news/politics/poll-shows-scottish-independence-support-surging-joint-record-levels-snp-set-majority-3070791 [accessed 18 January 2021].

88 Peter Walker and Libby Brooks, 'Why "Stronger than Ever" Union is Wishful Thinking from Boris Johnson', *Guardian*, 23 July 2020), www.theguardian.com/uk-news/2020/jul/23/why-stronger-than-ever-union-is-wishful-thinking-from-boris-johnson-scottish-independence [accessed 18 January 2021].

89 'Minister for the Union', *Gov.uk*, www.gov.uk/government/ministers/ minister-for-the-union; 'Boris Johnson "Called Scottish Devolution Disaster"', BBC, 17 November 2020, www.bbc.co.uk/news/uk-politics-54965585; Rajeev Syal, Archie Bland, and Heather Stewart, 'No 10 Wanted Union Flag on Oxford Coronavirus Vaccine Kits', *Guardian*, 27 November 2020, www.theguardian.com/politics/2020/ nov/27/no-10-reportedly-wanted-union-flag-on-oxford-coronavirus-vaccine-kits [accessed 18 January 2021].

90 'Scottish Independence has Never Been so Certain, Sturgeon Tells SNP', *Guardian*, 28 November 2020, www.theguardian.com/politics/2020/ nov/28/scottish-independence-never-been-so-certain-sturgeon-to-tell-snp [accessed 18 January 2021].

Conclusion

1 For three very good arguments of this character, see Rune Møller Stahl, 'Ruling the Interregnum: Politics and Ideology in Nonhegemonic Times', *Politics & Society*, 47/3 (2019); Milan Babic, 'Let's Talk About the

Interregnum: Gramsci and the Crisis of the Liberal World Order', *International Affairs*, 96/3 (2020); Helen Thompson, 'It's Still the 2008 Crash', *Political Quarterly*, 88/3 (2017).

2 Michael Savage, Toby Helm, and James Tapper, 'The Blue Wall: What Next for the Tories after a Shock Byelection Defeat?', *Guardian*, 19 June 2021), www.theguardian.com/politics/2021/jun/19/the-blue-wall-what-next-for-the-tories-after-a-shock-byelection-defeat [accessed 25 June 2021].

3 Craig Berry and Colin Hay, 'The Great British "Rebalancing" Act: The Construction and Implementation of an Economic Imperative for Exceptional Times', *British Journal of Politics & International Relations*, 18/1 (2016).

4 Andreas Chatzidakis et al., 'From Carewashing to Radical Care: The Discursive Explosions of Care During Covid-19', *Feminist Media Studies*, 20/6 (2020), p. 889.

5 William Davies, 'The Holiday of Exchange Value', *Political Economy Research Centre blog* (7 April 2020), www.perc.org.uk/project_posts/the-holiday-of-exchange-value/ [accessed 18 January 2021].

6 Helen Wood and Beverley Skeggs, 'Clap for Carers? From Care Gratitude to Care Justice', *European Journal of Cultural Studies*, 23/4 (2020), p. 644.

7 Nye Cominetti, Charlie McCurdy, and Hannah Slaughter, *Low Pay Britain 2021* (London: Resolution Foundation, 2021), www.resolutionfoundation.org/app/uploads/2021/06/Low-Pay-Britain-2021.pdf [accessed 25 June 2021].

8 Rupert Neate, '"Raise my Taxes – Now!": The Millionaires who Want to Give it all Away', *Guardian*, 3 April 2021, www.theguardian.com/news/2021/apr/03/raise-my-taxes-now-the-millionaires-who-want-to-give-it-all-away [accessed 17 June 2021].

9 Eric J. Hobsbawm, *Nations and Nationalism since 1780: Programme, Myth, Reality* (Cambridge: Cambridge University Press, 2012), pp. 1–13.

10 *Full Text of Keir Starmer Speech on A New Chapter for Britain*, Labour Party (18 February 2021), https://labour.org.uk/press/full-text-of-keir-starmer-speech-on-a-new-chapter-for-britain/ [accessed 17 June 2021].

11 Paul Gilroy, *After Empire: Melancholia or Convivial Culture?* (London: Routledge, 2004), p. 121.

Index